THE
EMANCIPATION
OF LIMITS

FIRST EDITION
Published in 2020

ISBN: 978-1-7356931-0-1

Library of Congress Registration
Turner, Richard Anthony
The Emancipation of Limits
Registration Number: TXU 2-224-026 | August 29, 2020

Category: Urban, Crime Fiction, Novel, Murder Mystery, Detective, Series

Author: A Paj Turner | **www.apajturner.com**

Editor: Marcia Garnett, Emerald Garnett Editing | www.emeraldgarnett.com

Cover Designer: Book Covers Art, Ivan | www.bookcoversart.com

Digital Formatter: Eli Blyden Sr. | www.elithebookguy.com

Published in the United States of America, Tampa Bay

To Philip Elliott (December 18, 1991 - January 6, 2020):
As you transition from this universe to the next, just know that your chill, million-dollar personality, and kindness left a huge void in everyone who knew you. The ancestors got a good one. You are truly missed. Until we meet again…

—

To Shantrell Reed (September 14, 1995 - June 13, 2020):
Your dad spoke of you often. I wish I had the chance to meet you. If my voice could travel across universes, I would tell you a piece of his soul left with you. That last hug you shared was everything to him. The ancestors have a fighter. You will be loved and missed forever.

CONTENTS

A. PAJ TURNER

Abbi,

Thank you for everything
you have done 4 my brand, website & the time spent doing this.
The journey is longer than desired
but I'm enjoying it. Enjoy the read!!! :)

A. Paj Turner

THE
EMANCIPATION
OF LIMITS

CHAPTER 1

It's 2 a.m. on December 29th, 2022. As he steps out the shower, Richie stares out of his 10-foot bathroom window overlooking downtown Chicago. He takes in the perfect view of the city's skyline, filled with skyscrapers, beautiful holiday lights, and tiny illuminations from the streetlights and cars passing by on Michigan Avenue, which is an expensive, prestigious area nicknamed the Magnificent Mile. Glorified with beautiful architecture, the Magnificent Mile is home to Chicago's most successful people, and it includes the latest attractions and many places to learn about Chicago's rich history. Richie nearly takes up the entire window with his six-foot-three athletic frame, and his caramel-colored skin, bald head, and thick beard are shown clearly in his reflection. In four more hours, Richie Swaggazine will be officially forty-three years old. He feels accomplished with this chapter of his life, but he still wants more for his family, his organization, and his community.

Richie walks over to the bathroom sink and utters, "Cold." The water turns on automatically. He cups his hands together underneath the water, lets it pool in his palms, and splashes the water onto his face. He grabs a towel, and the water stops as he pats his face dry. Richie then places his hands on the countertop and leans into the mirror to check his face for imperfections; he moves his head from side to side before stopping dead in the center. He zones out for a minute as he thinks about an incident that happened when he was a teenager. He can still see the tiny spot on his forehead where the barrel of a gun left an indentation. His chapter could have closed that night; just another inner-city statistic dead in the streets. The familiar sounds of gunfire going off in his head disconnects him from his past. He redirects his attention to the business he has to handle in his bedroom, and that he handles well.

He walks through the doorway to his bedroom. The flames from the fireplace, the fresh smell of candles, and the slow R&B music create the perfect ambiance for lovemaking. Lying face down, diagonally across his bed is Zuri, a woman he met at the 31st Annual African-American Film and Arts Festival nearly a week ago. She's a beautiful Ethiopian woman with hazel-colored eyes, shoulder-length sisterlocks, the body of a goddess, and skin rich with melanin. As he slowly approaches the bed, he scans her body, admiring her chocolate skin and voluptuous curves, finally getting the full view of it outside of her evening dress. He imagined this moment days before, and he's been preparing his mind to dominate her. Although he's confident, he feels nervous, wondering how she will take to his touch. He raises his right knee onto the bed, and he moves slowly as he gathers saliva in his mouth, preparing his tongue to be slippery, moist, and warm. He starts licking the heel of her left foot and continues up toward her calf. He simultaneously, lightly traces the fingernails on his right hand up her right leg, giving her the full effect of sensuality. When he arrives at her calves, he watches for her reaction. Her toes curl, her ass tightens, and her hands grip the sheets as she feels a tingling sensation shoot throughout her body. Her sweet nectar starts to seep from between her legs. His nervous energy is now gone, and his confidence swells, along with his depth. An invisible cape covers his back as he prepares for the level of lust, power, and control he will have over her.

Zuri's cheeks relax, and she spreads her legs slightly as Richie moves to licking and kissing on the back of her thighs. She understands his path and invites him into her core. His tongue moves toward her booty, which is shaped like an inverted heart, and he begins to make little circles and figure eights with his tongue across its entirety. Zuri lifts her head off the bed and moans as the tickling sensations are slowly overwhelming her. She reaches back and grabs his head to help control the feeling. He doesn't allow her to have control, so he grabs her arm and pins it to the bed momentarily. He slides his hands underneath her hips, lifts her up, and lightly licks from her pearl to the top of her booty.

Zuri knows she's being dominated, but her pride holds her steady. She hides her mini orgasms while still allowing him to do what he wants. Richie lightly taps the inside of her legs, prompting her to open them wider, and she does so without hesitation. She is soaking wet. He has her. She's now the puppet on his string. He lies between her legs and grips her cheeks firmly, spreading them apart. She squeezes them back at first but then willingly grants him access.

He no longer has to gather saliva because she supplies all that he needs. He licks her pearl and then he slowly moves upward past her queensway and plants his tongue in her tatti. Slowly, he moves his tongue in and out, up and down, and across the entrance. The perfect rhythm. She pushes back to receive more of his tongue. She can no longer hide her orgasm as she shakes uncontrollably. Reaching back, she grabs for his hands, trying to minimize the sensation and gain control. He moves back down and starts rapidly licking her pearl. She vigorously shakes her head to try and stop the tingling sensations that are overtaking her and radiating throughout her body. She moans and squirms with light barks of pleasure; her pride now irrelevant. Richie raises up as he licks the nectar of her sweet peach before he moves onto her lower back.

She moans as she feels his depth graze the inside of her leg. She presses her upper body into the mattress as she raises her hips upward, anticipating how he will feel when he enters her. He kisses and bites her back while moving up toward her neck; she reaches back, searches for his hardness, and gently strokes it. "I want you now," whispers Zuri as she attempts to turn over to receive him, but he presses her back facedown on the bed. He is now licking the back of her neck and kissing her ears, her shoulders shiver with pleasure.

He whispers in her ear, "You want this dick, don't you?"

Zuri replies, "Yes, yes!" in her Amharic accent. He turns her over and slowly thrusts his tongue into her mouth. She wraps her arms around him and squeezes tightly. He breaks loose of her clutch and proceeds to travel down to her breast. "This is my show. I control the curtains and when this movie starts," he says with authority. He grabs both of her breasts, pushes them together, and gently licks and bites her nipples. She crosses her ankles around his back, squeezing her thighs against his body, grasping for some form of control.

He pushes her legs apart and moves past her stomach to the sweet spot between her legs. He dives deep to taste her and moans from quenching his thirst. Her legs shake uncontrollably from the motion of his tongue, signaling the eruption of her long-lasting orgasm. She raises up on her elbows and tries to crawl away. The pleasure overwhelms her, and she looks for the end of the bed to aid in her escape. He stops, grabs the back of her knees, and pulls her back toward him. "This is a California King boo. You're a long way from shore."

He gently presses on her stomach, pushing her back until she's flat on the bed. He looks down at his throbbing manhood and then gazes into her eyes as he slides into her queendom. She takes a deep, exaggerated breath as he completely fills her. He thrusts in and out slowly, giving her time to adjust to the width and the curve. With each stroke, he goes deeper and deeper. Her eyes roll backward as her nails dig into his muscular back. Her mouth opens to let out a soft moan, and he slides his tongue inside. She eagerly sucks on his tongue. He withdraws his tongue from her mouth and says, "You like the way you taste, huh?" She smiles and says, "Of course," knowing how sweet her nectar tastes.

Bzzzzzz! The vibration of his phone briefly interrupts their sexual flow. It continues to vibrate while Richie continues his current business with Zuri. He glances at his phone and sees the name *BRICK* on the screen. As much as he would love to continue with Zuri, a call this late is possibly about a business gift he's been waiting on for a few days. Disappointed, he raises up and slowly slides from inside Zuri. She gasps softly then whispers, "No," with a pouty look on her face. "I know baby, I know. This is business, so I gotta get this." He kisses her on the forehead, crawls to the side of the bed, and grabs his phone. Richie takes a deep breath to switch to business mode and then answers the call. A voice that isn't Brick's cries out in desperation, and he quickly recognizes who's on the other end.

"Sheldon, how are you? Wait, don't answer that. Stupid question... my bad. I know you're probably tied up right now," Richie says smiling at his own joke, "so I'll make this quick. Listen, you had a great run. But all good things must come to an end, and bad things bring about the end much faster than anticipated. Don't worry; I'll take care of your kids. They'll go to college and have very successful lives. Alright, take care and happy travels. I hope you enjoyed your stay here."

As he moves the phone away from his ear, he hears Sheldon scream, "WAIT! WAIT!" He ends the call content that Sheldon is no longer a problem.

"Sorry, sexy. Should I start from the beginning?"

"Oh hell no!" They both laugh, and Richie slowly climbs back on top of Zuri, sucking her lips as he grabs a handful of her sisterlocks.

* * *

The next morning, Richie kisses his chocolate beauty and walks with her to the elevator with his arm around her shoulders. Zuri walks next to him with her arm around his waist, trying to stabilize her sore legs. Once the elevator doors close, he turns back to his condo and heads to his bedroom where he hears his phone ringing. He answers the call and hears a proud and loving voice on the other end.

"Happy birthday son!"

"Thank you, mother dearest," he replies with a loving grin.

"How do you feel?"

"It feels good to be twenty-five!"

"Honey, I wish you were twenty-five cause that would make me forty-eight."

"You're still forty-eight in my eyes, mom. Thank you for everything you've done throughout my life. I couldn't have gotten far without you, granddad, and unc. You need anything?"

"No, son. You're already a blessing to this family, and we don't have a need for anything. Do something nice for yourself for a change."

"I will, mom. Love you."

"Love you too, son."

Richie sits on the bed to briefly reminisce about last night and evaluate his performance. He smiles and yells in his best Snoop Dogg impersonation, "A plus is the grade that she gave me." He grabs his phone while continuing to rap a few more lyrics from "Murder Was the Case": "I can't die my Boo-Boo's bout to have my baby." He texts KAP and Brick and tells them to meet him at spot #2 at noon, so he can get an update on Sheldon's situation. They both reply within seconds with two black thumbs up. He goes to take a shower and get ready for the day.

Richie arrives ten minutes early at the spot, which is on the top floor of the Poetry Parking Garage less than a mile from where he resides. After he parks, he texts Damawi to give her a heads up that he'll be over soon to discuss his plans for his New Year's Eve comedy show and after-party. When he looks up from his phone, he sees a brand-new 2023 black on black GMC Yukon Denali coming up the ramp. Richie hops out of his 2012 BMW 750Li and walks over to KAP's SUV. He met KAP and Brick years ago when they all served in the military together. Brick, who is Richie's enforcer, opens the front passenger door to KAP's SUV and gets out. Brick is six foot eight, colossal in size, and as dark as a moonless midnight sky. He proudly greets Richie with a firm handshake, a long hug, and a pat on the back. Richie winces from the pain of the handshake and hops in the front seat of KAP's ride.

Brick hops in the back seat behind Richie, grunting as he struggles to get his legs in the car with his knees pushing into the back of the seat. Richie presses his back into his seat, adding to Brick's struggle. Richie jokingly yells, "Get your big ass back there!" Brick smiles and closes the door once he's finally seated properly.

"Happy birthday yo!" KAP says with coolness, reaching across the arm rest to give Richie a fist bump.

"I appreciate that, my dude," Richie replies. KAP, Richie's second in command, is a well-dressed, muscular playboy who keeps a plethora of women in his stable at all times. He runs the operations of Richie's "business" and is the mediator between Richie and the organizations they work with.

"So, we clear?" asks Richie.

"We clear," replies KAP.

"Sheldon's in the proper place?"

"That business is a done deal. He's at Lloyd's in a plastic bag waiting for disposal."

"Word, word," says Richie as he shakes his head with approval. "Was he in his car when you snatched him?"

"Yeah, we dropped it off at Smitty's. He'll crush it up in a day or so."

"H2H may try to pin his disappearance on somebody, so keep your heads on a swivel," Richie warns. "Regardless if they knew what he was doing or not, Sheldon was on his bullshit using counterfeit money in the club. Bringing unwanted attention. Either way, he was asking to be NyQuil'd."

"Without question," says KAP. "You think they'll want war over this?"

"For him... nah. He was sloppy, and his time was ending regardless. Prolly by his own people from what I've heard. So, let's see how this plays out. You get with his wifey?"

"I will tonight," says KAP with a devilish grin. "She wit it. Told me where he was and shit. She knows we got her back."

"Good...good," says Richie, rubbing his fingers through his beard. He thinks for a second, then adds, "I know she's your new boo thang and all, but if you get any sign that she's shaky..." He looks at KAP then at Brick through the rearview mirror, "Make room for her next to her man just in case. Feel me?"

Brick nods, tapping his gun holstered on the waist of his pants. KAP smiles again and nods in agreement. "Man, when are you going to upgrade that car?" asks KAP.

"That car has sentimental value to me," says Richie. "The wheels fall off, I'll put on some new ones."

"I hear you. You grabbing some lunch with us, birthday boy?"

"Nah man. I gotta go meet D to ensure errthang is good for New Year's Eve. Y'all have at it." He daps KAP up, then opens the door and hops out the truck. After Brick exits the back seat to get in the front, Richie hugs Brick, pats him on the chest and says, "Man, you squeeze my hand like that again, and you, Sheldon, and his ole lady gone have a threesome," as he throws a light punch into Brick's chest. Brick huffs playfully and smiles. Richie walks to his car and nods at the Yukon. KAP starts to leave once Richie's inside his car, and they both drive out of the parking garage.

About thirty minutes later, Richie arrives at Damawi's business, Josephine's, the hottest nightclub outside of Downtown Chicago. Richie felt weird walking through the front doors and not hearing the loud music playing or seeing the people packed in like sardines. Damawi's assistant, Octavio, greets him at the door, "Hey Swaggazine, she's upstairs in her office. She's expecting you, so just go on up." Richie nods, heads to the elevator, and takes it to the third floor. Damawi, known as D by the crew, owns the majority of Josephine's and was the best soldier under his command in the Army years ago. She's very high-strung and business-minded. After Richie retired from the military, he knew he needed her talents for his organization to run efficiently. Richie steps out of the elevator and turns to the right. Damawi's office door is open, so he stands in the doorway looking at her as she writes in a notepad unaware of her visitor. "Hey Damawi," he says with a smile. She looks up from her desk, then smiles when she sees Richie. She stands up from behind her desk, quickly walks over to him, and hugs him tightly. He hugs her firmly for a few seconds and then eases his grip, but she continues to hug him for a little while longer. She releases him and walks back to her desk; her neck-length bob swaying with each step.

Richie looks at her apple-shaped booty as she walks away and shakes his head. As Damawi turns the corner of her desk to slip on her heels, he notices Gina sitting over to the right on a love seat in the corner. She smiles, then looks away. Damawi walks back over to Richie with her hand extended toward Richie and excitedly says, "Come with me! I want to show you the set up." He grabs her hand, and they both head out of her office to the party room. As they leave the office, Gina puts the end of her pen in her mouth, shakes her head, and smirks before continuing to write in her notepad.

After a few steps outside Damawi's office, they release each other's hand and start chatting. "So," Richie says with an inquiring mind, "I know I don't have to ask, but I will ask. How's the logistics with…"

"The comedians are already here. Both shows at seven and ten are completely sold out...all 3,500 seats per show. As you can see," she points to the party room, "it's ready for the team to celebrate the New Year. The podium and microphone are ready, and the club is always ready. Between the show and the club, I'm expecting us to reach profits of just under one million. Just a little more than we made last year."

"See," Richie says, trying to come up with something to hide that he was micromanaging her, "I was just going to ask you what time the crew was flying in from Belize."

"Yeah, whatever! Arielle and the girls will be here the morning of New Year's Eve. And Phillip, as you know, can't get a visa because of all his pending murder investigations," Damawi adds, rolling her eyes.

"A visa?! He can't even get a debit card with all that BS he got going on!"

"Everyone else will be here," says Damawi laughing. "So, what do you think of everything?"

"Nothing for me to think about. The first time I saw you, when you came to my detachment, I thought, Now this soldier is a future officer." Damawi smiles. "You have always been on point, and your aunt Josephine would be proud of you. I remember when we purchased this building, and it was totally gutted. Now look at it! I'm glad you decided to cut your career with the military short to follow me and chase your dreams of owning a nightclub. Thanks for believing in me and my dreams, helping to make them come true, and believing in your abilities. Anything else you'd like to share before I leave?"

"No. Just happy birthday! Enjoy your day, and don't forget about your surprise tonight."

"Oh, I thought you forgot about my birthday. Thank you, and I won't forget!" Richie hugs Damawi and lifts her up onto her tiptoes.

"I'll see you later," says Damawi after they seperate. Richie heads toward the stairs and yells, "Everything looks great as usual." She smiles and watches Richie walk down the stairs.

* * *

On the south side in Chatham, Hand-to-Hand (H2H) has just finished a meeting led by Maurice Handley, the founder and leader of this twelve-person organization. Maurice, a six-foot-three, dark-skinned, bearded man with a muscular frame, is a certified street thug who has been involved with criminal activities since he was ten years old. He's always on the wrong side of the law, known as being grimey and evil, and very well connected to the streets, just like his father. Maurice asks Spree, Kolax, and Elder to stay back after the other members leave the room; they're his arms and legs of the organization. Spree, a five-foot-eight, skinny, light-skinned brother with hazel eyes, is Maurice's right-hand man and childhood friend who runs H2H when Maurice is away. Kolax is his muscle and hitman. Standing at six foot five with a muscular build and black as an alley with no streetlights, Kolax is a ruthless killer who shows no mercy to anyone who's in the way of the advancement of the organization. Maurice and Spree met Kolax when they were members in another crime organization as teenagers, and Kolax left that organization when Maurice started H2H. Elder is a six-foot, brown-skinned, bald-headed, clean shaven ole G who is still in great shape for his age. He was a close friend of Maurice's dad and became a father figure to Maurice after his dad was killed during a shootout with the police after a drug deal went south.

The room is all theirs now, and Maurice asks, "Anyone heard from Sheldon?"

Concerned, Spree replies, "Nobody's heard from that dude in nearly two days."

Angrily, Maurice stands up and shouts, "So no one has heard from or seen Shelly?!"

Silence fills the room.

"Has anyone stopped by his people's house to see if they know what's up?"

Spree stands up and responds, "Kolax, go to his people's house and see what it is."

Elder, who is a confidant and advisor to Maurice, says in a low, calm voice, "You know he had that package in the trunk of his car." Maurice closes his eyes for a moment as he clenches and releases a fist. He then runs his hands from the top of his head over his face, pulling on his chin hairs. Slowly, he asks, "Why the fuck would Jamal give that nigga something way out his league?! Half a mil just floating out there, huh?!"

No one answered.

"I tell you what. Kolax, after you visit Sheldon's people, find Jamal and put a bullet in his head. Then put his body on the ball court at Pirie Park so errbody can see what happens when you fuck up. And put a bullet in the head of whoever he stopped from doing what the fuck he was supposed to do. Find that fucking package!"

Maurice walks out the room, leaving everyone behind. Elder follows behind him. Spree says to Kolax, "After you leave his people's house, call Maurice and let him know the deal. And when you find Jamal, before or after, call me." Kolax nods and then heads out.

* * *

Sitting in his car outside of Josephine's, Richie receives an international phone call from someone he knows very well to wish him a happy birthday. He excitedly answers, "What's up A? What's goodie?"

"Hi Richie! Happy birthday! How do you feel?" asks Arielle, surprised that she got him on the phone.

"Feeling thirty-eight with the wisdom of a ninety year old, the pace of a toddler, and the back of a twenty-one year old." Arielle chuckles as she sees a flashback of one of their many times together.

"How's the crew doing?" asks Richie.

"Everyone is good. Listen, the reason I called you, besides your birthday, is because I have a grand opening for my third private school next week. The same week that T.K. and Tech will be here. You've helped me so much by motivating me and helping me get funding. I would be honored if you would come to the ribbon cutting ceremony."

"Third private school?! I'm proud of you. And I know the citizens of Belize are proud of the work you're doing for the youth." Richie pauses before answering as he watches Damawi, Octavio, and Gina get into Damawi's car and leave the club.

Arielle anxiously asks, "Sooooo?"

Richie thinks, I could use this opportunity to… "I'll be there, but I only have a few days open next week. Call D and give her the dates, and I'll see you New Year's Day and next week."

"Awesome! I'm so happy you can come! Thank you! I know you be so busy."

"No, thank you! See you soon."

Richie watches Damawi drive off and then waits a few minutes before he heads west. Thirty minutes later, he arrives in the heart of Buffalo Grove, IL, and turns into the driveway at his mom's house. He parks in front of the house, gathers his phone and key fob, and heads to the front door. He puts his key in the door, unlocks and opens it, and finds a dark, empty home.

He walks inside and yells, "Ma! Unc!" and then whispers to himself, "Where the hell is everybody, and why is it so dark in here?" He slowly walks into the living room. "I should've brought my gun with me." Suddenly, the lights turn on and he hears, "SURPRISE!!" Simultaneously, he sees a large group of people jump up. Stunned, he smiles wide and says, "Y'all got me. Y'all got me good. I can't believe it. Thank you, mom!"

Smiling ear to ear, he walks over and hugs his daughters, then turns to dab up KAP, T.K., Tech, and Brick. Finally, he hugs his mom and kisses her on the cheek. He looks at Damawi and winks at her to thank her for the heads up. He then walks into the family room with his arm around his mom and admires all the food in the dining area. Richie looks around the room at all his family and friends, and he thinks about how the day couldn't have ended more perfectly.

CHAPTER 2

The next morning, Kolax arrives at Sheldon's house and bangs on the door until Sheldon's lady Courtney answers.

"Who is it?" asks Courtney through the door.

"Open up!" yells Kolax impatiently.

"Okay. Damn!"

Courtney, a small-framed, five-foot-three, caramel-colored sista, opens the door, and Kolax barges in. He nearly knocks her down. He stops in the living room and scans the room for any clues as to where Sheldon may be.

"When was the last time you seen him?"

"He left out of here two days ago, and I don't know where he is or where he went to. Why? You don't know where—"

"Does he have another bitch on the side?"

"What do you mean? Who's the first bitch?" Courtney replies with an attitude.

"Is he fucking another bitch or not?"

"Don't be coming in my house—"

Without warning, Kolax backhands her and sends Courtney flipping over the back of the couch and landing hard on the floor. He walks over to her, places his right hand around her neck, and squeezes slowly. Courtney, terrified, stares up at Kolax, fixated on the vein throbbing in the middle of his forehead.

"You talking all that hard gangsta shit. If I wanted something hard coming out of it, I'd pull my dick out and shove it down your throat." Kolax hears some movement on the stairs and looks up to see Courtney's twin girls standing there watching him assault their mom. He releases his grip on her neck, throttling back his anger, and lets her go. He stands up straight and pulls at the bottom of his coat to straighten it out.

As he turns to leave the residence, he sees a pair of Howard University college applications on the end table next to the front door. He walks over and picks them up, looks over at Courtney with an evil grin, winks, then puts them back on the table and walks out. Once in his car, he calls Maurice and gives him an update on the Sheldon situation. Maurice listens intently, then responds, "That muthafucka can't afford no Howard University. Not from the paper Sheldon gets from us. He missing, and the package missing. How convenient. That bitch knows some shit. We gon see!!" Kolax pictures Maurice bouncing his head back and forth while he's talking. Before he hangs up with Kolax, he says, "The next order of business is Jamal."

* * *

Richie wakes up the next morning and walks into the kitchen to the smell of bacon and his family eating and chatting. He sits down to enjoy breakfast and catch up on old times. Right before he leaves, he stops in his Uncle Richard's room to chop it up. He was relieved to be on speaking terms with him again, even if his uncle was still bitter about the reorganization he did after he took over the business. He walks up to the door, knocks, and walks in.

"What's up, unc? How you holding up?"

"Hey nephew! Happy birthday boy!"

"Thanks. Just stepping in to holla at you. You need anything?"

"You remember Chet?"

"Of course, Chet the Jet. That was your man. I remember him."

"He died the other day. His family needs help."

"I'll take care of it, unc. How you holding up?"

"In this game called life, death is a big piece of it. How are you, nephew? What's the game looking like these days?"

"I'm working it. I'll be 100% legitimate soon enough and then I'm out."

Uncle Richard is known as Marble Head in the streets because he was stubborn and hardheaded back in his heyday. In his younger days, he walked tall in the streets where he was once feared. Now at sixty-eight years old, Marble Head's brown-skinned, skinny frame is confined to a wheelchair, and the medium-sized afro he once rocked was replaced with a bald head. He folds his hands in his lap and lets out a deep sigh before speaking, "Just remember, you got a lot of people who depend on you, on both sides of the spectrum. You're the middleman between the cartel and the streets. You got too much time invested to be in and out now. You've transitioned a ton of people onto the next life. Some deserved it; some didn't. This game holds on to you like slavery. It's been over for over a hundred and fifty years, but black folks still affected by it. What I'm saying is you may think you gone be free, but the game will haunt you mentally," says Marble Head as he taps his temple with his right index finger. "Now, the mental piece is the people you killed or had killed. The other is the tangible or the physical piece. Those who depend on you, like the cartel and the streets. The cartel wants to keep you below them, and the streets need you above them to service. Hence, leaving you stuck in the middle. They'll keep you in play regardless. Don't matter how far you run or how much money you got. This is a lifetime contract."

"I hear you, Unc," says Richie, "but you made it out."

Marble Head pauses, frowns, looks Richie straight in the eyes, and says, "If I was out, you wouldn't be seeking my counsel, but you do. So, if you in it, I'm in it." Richie thinks for a second, then nods and walks over to his uncle. He bends down, kisses his uncle on the top of his head, and says, "I love you, Marble Head. See you soon." Richie walks out of the room and heads to the front door.

Before he leaves, Richie hugs and kisses his mom and daughters, and he tells them that he will be out of town for a few days and will reach out to them when he returns. "Be careful son," says Richie's mom, JoAnn. He walks out the house and heads to his car. Talking to himself, Richie says, "Unc is real good at taking a shit on that bright light at the end of the tunnel." He starts his car, breathes deeply, and backs out of the driveway to head to his house.

* * *

Kolax, cruising through Chatham down Cottage Grove, is headed to Jamal's house. He sees Jamal's car outside of Harold's Chicken Shack and pulls over in front of his vehicle. Minutes later, Jamal comes out of the restaurant with a bag in his hand and heads to his car. He spots Kolax's Cadillac Escalade blocking his car, so he swiftly walks past his car and heads for the passenger side of Kolax's Escalade. Kolax lowers his passenger side window. Excited to see Kolax, Jamal rests his arm on top of the car door and sticks his head inside the window.

"What up, Ko?"

"J, my man. You chicken eat'n muthafucka. Where you going next?"

"To the house. What's good?"

"Maurice needs you to do something for him. Let's go to your spot, so I can tell you what the deal is."

Feeling important, Jamal replies, "Aight, follow me."

Jamal hops in his car, and Kolax follows him to his apartment. While driving, Kolax pushes the button to open his glove box, then he reaches in, takes out his silencer, and screws it onto the front of his 9MM gun. He places the weapon into his coat and pushes the button to close the glove box. After a few minutes, they pull up in the parking lot to Jamal's apartment. They both get out of their cars and head to the front door of Jamal's place. Kolax walks in and sits on the couch as Jamal heads to the kitchen with his bag of chicken. After a few minutes, Jamal heads back to the living room with his chicken on a paper plate and a soda in his right hand.

When he comes through the hallway into the living room, he finds Kolax standing with his arms crossed in front of his waist, wearing leather gloves with his gun in his right hand.

"Ko, what the fuck?! What's going on?!" screams Jamal as he puts his soda and plate down on the living room table.

"You fucked up. That package you gave Sheldon never reached its destination. Why did you give it to that dumb ass nigga?"

"The hospital called about my mom. Y'all know she sick man. I had to check on her," he explains nervously. "Come on, Ko! Let's call Maurice and get this thing straightened out." Kolax goes into his coat pocket with his left hand and throws Jamal his phone.

"The code is 6663." Jamal looks down at the phone. His hands are shaking violently while he's attempting to enter the code. He enters 6663, but the phone doesn't unlock. He looks up at Kolax to tell him the code isn't working just to see Kolax's arm fully extended with the gun pointed at Jamal's head. Jamal freezes, and his eyes start to water. Everything moves in slow motion as Jamal sees flashes of himself playing as a little kid at the playground where he grew up. Swinging in the neighborhood park. Looking up at the sky and squinting because the sun was in his eyes. Smiling and listening to the sound the swing makes from the steel grinding against steel. Hearing the voices of his friends pushing him in his back to propel him higher in the air. Then, his mom's face crosses his sight, smiling at him happy and proud, then in pain and struggling to survive.

He comes back to reality. His short film of life's moments is over. Kolax pulls the trigger, and within a millisecond, the bullet penetrates Jamal's forehead, sending his head back, spraying blood all over the wall behind him. His body thumps as it hits the floor. Kolax walks over to Jamal and watches Jamal's eyes blink rapidly until they slowly stop and become motionless. Kolax picks up his cell phone from Jamal's hand and calls Spree.

"Jamal's snoring," says Kolax.

"Did he say why he left the package with Sheldon?"

"He said the hospital called him about his moms. Saying she was sick. What you want me to do?"

Spree exhales loudly while rubbing his hand across his forehead. He knows Jamal's mother well because she was his fifth grade teacher and his favorite teacher at Pirie Elementary. She helped him through a very difficult time after his mom died that year.

"Leave it be. Put him where Maurice said to put him."

Kolax hangs up with Spree, then removes his coat and sits at the living room table. He grabs the remote control and turns on the television only to find that the cable service is disconnected. He turns around, looks at Jamal, and shakes his head in disappointment. He throws the remote control at Jamal's lifeless body, which is still oozing blood from the back of his head. He reaches for Jamal's soda, opens it, and grabs a chicken wing off the plate. He then leans back onto the couch and starts eating, waiting for nightfall, so he can close the loop.

* * *

On the South Side of Chicago, KAP is relaxing on the couch at one of his ladies' houses, Makala. KAP feels his phone vibrate on his hip and maneuvers his body to remove it from the holster. He sees Courtney on the screen, then goes to put his phone back in the holster, but something tells him to check the message. He raises the phone to his face and unlocks it. He sees a message that reads: "Kolax 911." He yells from the couch into the kitchen, "Hey boo, I got something to handle right quick. Where dem lips at?" He stands up to prepare to leave, and a beautiful five-foot-six redbone sista with the curves of a California freeway bolts out of the kitchen. Makala puts her left arm around his neck and moves her right hand down to squeeze his manhood. She then stands on her tiptoes to give him a deep but short kiss. When he pulls away, he smiles and says, "I'll see you in a few days, boo. You need anything?"

"I just grabbed it," she says flirtatiously.

"Then we'll be back," KAP says, kissing her again. Then he pauses and replies, "In a few days." She pouts and crosses her arms in disappointment as he heads for the front door. He hops in his GMC Yukon Denali, and soon, he arrives at Courtney's house. He reaches under his seat and pulls out a Glock 45, then lifts his butt up off the seat, pulls up his shirt in the back, and tucks the gun into his waistband at the small of his back. He opens the car door and steps out quickly, scanning the area before he shuts the door. He then fixes his shirt, hits the car alarm, and heads for the door.

Courtney sees him coming up the walkway and opens the door just as he reaches it. As soon as he walks in, she shuts the door and starts speaking in a panic. He puts his right index finger over her mouth, and she instantly goes silent. He then grabs the side of her face with his left hand, leans in close to her ear, and says calmly, "Take a deep breath. Where are the twins?" She's shook, but she follows his instructions.

"They're at my momma's."

KAP grabs her hand and says, "Come over here and sit down and tell me in detail what happened." She sits down on the couch and explains what transpired with Kolax. KAP sighs and responds, "When you started snapping on him about his questioning, he was looking for that kink in your armor. You gave it to him. He is a murderer! You hear his name all in these streets, and you bucking up to him?! Yo lil ass think you tough." He grabs her chin and twists her head to the right to look at her left cheek.

"The hole is right there."

"What hole?" Courtney asks.

"That little hole he slapped your soul through."

She knocks his hand down, irritated from the pain, and she replies, "Shut up! Shit!"

KAP smiles and continues, "Listen, I need you to lay low and chill out. In fact, go stay at your mom's until this thing cools down.

You've made it difficult for me to come here because now they watching you." He kisses her and tells her again to get to her mom's house and to call him when she's settled there. "I got you baby." She smiles and nods, feeling assured that he will protect her. They both stand up simultaneously, he wraps his right arm around her waist, and grabs her ass. With his free hand, he gently rubs her bruised cheek and says, "I'll see you in a few days," and then kisses her on the forehead. As he heads to the front door, he quickly glances at two college applications for Howard University on the end table. He doesn't give her any notice that he's seen them and doesn't break his stride as he leaves and closes the door behind him.

KAP scans the neighborhood again as he walks back to his SUV. He opens the door, removes his gun, and climbs inside. He places his weapon on his lap and pushes the ignition button. Before driving off, he rests his head on the steering wheel knowing that there's a possibility that Kolax saw him there. This could possibly give H2H a clue that Sheldon's disappearance was a hit orchestrated by Richie. Debating if he should tell Richie or not, KAP lifts his head and drives off angrily, knowing this could be a possible problem in the very near future.

As KAP stops at the red light on 87th Street and Martin Luther King, Jr. Drive, he hears police sirens coming up behind him, getting louder and louder. He puts his weapon under his seat and turns his music down, then he looks to his right and sees eight cop cars, three of which are unmarked, speeding east down 87th Street. He makes a right once everything's clear, wondering where they were headed. The cops turn left on St. Lawrence through a red light and pick up speed heading north and then make another right two blocks later. When they arrive, the neighborhood kids are standing around taking videos and photos of a dead body lying naked in the middle of the court at Pirie Park.

The patrol cops secure the crime scene while asking bystanders questions, and news crews and other unmarked cars pull as close to the yellow tape as possible. A tent is set up to cover the body from the public's view. Chief of Detectives Ronnie Watkins arrives on scene and exits his car wearing a dark gray tailored suit. He heads over to the tent, and everyone briefly stops when they notice him. Standing at five foot ten with a sturdy build, his presence demands attention in any room he walks into.

Detective Brian Coles greets Chief Watkins outside the doors of the tent. He's the lead detective in the department and Chief Watkins's best detective. He's a six-foot, light-skinned, clean-shaven brother with freckles who always keeps a nice faded hairstyle. As a patrolman, he had an athletic, slim build. However, after making detective, he spends a lot more time behind a desk, and his pot belly shows it.

Glad to see you here," says Chief Watkins. "What's the story inside the tent?"

In admiration, Detective Coles responds, "Chief, before we go inside, I would like to introduce you to our brand-new detectives who were recently promoted from the 6th Precinct. Detective Leon Russell and Detective Fred Neeley." They all shake hands as they head inside the tent and proceed briefing the chief on the situation.

"Sir, we have a young black male, age twenty-seven, birth date is…" Detective Coles pauses, looks up at the top of the tent, and closes his eyes to help him gather information on the victim. "October 26. Address is 8927 S. St. Lawrence, and his name is…" Coles snaps his finger once, then remembers, "Jamal Thomas."

The chief furrows his eyebrows trying to figure how this information can be so readily available. He asks, "And the victim was found naked at the scene, correct?"

"Yes, sir."

"Well Brian, I've always been amazed by your work. But today, you're a certified genius to have this information so fast."

"Not quite, Chief." Detective Coles hands Chief Watkins a zip lock bag with Jamal's driver's license inside. "Whoever did this wanted us to know who he was. His driver's license was found on the body."

Chief Watkins smiles and says, "You shouldn't have revealed your source; you nearly got promoted." Everyone smiles. Chief scans the body and the surrounding areas. "May I?" Chief Watkins asks.

"Sure," responds Detective Coles as he gestures respectfully and gives him the stage.

"This was someone who knew Jamal. Knew him well. Does Jamal have any priors?"

Detective Coles replies, "Not that I'm aware of, sir."

Chief Watkins continues, "To be able to put a single shot dead center in his forehead, Jamal had to have been comfortable being in the killer's presence. Stripping him naked and putting him on the court for everyone to see… Whoever did this or ordered this was sending a message. Look around the perimeter and see if you can find any footprints leading to this spot. I believe this was a one man carry, so if there are multiple footprints, look at the one that sunk in the deepest. Depending on the depth and the size, it can help determine the weight of the guy carrying Jamal. We can run it against our database and see what we come up with. I believe this person is in our system. You have to have huge balls to carry a body midcourt, unless you just that smart or that feared."

Chief Watkins looks at the new detectives and says, "You're going to learn a lot from this genius," as he heads out of the tent.

"I believe so, sir. Detective Coles has taught us a lot," says Detective Neeley with an attempt to brownnose.

Chief Watkins turns around, stares at Detective Neeley with disdain, and says, "I was talking about me." He then looks at Detective Coles, winks, smiles, and heads over to the news people to give a statement.

A patrolman opens the yellow tape to let the chief out of the perimeter. The news folks immediately rush to him with microphones and tape recorders ready to ask questions.

"Chief! Chief! Chief! Chief…" yells numerous reporters simultaneously.

Chief Watkins says, "I'll answer two questions, then I have to go. Go ahead, Susan."

Susan clears her throat and pushes her microphone forward. "Do you know who the victim is?"

"He is a young black male around twenty-seven years of age. That's all we have at this time."

"Chief," John from Channel 7 interjects, "Was this a murder and are there any suspects at this time?"

"We believe it to be a murder as well as sending a message. My detectives are on the case and will have more information within the hour. They are very good at what they do, and we will get to the bottom of this immediately. Thank you for your time." The chief walks away from the reporters, and the patrol officers make a clear path for him to his car. He gets inside his car and heads downtown to give the First Deputy Superintendent an update.

* * *

It's the morning of December 31st, and Richie is walking Zuri to the door. He kisses her on the lips, tells her he'll see her later, and watches her walk and get onto the elevator. She turns around and blows him a kiss, and he stands there watching until her body disappears behind the elevator doors. He closes his door and heads back to his bedroom, grabs his phone, and texts Damawi to confirm the Belize trip, ensuring all travelers were good to go and there are no issues. She replies: "Everyone is squared away ready for travel, and there were absolutely no issues."

He responds:"Great, see you tonight."

* * *

Still at Pirie Park, detectives Coles, Neeley, and Russell are looking for more evidence to help identify a possible suspect. Detective Coles asks Detective Russell, "Has the next of kin been notified of Jamal's death?"

"Yes. His mom is currently admitted at Michael Reese Hospital, and death is knocking at her door. Stage IV breast cancer, and I assure you this did not help her situation whatsoever."

"Aww, that's fucked up," replies Detective Coles.

Detective Russell continues, "We found footprints, which gave us a shoe size and possible height, and the depth from the print would make the person overweight, which supports the chief's theory that Jamal was carried. Leaving his driver's license on the body is pretty bold."

Detective Neeley eagerly chimes in trying to connect some dots. "About a year, year and a half ago, when I was working at the 6th, we had a guy that would call the dispatch and leave multiple messages on where we could find the body."

"Really, Fred?" asks Detective Coles. "What would he tell the dispatchers?"

"Um, well..."

"Fred, spit it out."

"Well, he would call dispatch and then say 'Come get this nigga!' and leave us the address."

Detective Russell, now curious, asks, "Then what?"

Detective Coles speaks with extreme confidence knowing the answer to Detective Russell's question. "My guess is...we'd go get that nigga at the address he left us."

Detective Russell chuckles. "If this is the same guy, I'm starting to figure out his personality." Detective Coles rubs his chin, figuring things out in his mind, while Neeley and Russell await a teaching moment from their mentor.

"He's the type of guy that would meet him a nice clean virgin. Beautiful girl! Take her out, wine and dine her, give her flowers. Bust out all the chivalry, and when he puts in enough time to finally be in the position to take her virginity, he goes and rents an expensive hotel suite. Top floor! California King bed and Jacuzzi. Takes her there, have flowers and champagne waiting in the room…" Detective Coles closes his eyes and tilts his head up toward the sky while rocking back and forth. "Kisses her softly, slowly removing her clothes and his. Gets her naked. Lies her on the bed oh so gently ready for the missionary position. Then aggressively flips her over and fucks her in the ass." Neeley and Russell look at each other, baffled and confused, trying to figure out the message and logic to his story.

"Detectives, get those recordings. I believe there's a connection," commands Detective Coles. They walk back together to their unmarked patrol car. Detective Coles stands at the front passenger door and asks Detective Neeley, "Do you like using the n-word, Detective?"

"Absolutely not, Detective," replies Detective Neeley sternly.

Conjuring up his best impersonation of Denzel Washington in *Training Day*, Detective Coles replies, "Myy Nigga," and gets inside the car. Neeley looks at Russell and finds him smiling wide. They all enter the car and head back to the station.

* * *

In one of H2H's conference rooms, Spree is telling Maurice his plans for New Years and how excited he is to head to Vegas and take a few days to just kick it and gamble some. Kolax walks up the stairs and sits at the table.

"Ko, you handle that?" asks Maurice.

"Yeah. The cops came and got him yesterday, B. Done deal."

"No phone call, right?"

"Nah, no calls." Kolax kept leaving Jamal's driver's license in his mouth to himself.

"What about the person he stopped doing what he was supposed to be doing?" Kolax didn't answer. He looked over at Spree, waiting for him to intervene and speak up.

Spree spoke up, hoping Maurice would show mercy. "He went to go check on his moms at the hospital. She sick. Stage IV breast cancer."

Pissed and irritated by Spree's news, Maurice responds, "Ion give a fuck what stage she on. I got niggas waiting on me to produce. I got they money, no package, and I don't have a clue where the fuck my merchandise is. Spree, it's on you. Get it done." Spree looks irritated and uncomfortable, but he agrees to take care of it before he heads out to spend time with his people.

"No word from Sheldon?" asks Maurice.

"Nobody has seen this dude?!" yells Kolax. "Nobody?!"

Maurice leans back in his chair, rubbing his chest. "Those college applications got me thinking. Sheldon can't afford that shit on what we give him. It's only one nigga I know who be out here giving out college scholarships and saving the world and all that shit. I'm convinced that clean-cut nigga and his corporate, military, fake ass gangsters is wrapped all up in this shit. I'd put money on that. Ko, we got somewhere to be tonight. Let's meet up just before midnight and head north. Dress nicely."

CHAPTER 3

It's the night of the comedy show, and the doors are about to open for guests. Richie has just arrived at The Chicago Theatre in Downtown Chicago. Visible from blocks away, the theatre's marquee reads: "Swaggazine Entertainment Presents The NYE All-Star Comedy Show hosted by Ric "Always Ready" Johnson, featuring: Timmy "The Punk Ass Cop" Hall, Big Sean Larkins, & Micah Bam-Bamm White." Seeing his name in bright lights never gets old.

Richie walks under the marquee and heads to the front doors, maneuvering through the crowd waiting in line for the show. The usher recognizes him, opens the door from inside the theatre, and says, "Mr. Swaggazine!" Richie responds with a head nod and pats the usher's shoulder. As many times as he has pierced the doors of this place, he never ceases to be amazed at the beauty of it; it's breathtaking. He stops just after the front doors to admire the architectural work of the historic Chicago landmark. Richie then heads over to the massive annex room where a cocktail reception will be held for patrons to take photos with the comedians after the show. He walks around to take a quick look at the booths for fifteen black-owned business sponsors who are showcasing their merchandise, which includes everything from African art, clothing, jewelry, artifacts, hair care products, and herbal supplements. There are also black investment companies, banks, and real estate investors who are ready to provide information and educate people on the importance of circulating the black dollar within the community.

Richie continues inside the auditorium. He enters and glances up at the ceiling lighting arrangement that perfectly illuminates the rows and rows of seats. Beneath the large stage is an oversized orchestra pit where the DJ is setting up to entertain guests before the show starts. Richie sees Damawi directing the theatre's staff to ensure the show flows as usual.

"D, what's goodie?" Richie asks, giving her a firm hug and a kiss on the check.

She looks at him infatuated. "Hey, Richie. Everything is going great!! The comedians are in the back relaxing, waiting for show time. Doors open in five minutes, and I expect we will have a full house by 6:45 p.m. We should be able to start the show exactly at 7 p.m."

"Cool. I'm going to head backstage to talk with my peoples. You need anything from me?"

"I do not. You and the crew are sitting in the same place as always." Richie heads backstage to talk with the comedians until showtime.

* * *

Spree pulls into the parking lot at Michael Reese Hospital and parks near the entrance. Before getting out of the car, he picks up his gun from the passenger seat, checks that it's loaded, and puts it in the glove box next to his switchblade. He gets out of the car and stands next to it to smoke a cigarette. He inhales deeply on the cigarette, then exhales; the Chicago wind pushes the smoke past the left side of his face.

Still smoking, Spree walks toward the entrance of the hospital. His anxiety is running high, and he feels his heart pounding in his chest. He's trying to play out in his mind how this will go once he's in the room facing her. A few steps before he walks through the entrance, he takes a long drag off the cigarette and flicks it into the bushes next to the automatic sliding doors. He walks in and goes to the reception desk.

"Can you tell me what room Ms. Evelyn Thomas is in?"

"Room 626. Take the elevator to the right, get off on the sixth floor, and the room is down the hallway on the left."

Spree replies, "Thank you," and heads toward the elevator.

* * *

It's showtime, and The Chicago Theatre is packed. Thousands of people are seated and waiting for the show to start. Richie's crew is seated in the front row, and Richie is backstage conversing with the comedians before taking his seat.

"I remember that show in Hawaii, man. That was my third show there and still the best one. Crazy to think that was ten years ago," says Richie reminiscing.

"It was a great show," says Micah "Bam-Bamm" White. "That was a 600 seat college theater. We've all grown over these last ten years and look at us now."

"Now we packing 3,500 seats," says Big Sean Larkins.

"For both shows," says Timmy Hall. "Thanks for having us to bring the New Year in with you."

"No doubt," says Richie. "Well, aight fellas, do what you do. It's showtime. One of my people will show you where you'll take photos with your fans after."

Richie heads to his seat in the front row with his crew. When the DJ spots him walking toward his seat, he stops playing music, indicating to the crowd that the show is about to start. His crew stands up as he walks past them, and they all sit down together as if it was synchronized. It's three minutes past 7 p.m. when Richie takes his seat. Once they're settled, the lights dim in the theatre, and the DJ resumes playing music. The DJ yells over the microphone, "Swaggazine Entertainment is in the house!!!! Give it up for our host, comedian Ric "Always Ready" Johnson!!" The crowd screams as the first comedian comes onto the stage.

* * *

The elevator arrives on the sixth floor, and Spree gets off the elevator and makes a right toward Ms. Thomas's room. Not many people are there visiting on New Year's Eve. Every hospital room he walks by, he only sees the foot of the bed or curtains swaying back and forth. He reads aloud the room numbers as he passes them, "620…622…624..." and then stops right outside the doorway of 626. He peeks into the room just enough to see a pair of feet pointed toward the ceiling. He listens intently just outside the room and hears only the rhythmic hissing of the ventilator and the beeping from the heart rate monitor. He takes a deep breath and walks through the doorway. The room glows a medium red tone caused by the dimmed overhead lights and the lights from the machines.

He walks slowly to the foot of the bed and stares at Ms. Thomas, who's wearing an oxygen mask. She's in the room by herself. Her hair and eyebrows are completely gone, her skin looks burned from radiation, and she weighs less than half of what he remembers. She was a large woman, very stern, caring, and a great teacher. The sound of Spree unzipping his coat makes her open her eyes. Their eyes meet, and he can see in her eyes that she's trying to recognize who's standing in front of her. She slowly reaches up to remove her oxygen mask. Struggling, she slowly removes it and questions, "Nathaniel?" Her voice is weak and feeble.

"Ms. Thomas, you still remember me?"

"Yes. I always remember my best students." Shocked that she remembers him, Spree begins to feel sadness overtake him as he remembers what he once was before the streets took everything innocent from him.

"That was a long time ago. I wish we could have reconnected under different circumstances, Ms. Thomas."

"Nathaniel, do you know what happened to my son?"

"No ma'am. I do not."

Saddened by his response, she replies, "I wish I could see my baby."

She coughs sporadically, but then it quickly gets out of control. One of the night nurses walks in.

"Ms. Thomas, why did you remove your mask?" As the nurse reaches for the oxygen mask, Spree immediately recognizes her.

"Kimberly?"

The nurse looks at Spree. "Oh my God, Nathaniel!" She puts the mask back on Ms. Thomas and checks her vitals before she walks over to Spree and hugs him.

"I haven't seen you since I left Pirie in the seventh grade. How have you been?"

"I been chillin," Spree replies. Gesturing toward the door, he asks, "Can I talk to you outside for a minute?" Kim follows him a few steps outside Ms. Thomas's doorway.

"So, how's she doing?"

"Not good. She was okay at one point, but the news about Jamal really took a toll on her. The doctors gave her less than a day or so before she passes. What are you doing here?"

"Just paying my respects, you know?"

"That is so nice of you to come. She doesn't have anyone. Jamal would come up here nearly every day and spend hours with her just holding her hand." Spree looks back into Ms. Thomas's room.

"I have other patients to check on, so if you need me, just press the red button on the wall next to the ventilator. It was so good seeing you." Kim walks away to tend to other patients. Spree walks back into the room, grabs the chair next to the bed, and takes a seat. He grabs Ms. Thomas's hand, and their eyes meet. The sounds of the ventilator and the heart rate monitor pierce the silence in the room.

* * *

Ric Johnson has finished his set, and Timmy Hall takes the stage. Sitting to the right of Richie is T.K., his right-hand man who's in charge of logistics. He always sits to the right of Richie, signifying their strong bond. Richie met T.K. midway through his military career in a Logistics Functions class on learning how to move supplies from the US to austere environments, war zones, and any places where the US logistics footprint was nonexistent. It was a very intense class with a failure rate of nearly eighty percent. T.K. never took one single note and would actually be day trading during class. For the final, the students had to showcase their skills in front of the class, showing their total logistics methods. Richie had been watching T.K. throughout the class and was eager to see if he would pass. He did. The instructors said his presentation was the best logistics networking and planning they had ever seen. Richie wondered, "Who the fuck is this dude?!"

Richie leans over to T.K. and asks, "So, you ready for Belize, T.K.?"

"Yes, bro. You know how much I love Belize. Nice women, nice weather. I'm staying there an extra couple of days after you leave."

"Nice. Well deserved. You should shoot over to Caye Caulker and stay at this beautiful resort by the beach. I can't remember the name, but I'll get it for you before we get there." Richie pauses to listen to Timmy Hall. "Hey, I've heard Timmy tell this joke a thousand times, and it's still funny as hell to me. Listen to this."

"There's a big difference between black cops and white cops. White cops love they fucking job. Dispatch calls a White cop, like squad car 1143… (He imitates a dispatcher's voice over the radio) '1143…We have a Black male' (He makes the sound of the feedback from the radio) '10-4, we're already there.' Not a Black cop. Dispatch be like, '1143… 1143… 1143… 1143.' Dispatch gotta call that nigga cell phone," Timmy puts the microphone to his ear like the Black cop is answering his cellphone. "Hello… This is dispatch. Answer your fucking radio!" The crowd erupts in laughter, and Richie and T.K. laugh at the joke, rocking back and forth in their chairs and relishing in the entertainment and energy from the crowd.

* * *

Nearly an hour passes before Spree finally releases Ms. Thomas's hand. He leans slightly closer to her and whispers, "I'll be back, Ms. Thomas." He gets up and heads to the lobby to stretch his legs and take a break from the inevitable. He walks into the bathroom, urinates, and goes to the sink to wash his hands. He pauses to look in the mirror, and he thinks about his mom and how he wishes he would've known more about her. She was a drug addict and alcoholic who would disappear for days, sometimes months at a time without any concern for him or his siblings. He would give anything to be able to sit at his mother's bedside and hold her hand while she slowly transitioned to the next life, knowing he had a relationship with her.

But he never had the chance. She was found dead from alcohol poisoning the summer before his fifth grade year. Ms. Thomas was a huge factor in his life during that time, and she was like a second mom to him for that year. He feels bad now knowing there was nothing he could've done for Jamal; his fate was unavoidable when he dishonored his responsibilities. The best Spree could do was to take Jamal's place by being there as Ms. Thomas takes her journey to the afterlife.

Spree looks away from the mirror and washes his hands. He then snatches a paper towel from the automatic dispenser, dries his hands, and tosses the used paper towel into the wastebasket. He walks out of the restroom and heads back to room 626.

* * *

The DJ plays Timmy's exit music, and Timmy receives a standing ovation from the crowd as he walks offstage. The crowd is hyped and ready for the next comedian to hit the stage. Ric takes the stage again to announce the next comedian, Big Sean Larkins. Richie turns around and looks at the crowd, pleased with the turnout. He can't wait to celebrate later at Josephine's with his business family. He turns his attention from the crowd and looks to his left at his family. The Belize crew is on the far end: Arielle, Ren, and Kay. Then there's KAP, Tech, Damawi, Brick, and T.K. He smiles, knowing that he has a team that is on one accord with making money from legit businesses and not so legit businesses. His whole team is committed to bettering themselves, the community, and the people around them.

Richie looks back toward the stage as the curtains open up, and Big Sean Larkins walks out to the center of the stage. He walks up to Ric and gives him a hug and a pat on his back. Ric then hands him the mic, and Big Sean Larkins is ready to take the crowd to another level of laughter and entertainment.

* * *

At the 6th Precinct, Detective Leon Russell has been searching the police database for anyone who fits the height and weight of the possible suspects. He figures it shouldn't be hard to find a 6'5"/6'6", 265-pound Black male in the system. The database pulls up thirty-two possible suspects who fit the description. Detective Fred Neeley walks over to Leon's desk and sits in the empty chair next to it.

"Hey Leon, listen to this." Detective Neeley plays a voice recording on his phone of a person calling dispatch to report where to pick up a body.

"911 dispatch, what's your emergency?"

A Black man's deep voice comes through the cell phone's speaker. "Come get this nigga at 8823 South St. Lawrence." The sound of the phone hanging up and the dial tone quickly follow.

"I have about nine other recordings just like this. Of the ten victims we got calls for, only one of the ten was a female. Same deep voice. No real emotion behind it. Same areas located in Chatham," says Detective Neeley.

"We need to find out who the victims are so we can cross-reference the areas, find any relationship to one another, any known associates, how they were murdered— How you know one was a female?"

Detective Neeley pokes out his chest and says in a deep voice, impersonating a Black man, "Come get this bitch!" They smile for a quick second, but then realize they have a lot of work to do to catch this guy.

Detective Neeley leaves and heads to the file room. He comes back over to Detective Russell's desk an hour later with all the victims' files connected to the murders that were called into dispatch. He tosses all the files on Russell's desk and says, "Let's find some kind of connection with these murders, then we can go through the database findings, examine everything, and present what we find to Coles."

"I'm with you, Fred. Seeing that we are the lowest ranking detectives on the totem pole working on New Year's Eve, apparently, we have all night." Both detectives are looking through the cases when they notice that all the victims were from the Chatham area and were all killed within three years of each other. Nine of the victims had gunshot wounds either in the head or the chest from the same caliber weapon, except for the female victim. She was strangled to death. All the victims except for two were involved with either gang activities or drugs.

Disappointed, Detective Neeley says, "I wonder why this wasn't identified earlier. These ten murders have been within a three-year time frame. The oldest from 2019."

"Hmmm," says Detective Russell looking up at the ceiling, trying to recall the reason for the lack of oversight. "I remember the department was going through some corruption cases back then. Internal Affairs was crawling up the ass of the entire precinct. Cops were getting suspended, fired, and a few went to jail behind the investigation. I don't think the people here were focused... People were hiding for the hills and trying to protect their necks. Let's see where this goes."

* * *

The first comedy show is over, and the comedians are in the reception room taking photos with their fans and enjoying the moment. Security is escorting the rest of the people out of the theatre while the ushers are handing out flyers for the New Year's Eve party at Club Josephine's. Richie and the crew are standing around talking when Damawi walks up to Richie. She tells him she is heading to the club, and her assistant Gina will take care of things for the second show. Richie gives a signal to Brick, and he escorts Damawi to her car. After the comedians are done with the photos, Richie walks backstage with them to the lounge area to relax for a few moments and talk business until the next show. They all sit together at a table where plates of grilled chicken, mac and cheese, and asparagus await them with some wine and water.

"I really miss doing your shows, Richie," says Bam-Bamm.

While admiring his food, Richie responds, "Me too. You my guys." Then he looks up and glances at each of the comedians around the table. "So, listen. You guys have your careers; all three of you came a long way and are doing quite well. It's time to expand y'all platforms and open some businesses in y'all communities or wherever. We can open private schools, youth centers, rehab centers, strip malls… Laughter is always good for people who have stressful lives. You give them an avenue to forget whatever it is they battling. I think it's time to give back to a community that can't necessarily afford to purchase a ticket to see you guys perform."

Timmy chimes in, "We have the names, but not the resources to start those businesses." Richie cuts in to kill any chance of negative energy taking over the conversation.

"I have the resources; I just need your fame. That'll help push the initiative. Maybe by you supporting your communities, other entertainers from our generation will follow suit." Sean looks amazed that Richie's mindset hasn't changed from ten years ago.

"You been talking like this for as long as I've known you. I'm with it." They all agree to have further conversations about pursuing this.

"I'll be in touch after the New Year. I'm heading to the club after the show starts, so I'll see you guys at the after party." Gina walks in while he's shaking their hands and heads out. "If you need anything, Gina is your contact."

* * *

Spree is sitting next to Ms. Thomas with his head lying on the side of her bed. He's drifting in and out of sleep, still holding her hand. He looks up at Ms. Thomas, who is in so much pain. Her pulse is slower than it was when he first got there, and this worries him. He reaches behind the ventilator and presses the red button to alert Nurse Kim. Within seconds, Kim comes into the room.

"Hi Nathaniel, what's wrong?"

"Is there anything you can do for her? She's in a lot of pain."

"Let me see…" Kim picks up Ms. Thomas's chart and looks at it. "Unfortunately, I'm afraid not. Her time is near. We can start a morphine drip to make her comfortable, but that will speed up the process."

"At least she'll be pain free."

"Well, I'll ask the doctor." Turning to Ms. Thomas, Kim asks, "Ms. Thomas, can you hear me?" Ms. Thomas moves her head slightly, and her eyebrows jump at the sound of her name. "Let me go find the doctor. I'll be back."

Kim leaves the room, and Spree walks over and stands at the foot of Ms. Thomas's bed. He gently grabs her feet, closes his eyes, and looks down. He then takes a deep breath and calls out, "Ms. Thomas!" Her eyebrows jump again. He continues, "Jamal was a good dude. Sometimes, with not having a father, the streets fill that void. We're the same in that way. What happened to him was he left the streets to see about someone he loved dearly, and he left his responsibilities to someone who wasn't as responsible. I couldn't stop it...even if I wanted to. That's what happened to Jah, and for that, I'm sorry. He didn't deserve that. If it was up to me, he would be right here beside you, holding your hand. He's waiting for you in heaven I'm sure. Thank you for being that mom for me. Thank you for caring."

He pauses, opens his eyes, and looks up at Ms. Thomas to see tears rolling down both sides of her face. He quickly closes his eyes to catch his tears, and he lowers his head again and says with a thinning voice, "Jamal was lucky to have you in his life." After a few seconds, he looks up again, turns his head toward the doorway, and sees Kim clutching her clipboard as a tear rolls off her cheek. She walks in closer and says, "The doctor will be here in about ten minutes."

"Thank you, Kim." She smiles, wipes the tear from her cheek, and looks at Ms. Thomas before she leaves. Spree is sitting next to the bed when the doctor walks into Ms. Thomas's room.

"Hello, young man, I'm Dr. Edmond Payne, the night doctor. How are you?"

"I'm good, Doc."

Dr. Payne looks through Ms. Thomas's file and asks, "Are you Jamal?"

Without hesitation and with a sense of pride, Spree responds, "Yes, I am. What's the problem, Doc?"

"I'm just checking her file. You are aware that she has elected a DNR order?"

"Um no, what is that?"

"DNR is do-not-resuscitate, meaning if her heart stops, she wants to be allowed a natural death. No CPR or any medical interventions. As her son, you are the proxy, the decision maker."

"I understand," says Spree sadly. "She's in pain, so I was wondering if there's something that could ease that? I don't want her to feel pain when she goes."

"We can start her with morphine. It will expedite her transition. Do you understand, and are you okay with that?"

"I do, and I'm okay with it."

"Okay. We'll get it going. My nurses will take care of everything." Dr. Payne pats Spree on his shoulder, then squeezes it with a look of sympathy on his face before he slowly walks out of the room.

* * *

Richie and Brick are nearly a block away from Josephine's for the after party. Security has already made a way for his car to park in one of the owners' spots by the entrance. He hears music playing as he pulls his BMW 750Li into the parking spot. As soon as he parks and shuts the car off, security opens their doors, and Richie and Brick step out of the vehicle. There's a line of people wrapped around the building waiting to get inside. It's 36 degrees in Chicago, and there are ten heat blowers lined up every ten feet, blowing hot air on the party goers awaiting to enter the club. This was something special to take care of the patrons in that way without his knowledge. He looks at Brick, shakes his head, and says with a smile, "She's a beast." Security escorts them to the door.

When security opens the massive entrance to the club, the base and the vocals of old school hip-hop and R&B music flows past Richie and Brick as if it's infused with the wind. The inside of the club is dark, but the flickering soft blue lights coming from the dance floor and the ceiling provide some visibility inside. The club is packed. As they travel around the right side of the club, they notice that all the loveseats and couches are taken. Some people are sitting on the laps of others, people watching, drinking, and having a great time. The bar against the wall has a line wrapped nearly around the entire first floor. All the bar stools are taken, so people are reaching over others trying to purchase drinks.

Security is wearing all-black suits and small earpieces for communication in case problems occur. The bartenders are all wearing money-green shirts. The waiters and waitresses are all in burgundy. VIP members and frequent club visitors are wearing wristbands that automatically charge their bank accounts when they purchase food and drinks and when they enter the club.

The dance floor on the second and third levels is made of thick glass with a dim blue light glowing throughout the floor. You can see the bottom of shoes and under dresses and skirts from the floor beneath. Security leads Richie and Brick to the elevators, which are also made of glass, and they give patrons visibility of the entire club at the top floor. When the doors open, they get in and take the elevator to the third floor. As the elevator passes the second floor, they hear Chicago house music playing through the elevator doors. The second floor is packed as well, just like the first floor, but the waiters and waitresses are all wearing purple instead of burgundy.

When the elevator doors open on the third floor, the sound of a live Jazz band floods into the elevator. Richie and Brick step out of the elevator and watch the dancers who are Chicago-style stepping all over the dance floor. The waitresses and waiters on this level are wearing red, and the party goers are outfitted with suits and dresses, stepping in the name of love. Brick and Richie head over to the party room where the whole crew is eating, drinking, and talking amongst each other. Brick opens the door to the room and holds it open for Richie to walk in. Everyone stands up to greet him as he makes his way to his seat at the head of the table.

* * *

Kolax pulls up to the front of H2H's office building at 11:20 p.m. Maurice gets out of his car and walks over to the Kolax's Cadillac Escalade, and Kolax opens the door to the passenger side. Maurice hops into the SUV and says, "What's up, Ko?"

"Where to?" Kolax asks.

"Let's head down to Club Josephine's. I got a few questions I need answered. You heard from Spree?"

"I texted him earlier. He was headed to the hospital." Maurice doesn't respond. He takes his weapon out of his coat pocket and opens the glove box. He sees Kolax's gun in there, so he closes it back, opens the armrest, and places his gun inside. Kolax pulls off and heads north to Club Josephine's.

* * *

Ms. Thomas has stopped responding to her name being called. She is minutes away from her last breath. Spree watches her with high anxiety, thinking about his life choices and how he hopes to do things differently in the future. He holds Ms. Thomas's hand, and it's not as warm as it once was. He wants to let her hand go because he's afraid of being in contact with death, but since he wasn't there for his mom, he continues to hold onto her. Gently rubbing the back of her hand with his thumb and resting his forehead on the side of the bed, he remains silent at Ms. Thomas's side.

* * *

It's 11:45 p.m., and Richie stands at the podium to speak to his organization before the New Year starts. He taps the microphone, and a thumping sound echoes throughout the room. "Can I get everyone's attention for a moment?" The room goes silent. "I'm not going to take up too much time. I know you want to party, eat, and call your peoples for the New Year, so I'll keep this short. But before I go on, I'd like to give a special thanks to D and her staff for coordinating everything tonight from the comedy show to the after party. Great job!" Everyone claps and whistles for a few moments. The waiters and waitresses are filling champagne glasses with Roederer Cristal Brut Champagne, which is $4,000 per bottle. "This has been a great year for us. We've all grown as people, businessmen and women, financially, and have helped the community a great deal. This year is special to me because the same faces that were here last year are still here today." Richie pauses as he gets choked up a bit. "I never believed in giving our organization a name, but I will tonight. It'll never go on any documents because we don't need documentation to tell us who we are. But what we are is a group of like-minded, common-goaled people working in secret to be the best for our families, each other, and our communities." Richie stops to look at his watch and sees that it's about thirty seconds before midnight.

"Raise your glasses to the Quiet Professionals!"

Everyone in the room raises their glasses and repeats, "Quiet Professionals!" Then they clink their glasses together.

"Everyone, please stand up and count down with me into the New Year!"

The room yells in unison, "10!"

Maurice and Kolax pull into Josephine's parking lot.

"9!"

Richie scans the room, meeting eyes with everyone and smiling wide, appreciative of the hard work and dedication from everyone.

"8!"

The pathologist at Michael Reese Hospital tucks Jamal's arms inside the body bag.

"7!"

"6!"

The Quiet Professionals look through the glass walls of the party room to view the crowd as they're counting down too.

"5!"

"4!"

Jamal's face disappears as the zipper moves past his head, and the body bag encases his body.

"3!"

Brick receives a text from the outside security: "Maurice and Kolax have just pulled into the parking lot."

"2!"

Detective Leon Russell is looking down at the thirty-two files of possible suspects for the murder of Jamal Thomas and the dispatch killer; the file on top shows the photo and full name of the primary suspect: Kolax Adongo Imanu.

"1!"

At 11:59:59 p.m., Evelyn Thomas, age 63, transitions to the afterlife, leaving behind her newfound son, Nathaniel "Spree" Green.

"Happy New Year!"

Brick walks over to Richie and hands him the phone so he can read the text message from security. Richie reads it, thinks for a second, and replies: "Show them up." He gives Brick back his phone, and Brick reads Richie's response and mentally gets into defense mode. Richie walks back over to behind the podium with

Brick close by his side, leans into the microphone, and asks everyone to please take their seats. "We have an important visitor that will be here shortly. Is everyone enjoying themselves? We still have enough champagne for everyone?" Everyone is checking each other's glasses, bottles, and what's left on the rack, reporting that they're good to go.

Brick taps Richie's lower back. Richie looks over toward the glass wall and sees security, Maurice, and Kolax just outside the door. The door opens, and they walk in with security behind them. The Quiet Professionals know of Maurice Handley. He started with stealing cars, then he worked his way up to robbing jewelry stores and drug dealers, pimping out prostitutes, engaging in identity theft, and pushing counterfeit money all over the Midwest.

"Everyone, we have a guest: Mr. Maurice Handley." Maurice looks bewildered, wondering why he's getting such a warm welcome into Richie's organization. "As you can see, we're still doing great things for the community. Just as soon as Mr. Handley walked into the room and the doors closed behind him, crime in Chicago went down thirty percent." Everyone laughs, but Maurice looks irritated from being ridiculed. Richie moves from behind the podium and walks toward Maurice and Kolax. They move forward toward Richie, security right behind them. Brick is walking directly behind Richie. T.K. and KAP wait until Brick passes and then follow in line behind him. They stop about three feet away from each other, and Maurice speaks first, "That was cute. I see you still trying to be a comedian."

"A comedian? Me? Nah. I tried it. All the traveling, people looking in your face on stage, gotta be funny all the time." Richie shakes his head and continues, "Just wasn't for me. So, I decided to become a mogul. You came all this way for something. What can you do for me?" Maurice stares at Richie and his crew behind him.

"I see you got your corporate gangsters with you and the mute." Angered, Brick steps forward, and Kolax moves toward him as well. Richie reaches back and places his hand on Brick's chest to stop him.

"What do you want?" Richie asks in a stern voice.

"I'm looking for an associate of mine. Sheldon. Word on the street is that your people might know of his whereabouts."

"Sheldon's whereabouts?" Richie replies with a dumbfounded look. He looks back at his team to see if anyone could answer regarding Sheldon's whereabouts. "I don't think anyone here would know. See, we don't deal in counterfeit money. Right team?" T.K. and KAP both pull out stacks of money wrapped in rubber bands. "He wouldn't have no business around us. But I will do you a solid since we go way, way back. I'll send KAP over to inquire with his peoples. He got a lady or something?" Maurice doesn't answer. "I'll send KAP over to talk to her and see if—"

Maurice cuts Richie off. "You could put his kids through college?" Maurice's response shocks him, but Richie's poker face is strong.

With a smile, Richie responds, "Well, I was going to say to see what he can pull out of her. If something terrible has happened to him... you know I love the kids. I will make sure they land okay. Is there anything else you can do for me?" He didn't give him a chance to answer. "No, well, Happy New Year! Take one of those bottles of... T.K., what's the name of that champagne?"

T.K. responds, mean mugging Maurice, "Roederer Cristal Brut. And he can take that half a bottle right over there."

"Nah, I'm good. We'll be in touch." Both crews stare at each other for a second before Maurice and Kolax turn to walk out of the party room, followed by security.

* * *

Spree leaves the hospital saddened by the passing of Ms. Thomas. He returns to his car and starts it up, then he places his head on the steering wheel, thinking about his life and what he's done with it up until now. Nothing to be proud of. He wants to do better for himself, his family, and his little girl. He thinks about getting out of the life, maybe going back to school, and leaving the senseless murders behind. When his little girl gets old enough to understand, he wants her to be proud of him. He grabs his phone and texts Maurice: "That problem is a done deal," and then he heads home. He later pulls up to the front of his house thinking about his upcoming vacation, which will give him an opportunity to change his current situation. But until then, he reaches in his glove box and pulls out his gun, ensures that it's loaded, puts it in his coat pocket, and exits the car.

* * *

After Maurice and Kolax leave the room, Richie turns to KAP and asks, "When you leaving town?"

KAP, already knowing where Richie is going, replies, "Monday. I'll handle that business on the way out." Richie nods, then walks off with Damawi to her office to calculate the day's profit.

Maurice and Kolax get into Kolax's Escalade, and before they drive off, Maurice looks over at Kolax and asks, "What you think, Ko?"

"He got a good ass poker face. I thought the college shit would show us something. It didn't though."

"Oh, it did. You were looking at the wrong one. That muscle head ass nigga standing on the left of the mute. He showed me they involved. Let's go to Courtney's."

CHAPTER 4

Kolax and Maurice stop on the street just outside Courtney's house. Her window blinds are open, and the living room lights are on, giving them a clear view inside. They can see that no one is home, so they drive off slowly and head back to the office. Before they pick up speed, a burgundy Kia Telluride full of women passes them; Kolax slows down his Escalade and looks in the rearview mirror to see if the Kia will stop at Courtney's house. It stops. A woman wearing a short gold dress hops out of the back seat, then Courtney hops out wearing a long black fur coat and black stilettos. They briefly hug, and the woman wearing the gold dress hops back into the vehicle as Courtney runs to her front door. Kolax drives around the block and parks a few houses away from Courtney's place. Kolax and Maurice then get out of the SUV and walk over to her house.

Maurice knocks softly on the door. Courtney, already upstairs getting undressed, hears the knock and thinks aloud, "Sheila must want her coat back." She runs down the stairs and opens the door without looking through the peephole. Frightened, she sees Kolax and attempts to close the door. Kolax shoves his arm between the door and the frame and pushes his way in. The force pushes her back. Maurice and Kolax walk into the house and lock the door behind them.

"Is that how you treat your guests?" Maurice asks with a grin.

"What are you doing here?" Courtney asks terrified.

"You already know why we here."

"Listen, my daughters are upstairs sleeping. Whatever it is you want from me, we can discuss it later. Please don't do anything to wake…"

"Shut up, bitch!" yells Maurice. "Kolax," Maurice says, nodding toward the stairs. Kolax brushes past Courtney and goes upstairs to see if what she said was true. Maurice and Courtney wait in silence until Kolax returns. Kolax comes back into the living room and stands behind her. From the look on his face, Courtney knew she wouldn't live to see another day.

"Yo, ain't nobody up there!"

Maurice laughs and says, "Another lie. You on a roll like a muthafucka, you ole dice ass bitch. Keep playing these games, and I promise you dem lil look-a-like bitches won't see no fucking college."

In a panic, Courtney cries out, "Okay, Okay. All I know is…Sheldon was using that counterfeit money all over the place, and some guy came by asking about his whereabouts…"

"What guy?!"

"This huge black guy. He was really tall, like 6'7", 6'8", bald…"

"You lying, disloyal ass bitch! That nigga can't even talk!" Maurice rubs his right hand over his forehead and slowly down his face until he grabs his beard.

"Where's my package?"

"What package? I don't know about a package. If I knew, I would tell you. Please just…"

"Aight, aight, aight," replies Maurice.

"So, we good?" asks Courtney.

"Oh, we good," replies Maurice as he walks toward the window to close the blinds. "Correction: I'm good. Kolax is good. Your daughters… Well, Richie say he loves the kids, so they good too. But you, not so good." When he's finished closing the blinds, Maurice walks toward Courtney, but she walks backward away from him until she's suddenly stopped by Kolax's body.

"What are you gonna do? Please! I'll do anything! Just let me live! Please!" begs Courtney.

Maurice thinks for a second. "Nah."

* * *

It's the evening of New Year's Day, and KAP has just turned into the driveway at Audrey's house, another girlfriend of his. He puts the car in park and says, "Who was I with last night?"

"Me boo."

"What did we do?"

"You handled my business."

"That I did. What time is it now?"

"It's 8 p.m., boo."

"What time did I drop you off though?"

"9 p.m." KAP raises his chin, and Audrey tries again. "Umm, 10?"

"That's my girl." He leans over, grabs her chin, and kisses her deeply. With a soft, sexy voice, she asks, "When am I gonna see you again?"

"In a few days, baby. Got to go see my peoples." He unlocks the car doors, indicating that it's time for her to step out. She kisses him again and gets out. He waits until she gets inside her home before he pulls off.

KAP then heads over to Courtney's house to close the loop before heading to Cleveland. He wonders if he should've told Richie about the college applications and the possibility of Kolax seeing them. He shakes his head disappointed, and thinks, *It is what it is.* He hears his phone vibrate and sees a text from Brick: "Did you open your gift."

KAP pulls up to Courtney's house to see if she's home. He can see that the lights are on through her window blinds. He drives past a few more houses and parks. He reaches under his seat, grabs his gun with a silencer, and places it inside his coat. He texts Brick: "I'm opening it in a few. I'll let you know what I think about it." KAP reaches into his armrest, pulls out a ring of keys, and looks for the key with Courtney's name written on it. He slides the key off the ring and puts it in his pocket.

When KAP gets to the door, he twists the knob, and the door opens. *It's not like her to leave her door unlocked*, he thinks as he walks in and closes the door. He pulls out his weapon and calls out, "Baby, where you at?" He walks through the living room looking for Courtney when he sees a foot sticking out just past the living room couch. KAP yells, "Courtney!" and looks behind the couch. He sees her lying on her side, and kneels down to grab her and turn her onto her back. Rigor mortis was setting in, and her body was beginning to stiffen. Looking at her face, he sees her eyes and mouth still open. "Fuck!" Multiple emotions quickly fly through his mind. He was sad she was dead but happy he wasn't the one who had to do it. Although he used her as a pawn, he liked her feisty attitude in such a small frame.

KAP rolls Courtney's body back to how he found her, and he gets down on his hands and knees and tucks his weapon into his waistband at the middle of his back. He then removes his coat and pushes it over the floor to remove any of his footprints from the carpet. He continues to move backward over the floor until he gets to the door. Once he makes it to the door, he stands up and opens the door with his coat. He then wipes both sides of the doorknob with his coat before putting it back on. He flips his hoodie over his head and heads back to his Yukon. He immediately drives off while texting Brick: "Somebody already GOT this present for me."

About ten minutes later, KAP receives a call from an unknown number. He answers, "Who dis?"

"What's goodie?"

Relieved to hear Richie's voice, KAP responds, "I'm good. That shirt was already stained."

"I knew that was a possibility. Did you clean the area?"

"Yeah."

"Was it spotted?" Richie asks curiously.

"I don't think so. Should we get our cleaning service to handle that?"

"No, it wasn't our fault. Leave it be. Can somebody vouch for you saying that shirt came like that?"

"Fa sho."

"Sounds like we should get a refund."

"You got plenty of shirts in your closet. Enjoy the fam and tell moms I said Happy New Year."

"Will do. Enjoy your trip!"

* * *

Detective Coles returns to work from vacation to find Detective Russell working diligently to find Jamal's killer.

"Welcome back, Coles!"

"Thank you, Leon. What do you have for me?"

"Fred and I narrowed the suspects we gathered from the system. We initially had thirty-two possibles a couple days ago. We narrowed it down to five based on these facts." Detective Russell hands Detective Coles the files. "Seven of the thirty-two are deceased, ten are currently incarcerated here in the city or elsewhere, and four live in different states. Six of them fit the height and weight requirement but went to prison for nonviolent crimes, which leaves us with five suspects who went to prison for drug activity, violent crimes, or both. Looking at Jamal's juvenile records, which weren't in our system, he was charged with possession of a controlled substance when he was 16."

Detective Coles shuffles through the five files and says, "I'm not familiar with any of these mopes. I got your emails with your findings and the recordings on the dispatch caller. Very interesting. I'll talk with the chief and see if we can start surveilling these guys. Great work!"

"Detective, I have a question for you. Fred and I were discussing why those murders were never connected. Ten murders in a three-year time frame. Then I heard about IA conducting an investigation during that time. What happened?" Detective Coles looks around before speaking.

"What are you doing after work?"

"No plans," replies Detective Russell.

"Let me know when you're leaving for the day."

"Okay, boss."

Detective Coles heads to his office with the files under his arm.

* * *

Richie arrives at his condo in Belize, just four miles from the Port of Belize. In a secured port inside a private warehouse, T.K. and Tech are overseeing the off-loading of the product that'll be heading to the US in a day or so.

"Is it me, or does it seem like we have a lot more than we normally get?" asks T.K.

"If that's the case, how much more do you think we can hold? And with the additional weight, how will this affect the arrival date?" asks Tech.

"I was wondering the same thing," replies T.K. "We'll be able to handle the weight. Off the dome, I would say it'll push it back about three days only because we'll have to slow down to arrive during the cover of darkness. This'll throw the logistics off. Go ahead and load the normal load, and I'll get with Richie to discuss the way forward. We're getting more every month instead of less like we planned."

T.K. leaves Tech in the warehouse and heads to Richie's condo. When he arrives, he's met at the door by Phillip.

"Phil, what up?"

"Nothing much," Phillip replies as they shake hands.

"Where's Rich?"

"He's in the back on the balcony."

T.K. walks onto the balcony to see Richie on the phone. Richie holds a finger up to T.K. while he's in the middle of a conversation.

"What time? Okay, Phillip will be there to pick you up and bring you to me. I gotta go. Got an engagement I've got to get to. See you this evening." Richie ends the call and puts his phone on the table. "T.K.!" he says as he walks over and gives T.K. a pound before inviting him to sit down.

"So, you going to go through with it, huh?" asks T.K.

"Yeah, it's the best move to make for us to help the community," replies Richie.

"I agree."

"If it works. We still have the other piece needed to complete the puzzle. What's up, T.K.? We got an issue?"

"True. It's more than we got last month."

"More? What the fuck!" Richie replies with anger. "Can we handle it?"

"We can, but it'll get there nearly three days later, which will throw off the rally point time frames."

Richie stands up and walks over to the bannister. "See how much more and divide it up amongst the organizations on consignment. 70-30 split their way for being late, loyal, blah blah blah. Get the word to KAP to put it out. When I'm done here, I'm heading to Mexico to talk to Felix."

"Okay, I'll let you know tonight how much excess," replies T.K. "You need me to go with you?"

"Nah, brother. I'll take Phil. Enjoy your time in… my bad. I forgot to tell you about that resort in Caye Caulker."

"It's cool. I'm going to San Pedro to chill. Maybe next time. Tell Arielle congrats for me." They shake hands and bump shoulders as T.K. heads back to the Port of Belize.

Richie and Phillip arrive at the grand opening of Arielle's private school, Those to Inspire Academy. "I'll hit you when I'm ready to leave," Richie tells Phillip. Kay meets Richie out front by the curb.

"Hey, how's it going?"

"I'm good," Richie replies as they share a hug and walk to the front of the school.

The school is a beautiful four-story, canary yellow building with white borders around the windows. It nearly takes up the whole block.

"Man, she really did it this time. Four stories? How many kids does it house?" Richie asks.

"Three hundred and fifty students, twenty-five teachers, ten staff, and about four security guards," replies Kay.

"Wow."

"Let me take you to your seat."

Richie walks past the empty seats, looking at the positions of the invited guests on the back of the chairs. "A government-appointed senator, four ministers from the executive branch, and then my seat," says Richie. On the stage are Arielle, Ren, and Kay seated next to the podium. Richie met Arielle years ago at a gym just outside of Belize City. All the men watched her every move and was after her. She's a beautiful, dark-skinned, ex-model with full lips and long braids, and most importantly, educated. At the time, she was the lead news anchor for the Channel 3 News at 5 p.m. She was the person who connected Richie to Felix, which catapulted Richie's organization into the powerhouse it is today. Richie and Arielle were in a situation-ship during his time in Belize, and they decided to go their separate ways because having a relationship with someone with the drug cartel in between would make Richie way too vulnerable. As the host welcomed her to the podium, Arielle's eyes met with Richie's, and they both smiled at each other as she started her speech.

After the ribbon cutting to open the new school, the politicians and invited guests toured the school along with news reporters with their film crews.

"Thanks again for coming, Richie," says Arielle.

"This is really going to open doors for you, A," replies Richie. "Your future is bright, Ms. Prime Minister."

"Whoa, whoa, whoa now. Let's slow down, playboy," Arielle replies smiling.

"I'm just saying. Your popularity grows by the day. Look around. Look at your guests. Don't shy away from your calling, A. Besides, you would look good on that wall…" They both look at the wall with portraits of Belize's government officials. He looks at her, and they both smile. "I'm just saying. Don't close no doors." Richie looks at his watch. "Let me text Phil. I gotta get back. I have a visitor who'll be here soon."

"Richie, you ever wonder what could've happened with us?"

"Yes, more than you'd think." Richie grabs one of Arielle's wrists, brings it up to his lips, and kisses it. "Congratulations, A." He then heads downstairs to meet Phillip by the car.

* * *

Back at the dock, Richie waits for T.K. to calculate the final figure for the product overage and the journey back to the US.

"We have about 500 kilos over, which is a little over 1,100 pounds of added weight. That'll slow us down about 1.5 knots and will delay us about two days, eleven hours and twenty-six minutes. So, it'll arrive in Louisiana at 4 p.m. exactly six and a half days from now. We'll have to either slow down to reach the destination during the cover of darkness or get there and sit with confidence," says T.K. Richie pulls the hair on his chin.

"Did KAP get feedback from the organizations?" asks Richie.

"Yeah, we good there. You good to them, so they behind you."

"Good," says Richie. "Let's slow it down to get it there by dark." As he looks down the dock from inside the warehouse, he sees Phillip driving toward him. He walks to the road away from the warehouse, and the car stops perfectly so Richie could open the back passenger door. He opens it. A voice comes from the back seat with excitement.

"What's up, big homie?!"

Richie smiles sharing the excitement. "Nathaniel 'Spree' Green. What's the business?" Spree gets out of the car, and they shake hands and hug as Phillip drives further up the road and parks.

"How was your flight?"

"It was good. First class," says Spree.

"I know you used one of your fake ass passports to get here." Spree reaches in his pocket and gives it to Richie.

"Check the name out." Richie looks at it.

"Samuel L. Jackson? Get the fuck outta here."

Spree laughs. "I got another one if it didn't work that says McLovin on that bitch!" Shaking his head, Richie laughs. They walk slowly toward the warehouse at the end of the pier.

"I appreciate you giving me the heads up with Sheldon."

"Yo, Richie, he had a package with him that Maurice is scouring the earth for."

"A package? My people never told me about him having a package. What was in it?"

"Passports, credit cards, driver's licenses, counterfeit money, diamonds... You name it."

"We took his car to Smitty's to dispose of it." He reaches in his pocket and grabs his phone to text Brick: "Yo B, see if Smitty got something of ours."

Spree continues, "Maurice got gang lords and some Arab muthafuckas all in his ass for this shit. The heat is on him."

* * *

Detective Russell stops by Detective Coles's office to let him know he was headed home. Detective Coles grabs his car keys and his coat and says, "Let's go rook." They head to the parking garage, and once inside the car, they drive out of the parking garage to talk while driving around the South Side of Chicago. Detective Coles turns down the music and says, "Now the Internal Affairs investigation. What I'm telling you stays between you and me. Follow me?"

"Of course," replies Detective Russell.

* * *

"Spree, have you ever asked yourself why I'm in the game? I mean, I do twenty plus years in the military and come home just to push dope."

"To be honest," Spree replies, "the hood looked at you as someone who made it out clean. Your uncle was running shit; niggas was surprised you came home to take it over from him."

"I been all over the world, twice. Everywhere I went, our people was knee-deep in poverty, living like animals in some places. No opportunities while whites prosper from what their ancestors did to us. And when we try to grab our own bootstraps to put in work toward being self-sufficient, then shit happen to us like Rosewood, Black Wall Street, and being killed on the streets by White cops, White folks, and white hoods. Can't find jobs, poor education, and their bullshit religion. They constantly destroy our progress. We can't even survive a pandemic because of these systemic inequalities."

* * *

Detective Coles continues, "About two years ago, the 'powers that be,' if you know what I mean, were noticing that the black communities in Chicago were thriving big time, and they couldn't figure out how. The big businesses were suffering because the black dollar was being spent in the black community, circulating and staying within the community. They used to say that the black dollar stays in the black community for six hours while other communities keep their dollar for six days. The black dollar now stays within its community for nearly ten days."

* * *

Richie goes on, "That's when I figured I can change things. I took that element that was already destroying black families and used it for good. So, I got in the game to uplift the community by taking drug money and investing it back into the community. Most dealers only like to benefit themselves and the people that's close to them, not me. What I do goes in line to what Sou-sou does for a community. You ever heard of Sou-sou?"

"Nah," replies Spree.

"Sou-sou started in West Africa and the Caribbean. It's a savings club where a group of people get on one accord and pour an equal amount of money into a fund. It's then paid to one of the members of the group, and it keeps revolving until everyone has been paid and the cycle continues."

"Oh, that's what them Jews been doing for years," says Spree.

"Yeah, but they got it from us, like every other race. But what I do is find people in the community who are business-minded, talented, and motivated. I help them start their business, and I have other motivated people work for them until they ready to start their own. Once the businesses start cycling, I put some distance between them and the drug money. I provide the foundation, but the motivation from our people is what keeps it moving. Then I move this concept to different neighborhoods, cities, and states. The drugs destroy no doubt, but I use the profits to rebuild."

* * *

Detective Coles continues, "Strip malls, banks, private schools, clubs, daycare centers, youth centers, rehabilitation centers, movie theaters...You name it. These businesses were popping up in the black community all over the fucking place. And they're legit. No trace of illegal activity."

* * *

Richie explains more, "I pay less than half the price of what a kilo of coke would cost in the US because I saved my connect's ass years ago. My last few years in the military, I used to work for the Embassy here in Belize supporting Counter Narcotics Operations. I knew the US and Mexican governments were about to raid his entire operation. I needed the connect, and I knew someone who could make the connection; so I met with him and warned him. When they raided his fields, stash spots, and where he was hiding his money, it was all gone! And so was he. He then gifted me the prices, transportation, land, pier, and warehouse. Belize officials are paid off, so it's untouchable." Richie opens the door to the warehouse showing Spree his two seventy-five-foot fully submersible submarines docked inside the warehouse.

"The fuck!! Nigga, are you serious?!" Spree asks, surprised. "You on some 007 shit."

"Our product is brought here in trucks, loaded up, and we sail it to the US. When I got back home after I retired from the military, I went to all the leaders of the drug organizations in Chicago and offered them cheaper prices per kilo than what they were paying, but with one stipulation: They had to put some of the profits into building the black community. Those who agreed continued to operate. Those who didn't, well..."

* * *

Detective Coles continues to enlighten Detective Russell: "There was a plethora of murders going on all over Chicago before the calm. Not regular citizens, but drug dealers, organizations, gangs. All the countless man-hours and taxpayer dollars we spent to investigate these fuckers, and they were wiped out. Seems like it was overnight. Then things were quiet for a long while. There's still crime, but it's been reduced a great deal.

"So, the 'establishment' tried to reverse what was happening in Chicago's black community. The force started recruiting more white officers and transferring white cops to patrol black communities, patrolling with the intent to harm. They started leaving assault rifles on the streets, supplying different gangs with weapons, and actually killing certain gang members to kick some shit off between rival gangs. But they underestimated Commander Watkins in Precinct 6. He grew up in those streets and went to high school with a lot of the gang leaders' families. They respected him. Once he started hearing the whispers from the streets, he knew the gangs would never snitch because of the street code. He hired private investigators to watch his cops. They started recording and catching these cops in the act. He contacted IA once he collected all the evidence, and they had no choice but to investigate. Those crackers were running for the hills."

Detective Russell, astonished, asks, "Is that how he got promoted to Chief of Detectives?"

"Yep! Not only because he's extremely smart and loyal with flawless integrity but also because they wanted him in a position where they could keep an eye on his black ass. Then this trend started in other states."

* * *

"So," Richie continues, "after months of building businesses, educating people, and providing jobs, crime dropped because opportunities were available. Once we saw how we could positively affect the black community, we expanded this movement to different drug organizations all over the Midwest. Before you know it…"

* * *

Detective Coles puts both hands up and touches his fingers as he lists some states: "In Indiana, Michigan, Missouri, Ohio, Nebraska, Kansas, Wisconsin, and Minnesota, black businesses were popping up all over the place, mimicking the same movement in Chicago. Such a beautiful thing."

"So, all these black businesses popping up all over the Midwest, and you believe it's all legit?" asks Detective Russell.

"As much as I would love to see black folks finally getting our shit together, it's too good to be true." Detective Coles looks at Detective Russell with a look of disappointment as he heads back to the station's parking garage.

* * *

Ms. Debra hadn't heard from her daughter, Courtney, in nearly three days. She called her cell phone several times with no luck. She yells upstairs to her granddaughters, "Get dressed! We going to your mama house to see why she ain't returning my calls." After a twenty-five-minute drive, they pull up at Courtney's house.

"Is mom home, grandma?"

"Her light is on in the living room. Take your seatbelts off. But stay here, okay? Y'all don't need to hear me yell at ya mama."

Ms. Debra gets out of her car and walks up to the door talking to herself. "Makes no damn sense. Got me here with these damn kids.

Shit, I wanna go out too. Working my damn nerves." She knocks on the door. When she doesn't hear anything coming from inside, she twists the doorknob and pushes the door open. She smells a strong stench that deeply penetrates her nostrils. She steps inside, covering her nose. "Courtney! Courtney! What the hell you got going on?!" She sees Courtney's foot sticking out past the corner of the couch and yells out, "Courtney!!" Ms. Debra walks past the couch to see her daughter's body decomposing. "OH MY GOD!!! MY BABY, MY BABY!!!" She runs out of the house, crying hysterically with her phone in her hand as she struggles to dial 911. The neighbors run outside of their homes to see what's going on.

* * *

Detective Coles and Detective Russell return to the station. "Leon, listen. Black excellence doesn't always mean that there's something negative behind it. Just be grateful knowing that your kids will have opportunities to flourish in the black community instead of living in fear."

"I'm not saying that there's a negative background, but don't you find it funny—"

Detective Coles's cell phone rings, interrupting Detective Russell mid sentence. "Detective Coles, homicide. Uh huh. Where? I'll be right there." He hangs up and looks at Detective Russell. "Possible homicide. You coming with or following?"

"I'll follow you." Detective Russell hops out of the car and gets into his own.

* * *

"So," Spree asks curiously, "why am I here?"

"Great question," replies Richie. "I want you to run H2H. I need you as the head in order to help push the agenda."

"You know, if you'd asked me this about two weeks ago, I would've shut you down. But I'm not exactly happy where I'm at. Maurice, well, he murked someone who didn't deserve that shit. I'm done with the killing, man. No more. But you know killing that dude will be harder than you think. He has a connection with the gang lords. You kill him, and no fake identities for their peoples, no cars, houses, and whatever else they do. Then they'd be after you for his death and that connect. If you two could somehow make peace, with his connections in and out of Chicago, you guys would be unstoppable. With what you're trying to do, you're going to need soldiers, his soldiers!" Richie turns his back to Spree and thinks.

"Okay, I agree. But I'll give him the opportunity to get with my agenda and get him on his feet. But agree with me on this: If it doesn't work, you'll do whatever it takes to help me put six feet over him, and you take over." Spree nods, and they shake hands.

* * *

Detective Coles, followed by Detective Russell, reaches Courtney's house. The patrolmen already have the scene secured when the detectives arrive. They exit their cars and head into the house.

"What do we have here, Sergeant?" asks Detective Coles.

"The deceased is Courtney Chambers. She was found dead by her mom; twin daughters were waiting outside in the car. The mom stated that she hadn't seen her daughter in a couple days, came by to check on her, and found her like this."

Detective Coles reaches into his coat pocket, pulls out some Vicks Vapor rub, rubs some under his nose, and hands it to Detective Russell to place some under his nose too.

"She's been dead a little over three days," says Detective Coles as he pulls some surgical gloves out from the inside of his coat and kneels over Courtney's body, looking for clues on how she died.

He scans her body from her toes to her head and notices the marks on her neck. "She was strangled to death. Come closer, detective." Detective Russell's eyes are watering from the smell of the dead body. He kneels while rubbing the Vicks under his nose.

"See the marks, and how her eyes and mouth are wide open? She was gasping for air," says Detective Coles.

"It may be a coincidence, but the female victim from the dispatch caller was strangled to death as well," says Detective Russell.

"Connection?"

"Possibly, pos-si-bly."

"Sergeant, any eyewitnesses?" asks Detective Coles.

"The neighbors are being questioned now," replies the sergeant.

"Good, good. Have forensics sweep the house, and let's get the body to the Medical Examiner. Russell, let's get you some air. Follow me." As they step outside, one of the detectives calls Detective Coles over to him. "Detective Coles, this is Ms. Hattie Mae." Detective Coles reaches his hand toward her, and they shake hands.

"What can I do for you, ma'am?"

"Well, detective, I live right across the street, and I saw a black truck leave Courtney's house a few days ago. Look like a Black man was inside. He sat for a few seconds and drove off."

"Do you know around what time?"

"Well, I was cooking some greens that night because I'd been constipated lately. So, I put a little vinegar in my greens to help me with that, ya know? So, after that, I went to turn on the TV and watch my old shows when I looked out my window…"

"And what time do you turn on your TV to watch your old shows, ma'am?"

"Well, I watch Matlock and that comes on right before I need to take my pills for my high blood pressure because it runs in my family…" Ms. Hattie Mae rambles on. Detective Coles looks at the detective and says, "Thanks," and then mumbles, "fucking shit nugget." He slowly walks away with Detective Russell. He was about to start up another conversation when he hears Ms. Hattie Mae say, "The black truck license plate read KAP216." He turns around and walks back to her.

"Ma'am, did I hear you say KAP216?"

"Yes, that's what I said. You don't listen too good, do ya? I remember 216 because I played it in the pick three the next morning after I saw it. I didn't win because my friend Barbara Lee..." Detective Russell writes the information in his notepad.

Detective Coles smirks and replies, "Thank you very much for your help, ma'am," then they walk back into Courtney's house.

* * *

Richie walks with Spree over to see what Tech's doing. He has all these computers and drones scattered around. Richie, then a Chief Warrant Officer, first met Tech, Specialist Parks, the biracial nerd, when Tech was sitting outside of General Warrington's office. Richie had an appointment with General Warrington to go over some logistics for vessels throughout the Pacific, and Specialist Parks was sitting outside General Warrington's office with his chain of command.

After Richie finished his short meeting with the general, he asked, "G.W., who is that outside?"

"That's Specialist Parks. He's awaiting punishment," said General Warrington.

"What did he do?"

"Well, Chief, he allegedly set up video cameras in all fourteen of the female showers within the Sustainment Brigade and was charging soldiers money to come in his room and watch. Needless to say, he made a killing. One of the soldiers who was watching saw his girlfriend in the video, and he told the Criminal Investigation Division and here we are."

"How old is he? Twenty? Twenty-one?"

"That would be my guess."

"Well, sir, before you decide to kick him out, the Army could really use his 'IT' knowledge."

"What are you saying, Chief?"

"I'm saying wipe your ass with his career but don't flush it. I remember you as a young captain, sir. What was her name again?" The General smiled.

"Okay, Chief, you owe me."

Richie stood up and started walking out of the general's office, but then he turned and said, "Not sure what score you're keeping Chris, but you are down two." They both smiled. As Richie walked out, Specialist Parks's chain of command walked into the general's office, leaving Parks outside the office. Richie walked over to him and said, "You'll lose money and rank, but not your career. We can still use your talents. Here's my card. Give up the videos and hone your skills. Call me once a month to let me know how you're doing." Parks smiled, relieved, and replied, "Yes, sir."

Richie leaves Spree with Tech to chat while he walks to the other side of the warehouse to check his emails and text while listening to Spree and Tech's conversation. "What's up, man? My name's Spree."

"What's up, Spree. I'm Tech. They call me that cause I run the technology up in this piece, and I'm the most important mickey fickey in this jooiint!" he says as he smiles. "Don't tell nobody I said that."

"So, what is all this stuff?" Tech looks across the warehouse at Richie, who nods giving him the approval to explain.

"So, I'll give you the what I do 101. The submarines are solar-powered and gas-propelled, and I can control them from my computer or my cell phone. These," Tech explains as he points, "my newly acquired friend, are drones that are waterproof, of course, and they ride on top of the subs. They're the brains, the bread, and the butter of the whole fucking operation. Whoop, whoop!

"Each submarine has four drones. I load the GPS coordinates into all of them and synchronize each of them when it's their shift. One goes on the front, which is the eyes and ears or the driver. It can see about ten nautical miles on the surface. What it sees, I see. It's stationary, but it can fly as a last resort to do what the other three do. Drone two, three, and four are scouts, and they rotate to take photos night and day. They then dock back on the sub and give me data, which tells me if I have to change course, dive, or stop because of a surface object.

"You see these poles? They extend up to fifteen feet out of the water, and that's how the drones charge and take flight, and that's what they land on. It connects with the bottom of the drones and re-submerge them back onto the sub. They charge once they dock and have an eight-hour battery life. If all three drones go to shit, which will never fucking happen, then the one on the front can do everything the other three can do, but we'd just dive deep and keep it moving. So, I get everything, data, visual, and sound from all the drones, and I can see it all on my computer and cell phone. I can be at the club with a hooker—"

Richie interrupts from across the warehouse, "No hookers!"

"That's right, boss! I don't do hookers anymore." Tech whispers to Spree, "Since last week, chicka chicka bow wow," and humps the air. Spree smiles and looks across the warehouse at Richie, who shakes his head in disappointment.

Tech continues, "All this is super secure through a satellite with so many fucking firewalls and protections around it… Come on, Spree, ask me how secure."

"Okay, how secure?"

"Spree, that's a great fucking question. Funny you should ask. My setup is so fucking tight that if it was an asshole, and you farted, you'd shatter glass from ten feet away!" Spree snickers at Tech's analogy. "Any questions, Spree?"

"Well said," Spree said jokingly. "Before you said something about hookers, I was gonna ask if you get pussy or not?"

"Hell to the yeah…cause I'm a fucking millionaire!!"

Richie grabs his phone and calls Felix. The phone rings a long time, which is normal, before anyone picks up.

"Richie, my friend. How are you?"

"I'm good, Felix. I'm next door and wanted to see if you had time to meet up tomorrow?"

"Sure, Richie. I will send a jet to Belize to get you and…"

"Phillip, I'm bringing Phillip with me."

"Sounds good, Richie. Plane will be at the airport tomorrow at 1 p.m. See you then."

* * *

Before he walks back into Courtney's house, Detective Russell calls over a patrolman. He gives him the license plate number to find out who's the owner of the tag and if it matches the vehicle. When he walks into the house, he sees Detective Coles going through mail in the kitchen hallway and looks over his shoulder.

"Who's Sheldon Bradley?" asks Detective Coles. "Husband or baby daddy?" He flips through a couple more letters. "Jasmine Bradley, Jalynn Bradley, and Courtney Chambers." They look at each other and reply in unison, "Baby daddy."

"Well, Sheldon Bradley," says Detective Coles, "we're looking for you buddy."

The patrolman comes into the house and moves to the side as Courtney's body is carried out in a body bag. You can hear her mother, daughters, and other family members cry out as forensics personnel carries the body to the van. The patrolman heads straight to Detective Russell with information pertaining to the license plate and truck details.

"Detective, the license plate comes back to a 2023 GMC Yukon Denali, and it belongs to a Kali Allen Pettaway. He's clean. No priors, not even a traffic ticket. No known aliases. Car is registered in Cleveland, but he owns a place in the city."

"Thank you," says Detective Russell. "We now have two possible suspects. Let's find them."

* * *

The submarines are all loaded and ready for sea. From his computer, Tech conducts some pre-sail checks to ensure everything is powered and operating correctly. He starts the engines, steering system, rudders, and the rest of the auxiliary systems from his computer, then he switches to drone control to see if the readings were identical to the drones.

"T.K., we are a go on systems check."

"Very well," says T.K. "Open the ballast tanks." Tech pushes a couple of keys on the computer, and the submarines slowly go underwater about five feet. After ten minutes of being submerged, Tech conducts another check to make sure the integrity of the hull is intact. Once this is satisfactory, T.K. looks at Richie, and he nods. The warehouse doors open, and the first submarine slowly moves forward. After the first submarine is completely out of the warehouse, Tech syncs the second submarine with the same speed, depth, and coordinates as the first one.

"You got it, Tech?" asks T.K.

"Yes, sir," replies Tech. "I'll be here another two hours or so. I'll let you know when we're all clear, boss." Richie, T.K., and Spree head to T.K.'s truck, passing Phillip as he parks outside the warehouse to wait for Tech to finish up. T.K. drops Richie and Spree off at Richie's condo, and they take the elevator to the third floor. Tech stays in the warehouse until the submarines are in open waters before he shuts down his computer and heads to his condo.

"You can stay here until you're ready to leave, Spree," Richie says as they head into his living room. "Phil is going with me, so one of the girls will take you to the airport."

"Man, Richie, I see your vision, and I hope it all works out with Maurice, man. He envies you for real, and I hope he can see past his jealousy and get down with you. If he doesn't, I'll proudly work with you, no doubt."

"Thanks, Spree, that means a lot. Your room is off to the right. Mi casa es su casa. And, uh, I'll soon be giving you two more reasons to get down with the cause. Good night and have a safe trip back." They shake hands and bump shoulders as Spree looks at Richie in admiration before he heads to the guest room. He walks into his room and closes the door behind him. It's a very spacious, king-sized suite with a Jacuzzi and a wet bar. "Man, this what I'm talking bout right here. This shit is nice." Spree opens the closet, grabs his suitcase, and goes into the bathroom. "Damn!" He hears a knock on his bedroom door and hurries to open it to see if Richie forgot to tell him something.

"Yo, Richie, what up?" As he opens the door, he's surprised to see two beautiful, mocha-colored, Belizean women wearing see-through lingerie and holding towels. He smiles big and steps to the side to let the ladies in, looking at them from head to toe. They enter, and he closes the door behind them.

* * *

After spending time with his family in Cleveland, KAP returns home late in the morning, and he's now ready to rendezvous with his stable of ladies and get back to business as usual. When he gets close to his house, he calls his building manager to discuss some properties he's looking to purchase for the New Year. "Glover, you know that multi-unit off 79th and Sangamon? I gotta have it, baby! Get the 411 on it and see when the bid is, so we can be ready. I need you to walk through it to see what kinda shape it's in. Feel me?"

"I hear you, boss," says Glover. "I'll have that information for you by the end of the day."

KAP slowly backs his car into his garage as his garage door rises. Once his truck is fully in the garage, he lowers the garage door, turns off his truck, and gathers his things to enter the house. He then remembers that he was supposed to stop at the store to pick up some wine for tonight. He runs his suitcase in the house after turning off his security alarm and heads back to the truck. He gets back inside, starts his truck, and opens the garage door while texting Makala to let her know what time to stop by. When he looks up, he sees three cop cars waiting for him in his driveway.

He raises his phone up in both hands above the steering wheel, so the cops can see what he's doing. He texts "911" to Richie, Damawi, T.K., and Brick, then he uses his left hand to open the door before he steps out of the vehicle.

"May I help you?" asks KAP.

"Are you Kali Allen Pettaway?"

"I am. What's the problem?"

"We're Detectives Russell and Neeley. We need you to come with us to the station. We have a couple questions concerning Courtney Chambers."

With a concerned expression, KAP asks, "Couple questions... is she okay?"

"Just come with us please, sir," says Detective Neeley. "Leave your vehicle in the garage and lock up your house. An officer will take you to the station." KAP shuts his car off, locks his truck, and closes the garage door with his phone. He then texts the group: "Headed to the station."

* * *

Richie and Phillip arrive at Philip S.W. Goldson International Airport ready to depart to an unknown destination in Mexico. Airport security escorts them through the airport, and they see Felix's beautiful pearl white private jet parked with the engines running. Richie's phone vibrates in his pocket, and he pulls it out and sees a text message from KAP: "911," followed by another text, "Headed to the station." He checks to see everyone who's included in the message and immediately sends a message to Damawi: "D, contact Alex and get him to the station ASAP!" Richie is a bit concerned because although KAP didn't commit the murder, he could've been seen leaving Courtney's house, and this could bring unwanted problems that he's managed to avoid. "Fuck!" yells Richie. He knows KAP extremely well and knows that he will stick to his guns; he also knows that KAP will be a true soldier even if he committed the act.

Richie met KAP when he first joined the Navy nearly thirty years ago. They were great friends from the beginning and had similar interests: women, rapping, club fights with the locals because of women, and oh yeah, women. They even transitioned to the Army together to become officers. Brick and KAP are Richie's closest friends, but KAP had some issues with being his number two guy. However, Richie knew KAP's thirst for women was sometimes more important than handling business. T.K. is extremely business-oriented, but he lacks the people skills needed to lead. As a former combat medic in the Army, T.K. witnessed some horrible things that subtracted compassion and patience from his personality and added PTSD to the mix.

Richie feels his phone vibrate and looks at it to see Damawi's reply: "He's aware and headed to the station." Outside Felix's jet are a few of his security guards in suits and armed with M4s, waiting for Phillip and Richie to board. They walk inside this plane of pure luxury. It's fully carpeted with wood grain all over the cabin and plush and spacious leather seats. There are two beautiful flight attendants aboard the jet and a huge liquor cabinet on the left side near the entrance. As they take their seats, the doors close behind them, and the plane prepares for take off.

CHAPTER 5

KAP arrives at the police station with Detectives Russell and Neeley, and Detective Neeley takes KAP into a small interrogation room. Being inside a police station is not unfamiliar to him. Before joining the military, KAP was a wild child. Like Richie, he was involved with the world of drugs since he was a youth. At age 17, he was nearly charged with assault and battery against a forty-year-old man who tried to cut him with a beer bottle. The man accused KAP of sleeping with his daughter and threatened him. KAP fought the man and was arrested for assault. Back then, judges were sending "troubled youths" to the military for a chance at life and to avoid jail time. When KAP asked the judge, "How much jail time?" the courtroom was so quiet you could've heard a pin drop. The judge replied, "After that remark, you'd retire from the military twice before I'd let you out. You have two weeks to sign up and another two weeks to be in somebody's boot camp." KAP's record was sealed, and he was in Orlando, FL, in basic training for the Navy a month later.

KAP sits down at the table inside the room. "So, where's my strawberry soda and chips at? I don't like talking on an empty stomach."

"That's a good sign for us because it sounds like you plan to be here for a while," replies Detective Neeley.

"Nah. Maybe another fifteen, twenty minutes. So, what's the business?" Detective Russell walks into the room and drops photos of Courtney's deceased body in front of him.

"We got a witness seeing you leave her place Monday night," says Detective Russell. "Is this your work?"

KAP looks at the photos and responds, "This is terrible to look at man," then pushes the photos to the other side of the table. "I was at her place. I rang the doorbell, and no one answered. So I left and drove to Cleveland to see my peoples."

"Was she your girlfriend?" asks Detective Russell.

"Yeah, one of em. I would never harm her though. Never. She was special."

"Special how?" asks Detective Neeley. KAP looks at Detective Neeley with a serious face and leans forward in his chair.

"She's the only woman that could make me cum back to back from head, twice," KAP explains, holding up two fingers to show both detectives. "And I'm almost fifty. She wasn't just a mother of two; she was a fucking unicorn. I needed her here with me. So you got the wrong guy, fellas. I mean, do I look like the type of dude that'll kill a female?" The detectives look at each other, astonished at his reasoning for wanting her to live.

"So, you're saying you would kill somebody?" asks Detective Russell. KAP relaxes back in his chair.

"I'm a twenty-plus-year war vet. You damn right I would, but I don't wear the uniform anymore." Looking back and forth at both detectives, KAP asks, "Is my strawberry soda coming?"

"Wait here, smart ass," says Detective Russell. Both detectives step out of the interrogation room to talk when they see Detective Coles walking toward them.

"Detectives. You guys ready?" asks Detective Coles."

"We've already started questioning him."

"What the fuck?! You two amateur night at the Apollo, green ass rookies question a possible murder suspect without me or a seasoned detective present?! You two are as fucked up as a football bat. Follow me!" Detective Coles takes them to the room that sits on the other side of the interrogation room.

"So, what do you think?" asks Detective Coles, looking through the two-way mirror. "Is he our guy?"

Russell and Neeley look at each other, and Detective Russell says, "I don't think so."

"Why?"

The rookie detectives look at each other.

* * *

A few hours later, Felix's private jet lands just outside of Puerto Vallarta, Mexico. After traveling for an hour on a long, freshly paved road, the plane finally comes to a stop, and the flight attendants open the doors. Walking behind security, Richie steps off the plane and is surprised to see that the landing strip is located in the back of Felix's home. A castle. "This shit is crazy!" says Phillip. "I ain't never seen nothing this massive and beautiful."

A jeep is parked next to the jet to take them to Felix's mansion. Richie and Phillip hop in the jeep while their luggage is loaded into the back. Riding in the jeep as the air hits his face, Richie has a flashback to when he was attacked from behind, and a thick black cloth hood was placed over his head before he was thrown into the back of a truck. His hands and feet were hog-tied, and he was beaten to shit, feeling all the bumps, ditches, and high-speed turns. That was his moment of truth. When you ask enough questions on where to find a drug lord, one will definitely come looking for you. After a thirty-minute ride, Richie was snatched out of the truck by his feet, and he hit the pavement face first before they carried him inside. There were two men on each arm and two on each leg. He felt like a black taco headed for execution. Once inside, they threw him inside a room with cold marble floors. Then they sat him up in a chair and left shortly afterward, leaving him alone and locking the door on their way out.

Ten minutes later, he heard the door open and some people walked in. They were speaking in Spanish, so he couldn't make out everything they were saying. Suddenly, his hood was snatched off, and standing before him was Felix Antonio Navarro, also known as El Oso Blanco, "The White Bear." Richie later found out that Felix got his nickname because he was known as the largest predator in the drug game, killing off opposing drug cartels. Felix pulled a chair in front of Richie and took a seat.

"Hello, Chief Warrant Officer. Yes, I know all about who you are, who you work for, and why you're in Belize. What can you do for me, Richie?"

* * *

Detective Coles walks into the interrogation room and sits down next to KAP. KAP looks at the detective's hands and says, "Still no strawberry soda?"

Detective Coles smiles and responds, "No, we only give soda to potential murderers and drug pushers."

"Well, no soda for me then," replies KAP.

"Let me ask you a question, Mr. Pettaway. Do you know Sheldon Bradley? He's Courtney's baby daddy."

"No, never met him nor had any interest in doing so."

"I understand the situation," says Detective Coles. Detective Russell comes into the room with Alex Scott, KAP's attorney.

"Gentlemen, any more questions for my client will come through me. If there's no evidence that links my client to this investigation, we're done here. Let's go, Mr. Pettaway."

"Fellas, it's been fun. I hope you find the asshole who did this, and please, no sodas or chips for them," KAP says as he follows his lawyer out of the interrogation room.

* * *

Richie is stepping out of the jeep in front of Felix's massive home when he feels his phone vibrate. It's a text from Brick: "I have that package. What do you need me to do?" Richie texts back: "Cool keep it close. We going to use that for leverage." Felix walks up to Richie as he's returning his phone to his pocket.

"Richie, my friend! How do you do? Walk with me." Phillip heads for the house with the flight attendants and a security guard. The other security guards follow behind Felix and Richie.

"Felix, you're creating a problem for me with the excess keys. We agreed that we would decrease the keys over time, not increase. It's getting difficult for me to move it and get the return on our investment sooner."

"Richie, life is difficult, and there are people who wish they could be in your position. I have no pity for you. You will get the amount I send, and you will move it."

"Really, Felix?"

"This is where we are."

"We've already discussed my plans and my timeline on this and my replacement."

"Richie, I understand. What you have done for me in the past is not relevant today. I was grateful, but you have been well compensated for that. Things always change. There will be no replacement for you unless I approve it."

"Felix—"

"Richie, I am being patient with you. Anyone else would have already had a bullet in their head for this conversation. You may be Black Jesus to your monkeys in the United States, but here, you are who I say you are. Comprende?" Richie looks defeated and feels betrayed. There was no way he would tell Felix that he comprehended what he just heard, so he just stared at him and waited for him to speak more of this fuck shit.

"Richie, I had my chefs prepare a meal for you and Phil. I hope you are hungry," says Felix. Richie doesn't respond. "I understand you don't like what you have heard. So, who is your replacement? KAP?"

"No, not KAP," replies Richie.

"Good, KAP would be perfect if we were in the pussy business," replies Felix, smiling as he puts his arm around Richie's shoulders.

"His name is Chris Warrington. He's currently a General Officer in the Army. I served with him for about twenty years. Great leader, he understands our business, and we won't skip a beat once he's on board," Richie says with confidence.

"When will I have the opportunity to meet him?"

"Soon. He's in the process of retiring and will be free to meet you in two weeks."

"Bueno. Text me when he will be coming. Can't wait to meet him."

* * *

Damawi arrives at the police station to pick up KAP. He spots her as soon as he walks outside and heads to her car. "Don't I feel special," says KAP as he opens the door and hops in. "Thank you, D!" He leans over to give her a kiss, but she quickly dodges it as she pulls away from the curb.

"Ahh, no sir! You just left jail. Ion know where your lips been. I heard the rumors on what goes on in there."

"You got jokes," says KAP, feeling rejected. "Just get me home, Ms. Daisy, and drive fast. Anyway, how's the club doing? Or should I say your whole life."

"Well, you see what hard work will do, okay."

"Do you do anything else besides being in that club? Where's your man at?"

"Don't worry about my man. You worry about all your women and leave me be."

"I don't know why they call you D cause you ain't getting none. Huh, Amawi?"

"Whateva jail bird!"

"I'm just playing wit you. What you doing tonight?"

"Amawi's working, that's what I'm doing."

"Let me take you out… get a few drinks."

"Take me out?" asks Damawi, curiously.

"Yea, I know a nice spot."

"Where?"

"Josephine's! You should check it out! It's the hottest club in the Chi."

"Funny, but I'll be there to have some drinks with you about six." KAP guides her to his house, and after a short drive, she pulls into his driveway to let him out. "Thanks, D! I'll see you later! Drive safe."

"Okay, KAP! Be safe." She drives off as he heads into his house.

* * *

Detectives Coles, Russell, and Neeley walk into forensics to find out if there's any newfound evidence that may get them closer to solving Courtney's murder or reveal a connection to the dispatch call murders. "Here's my favorite forensics person! Mr. Deans, how goes it brother?"

"Detective Coles, it goes well. As you can see, I'm in a grave situation." The detectives smile at the off-colored joke. "How may I help you?" asks Mr. Deans.

"Well, since you're working on Ms. Courtney, we were wondering if your findings are similar to a vic we had just over a year ago who was also strangled," says Detective Coles as he hands Mr. Deans her file. Mr. Deans looks at the file, then he grabs his clipboard and shuffles through the papers looking for the measurements of the marks on Courtney's neck.

"Here we go. Let's see what we have, Detective." Mr. Deans flips through the other file and locates the measurements for the markings on the other victim's neck. He reviews the documents side by side, and remembers, "Oh, I did these as well." Scanning both files, he continues, "As you can see, the bruising patterns are the same on both victims. The person who did this was a rather large man. There were leather fibers on both victims' necks. They're identical. If I were a betting man, I'd say both victims were done by the same person. Only way to be sure would be to get those gloves. I could possibly match the fibers I have with the inside of the gloves. I wish I could be of more assistance."

"No, Dean, you've been great as always. Until we meet again, my good man," says Detective Coles. "Then again, it would be better if we didn't, Mr. Deans."

"Touché, Detective Coles, touché." The detectives exit the forensics room and walk to the elevator.

"Let's narrow our five suspects down to one or two and get the chief's approval to surveil them," says Detective Coles to Russell and Neeley as they step onto the elevator to head back to their desks.

* * *

Richie finishes the dinner prepared by Felix's chefs and listens as Phillip raves on about how good it was. Even though he told Felix it was the best meal he'd had in a long time, everything tasted bland to Richie. His mind was focused on the disrespect from earlier and how he should be thankful that the length and content of the conversation didn't warrant a bullet in his head. Richie heads to his room for the night and to prepare for an early departure back to Belize. As he's walking, he softly wonders aloud about why he's getting more product. "Felix is normally transparent with everything that affects the logistics and turnaround time for repayment, and he's never said anything so off-color to me before. Something isn't adding up. How do you go from threatening to kill me to you can't wait to meet my replacement? Only time will tell I guess, but my time is running short."

Richie must expand his operations to keep up with Felix's demands and timeline for payment. As much as he hates to admit it, he needs Maurice's connections to the East Coast for this to happen. Once he's in his room, Richie sits on the bed, kicks off his shoes, and thinks about how this is going to pan out. He then lies back with his right arm under his head and reminisces about how his relationship with Maurice has been bad since the sixth grade when Maurice transferred to St. Kilian grade school in the middle of the school year. He probably came from some place for juvenile delinquents where they learn lies and deceit and specialized in the art of being an asshole. When Ms. Paul introduced Maurice to the class, Richie had a strange feeling that he would be kicking Maurice's ass over something in the weeks to come. He was slightly wrong. It took two months, and it led to Richie's first suspension.

Ms. Paul required all students to turn in all their assigned homework every morning. Richie hated school. He wasn't the best student, but he did what he was told. Although Richie had been turning in his assignments for nearly three weeks, he never received any of them back. Eventually, Ms. Paul called Richie's mom one night and told her that he hadn't been doing his homework. Richie's mom snatched his Atari 2600 from the television and chewed his ass out. With her index finger inches from his nose, Richie tried to tell her that he turned in his homework, but it was useless. A few days later, Ms. Paul passed the graded homework assignments to the students in the front of each row of seats, then each student took their assignments and passed the remaining ones to the students behind them.

Maurice sat in front of Richie, and the homework assignments were sitting on Maurice's desk. Since Maurice had gone to the restroom, Richie got up and grabbed the stack of papers to look for his work. "Missing!! What the heck!" shouts out Richie. He shuffled through the papers again, reading the names on each paper. "Felicia, John, Robert, Shawanna, Maurice, and Terrence." He looked one more time, frantically, but more slowly and carefully. "Felicia… John… Robert… Shawanna… Maurice and— wait a minute." Richie stopped and looked closely at Maurice's homework. His name was on the top of the paper, but the work was in Richie's handwriting. Richie was confused for a second, then it hit him. That fucker erased his name and put his own. Oh Richie was pissed!

When Maurice walked back into the classroom, everything switched to slow motion. All Richie could think about was his mom yelling at him, waving her finger in his face, and snatching his Atari 2600 out of the TV. As soon as Maurice got close enough, Richie punched Maurice dead in his right eye. When the punch connected, Maurice fell to the floor, holding his eye. Richie then stood over Maurice, yelling at him for forging his name on Richie's C-level work. Maurice kicked Richie in the family jewels, bringing him down to the floor right next to him. They wrestled on the floor until Ms. Paul broke them up. Their dealings with each other haven't changed to this day.

After reminiscing about the old days and what he would have to deal with to get Maurice on board, all Richie could do was roll over and say, "Fuck!"

* * *

Damawi was in her office reviewing paperwork for a cigar lounge she was adding to the back of the club when Gina walks into the office in investigation mode. "Damawi, KAP is here asking for you to come down and have some drinks with him. What's going on here? The way you and Richie be looking at each other, I thought he was going to be your new boo bear. I mean... KAP is cute with that sexy body—"

"First off," replies Damawi, "If you paid more attention to the bartenders giving away free drinks to females for sex on the beach instead of sherlocking, we would be okay. Secondly, sometimes you need to use a smaller fish as bait to catch the big fish, okay?" Gina laughs out loud and raises her hand up to give Damawi a high five.

"You go girl!"

Smiling, Damawi high fives Gina and replies, "You go girl… downstairs and tell them bartenders to straighten the hell up."

Gina frowns and walks toward the door. "You know you get on my nerves, right?"

Damawi smiles, then she wraps up what she's working on before she heads downstairs. She smiles and walks right over when she sees KAP at a table waiting for her to join him. "Hey, KAP! You came! I thought you were just talking when you said you were coming."

"Nah, I told you I was coming. Have a seat." The waitress comes over to the table, takes their drink orders, then leaves.

"So, what's up, KAP?"

"We've never really had a chance to talk and really get to know each other."

So, what do you want to know?"

"First off, I want to apologize to you about my little joke in the car earlier. You know I was just joking, but is this club it for you, D?"

"No, KAP. I'm just focusing on work, and that's what it is right now. I'm trying to do more to this club to bring in more money, so we can clean more. That's my focus. I'm fine for right now."

"Oh, okay."

"Why are you so interested in what I'm doing or who I'm doing all of a sudden?"

"Well, the interest has always been there, but you know Richie's rules."

They recite the rule together: "Don't mix my business with your pleasure. Keep it locked da fuck up." They both laugh.

"Is that why you two never got together?" asks KAP.

"Not at all. I gave you my reasons."

"Well, I can change that rule once I take over when Richie walks away from the game."

"Do you think he'll actually walk away? And what makes you think he'll leave you in charge?"

"Man, Richie and I have been putting in work with each other for over thirty years. I know the business, the connects, I'm handsome, cute, sexy, gorgeous all rolled up into—"

"Boy, whatever! None of those are good reasons to believe you'll take over everything."

KAP leans closer to Damawi and says, "But you don't disagree that I am those things?" Damawi smiles, and the waitress brings their drinks over to the table, interrupting the moment.

"No, I won't disagree with you. You are those things, but there has to be more to a person to move me. Thank you, Kelly!" The waitress nods and returns to the bar.

"True that," says KAP. "All I'm saying is when I'm king, I'm going to need a queen."

* * *

Richie's flight lands in Belize, and he heads directly to his condo. Once he's inside and puts his bag down, he walks into the kitchen and sees a note left by Spree on the kitchen counter. He picks it up and reads it: "Richie, thank you for everything my G. I'm ready to put in the work. Give me the word when you ready to meet with Maurice. I'll work it out. Peace, Spree." Richie puts the note back on the counter, grabs a bottle of wine, and pours himself a glass before he heads out onto the balcony. He sits down and leans back in his seat, then he takes a sip of wine and thinks aloud,

"He's giving me more for a reason. His other dealers must be having issues, so he has to push the product to someone in order to pay his connect. He must be stressing me out cause he stressed. Or he keeping me in play until he has other dealers, and he can push the excess over to them. I mean, if he don't want me to leave now, then why is he willing to meet my replacement?" Richie takes another sip of wine and sinks deeper into his chair. Richie grabs his phone and calls Damawi. When her phone rings, Damawi looks at KAP and says, "The boss is calling."

"I guess this would be a good time to take a bathroom break," says KAP. He smiles, stands up, and walks away. Damawi waits until KAP is far enough away before she answers. "Hey, Richie! How are things?"

"Things are well," says Richie. "How are you? Did KAP make it out okay?"

"He did! He's over here at the club; we having drinks and catching up."

"Really? Hmm... okay. I'll be back tomorrow. Everything cool?"

"Everything's fine. You didn't tell me how funny KAP is. He's a trip. Anyway, is there anything you need me to do for your arrival?"

"I didn't drive, so can you have someone pick me up."

"I'll have KAP pick you up."

"Cool thanks." Richie hangs up abruptly. Damawi snaps her head to the side and looks at her phone, shocked at how Richie got off the phone. She then smiles and sips her wine, knowing she's casted her line with the bait she needs to catch the bigger fish. KAP returns from the restroom, sits down, and grabs his drink.

"Everything cool?"

"Yep! Richie wants you to pick him up from the airport tomorrow. He lands at 2 p.m. Delta flight 3433."

* * *

As soon as Richie's plane lands in Chicago, he turns on his phone, and he sees a text from KAP: "Hey, let me know when you get to baggage claim, and I'll be outside to scoop you up." While he's walking through the airport, Richie gets another text from a number not programmed in his phone. Although the name wasn't in his phone, he knew the person well. "You flying in today?" reads the text.

Richie responds: "I sure am. What do you need?"

"I need some information from you. Can you meet me at the ticketing level?"

"I'll be out in a few minutes." Richie then texts KAP and tells him to park because he has something to handle. "Give me fifteen minutes."

KAP replies, "Cool, let me know." Richie walks outside of ticketing to see an old friend pulling up. Richie opens the car door and gets inside. "Detective Coles, Chicago PD's pride and joy," says Richie. "What's good?"

"Let's pull in the parking garage," suggests Detective Coles. He pulls into the garage and parks where there are only a few cars around. "Question, Richie: are you familiar with any of these guys?" Detective Coles hands Richie five files of possible suspects involved in the ten dispatch call murders, Jamal Thomas's murder, and Courtney's murder. Richie looks through the files and comes across one on Kolax. He looks up at Detective Coles and asks, "How the hell did you know to find me here?"

"Although we released KAP, the higher ups wanted to see where he'd go and what he'd do. I took the task. Didn't want anybody else following him. Don't worry. He handled himself like a soldier when we questioned him. I let my two overzealous rookies question him first. I knew they would fuck it up."

"I appreciate that." Richie continues looking through the files. "Let me get back to you on this. Can I keep these?"

"Sure. Those are copies. Let me know if you find something out. We're trying to get the asshole responsible off the streets." Detective Coles then pulls out his phone and plays three of the voice recordings of the suspect calling into the dispatch. "We think he's..." The detective pauses as he pulls Kolax's file from Richie's hand and then continues, "our guy. We have to keep pushing this movement forward."

"Indeed," says Richie. "Give me a day or so, and I'll get back to you."

"Great." Detective Coles drives Richie back to ticketing. They fist bump as Richie exits the vehicle. Once Detective Coles drives away, Richie texts KAP to meet him at baggage claim. While walking to meet KAP, Richie smiles knowing Kolax will soon be off the streets. As soon as KAP pulls up along the curb, Richie opens the back door and puts his carry-on luggage in the back seat, then he hops in the front passenger seat and shuts the door behind him.

"What's up, my G?" asks KAP.

"What up, fam?" replies Richie. They fist bump as KAP drives off. "So, how did that meeting with Felix go?"

"It went," replies Richie. "He's giving us more product and shit, and I can't figure out the reason behind it. I will though, in time. But what's good with you? How was your little time at the precinct?"

"Man, you know they can't fuck with me, dude. Rookie ass cops in there... I threw curve balls like a muthafucka. They asked me what my reasoning was for not killing her. I told dem clowns that she can make me cum twice from head, back to back, and I'm fifty. She wasn't a mother of two; she was a fucking unicorn."

"You told dem that shit!" Richie bursts out laughing. "What they say to that shit?"

"Man, dem niggas just gave each other the deer in headlights look and shit."

"Bahahaha. Oh, shit!" says Richie. "But dawg, twice tho?"

"Twice!" says KAP, holding up two fingers.

"Dawg, you almost fifty," says Richie. "You right. She is a unicorn. Damn! Too bad she dead and gone. We should wipe out Maurice and his whole crew for that shit. Da fuck they thinking." They both laugh as they head down the highway to Richie's condo.

"On the real, KAP, you know I love you, and I am telling you this outta love. You gotta curve how you deal with these broads, man. You throwing dick outta both pant legs. I been there. But you gotta be careful. If you ever get caught up with one of them, and they put you in a situation where they can expose you... After they get you fucked up, they'll regret it later, but then it'll be too late. Get you maybe one or two dawg and chill."

"You right, B. I will," replies KAP with sincerity. "I got my eye on a queen. That will come later tho." Richie wonders if he's speaking about Damawi. He looks out the passenger side window, frowns for a quick second, and gets back to business. "The shipment will arrive in Louisiana in another four days. When you heading out?"

"I been getting position reports from Tech, so all is well. I'm heading down there with Tech and the crew tomorrow. Dem cats from Marble Head old crew is getting too old for this shit, Richie. They breathing all hard after the first fifteen minutes of unloading."

Richie smiles. "I know, but they loyal, tight-lipped, and can drive without getting pulled over. Tech working on them fully autonomous cars. Once we get those up and running, the only thing we'll be vulnerable with is during unloading and loading at the drop-off spots. Other than that, there's nothing that can be traced back to us unless we make it possible. Hopefully in the next few weeks, Tech and his crew can have us straight."

"Man, that's what's up," says KAP. "Have you figured out who you gone have replace you when you get out the game?"

"Not sure yet. Hopefully, I'll know soon."

"You know I'm ready! You know I'm ready!"

They pull up to Richie's place, and Richie removes his seat belt, getting ready to depart the vehicle. "Aight, my G," says KAP.

"Aight, fam. Text me and let me know when you land in Louisiana." They fist bump. Richie exits the vehicle, grabs his carry-on from the back seat, and nods as KAP drives off.

* * *

Maurice is in the H2H office meeting with the most powerful gang lords in Chicago. Every major gang from the city is represented, all wanting to know why there's a delay on the merchandise they should've already had in their possession. "Handley, we've been waiting patiently on this merchandise for over a week now. What gives?" asks Jose Rayo, the lord of the Cobra Stones from the north side.

"Jose, be patient," says Maurice. "You know I've never been late, ever. My supplier is having some shipping issues. I'll get it to y'all personally once it comes in. You know my word is bond."

Derrick Brooks, lord of the Gangster Disciples from the west side, speaks up, "We know you bout business, but if the shipment doesn't come, what then? We all got moves to make with them passports, and we trying to get our people a fresh start. Know what I'm saying?"

"I hear you, D," says Maurice. "If I don't deliver within the week, I'll pay you back your money with interest.

"We got plenty money, Joe," says Kenyatta White, lord of the South Side Vice Lords. "It ain't bout the money. I ran with yo dad back in the day, Maurice. He was my #2. You know this and how I felt bout him. This business tho. As soon as you get word, we need to know the deal. Put some fire to them Arabs' ass to get them shits here."

"Yatta, I got you. That's my word." The meeting adjourns, and they all stand up and shake hands. The H2H crew stays back to discuss a few things. "I think that package gone," says Maurice. "We gone have to ante up the bread to pay this shit back. We gone have to figure out another way to get em here in the future. This can't happen again."

"True," says Spree. "Let me reach out to Richie and his crew. We all go way back. Let me see if I can chop it up with him and if he knows something or can push us to someone who do."

"I got no faith in that shit, but that's on you," says Maurice. "If you suspect something, then one of them niggas is paying the price for fucking up my money."

"Aight," says Spree. "I'll let you know."

* * *

Richie drops his bags off inside his house and then he jumps in his car and heads to his mom's house to seek counsel from his uncle on his next move. Richie's phone vibrates, and he sees a text from Spree: "Big homie, this would be a good time to bring that package through and talk to Maurice about linking up. At this point, he wouldn't give a fuck how you got the shit. Let's meet up." Richie puts his phone in his pocket as he pulls into his mom's driveway. He walks through the door, and his mom comes into the foyer wiping her hands off with a kitchen towel. "Hey, son! Happy New Year! How was your trip?" He hugs his mom and kisses her on the cheek.

"Happy New Year, mom. It was good."

"You okay? Seems like something's bothering you."

"Got some business stuff on my mind, mom."

"Did your comedy show go okay?"

"It did."

"Your daughters left for Connecticut yesterday. Their aunt isn't doing too well."

"Okay, I'll call them later. Is unc upstairs?"

"Yeah, he up there watching cartoons. I cooked if you want something."

"Okay, mom." Richie heads upstairs to his uncle's room. He knocks on the door and calls out, "Unc, you good in there?"

"Nephew, come on in!" Richie walks in and waves the weed smoke from his face as he takes a seat. Marble Head smiles and hands Richie the weed, so he can take a hit. "You know better, unc."

"I know, nephew. What's up?"

"Felix is upping the product. Eight hundred more than what we agreed on."

"Eight hundred?" replies Marble Head, looking shocked. "That's a lot of snort. Did he say why he giving you that much over?"

"Not at all. He felt disrespected that I even asked. Told me if I was anybody else, I would've had a bullet in my head. And he say he gotta approve my replacement and some ole racist bullshit."

"Really? Well, I'll tell you this: Any connect that increases your output means two things. Whoever else he's supplying is unable to push product, which disrupts the supply chain. Felix's connect isn't trying to hear about no low-level problems. That's Felix's issue. Or, Felix's connect has someone who's on the same level as Felix and is having trouble, and he's forcing more product on Felix. Either way, you safe cause they need you more than ever. They won't kill you, but they'll hurt the people close to you to get you to act accordingly."

Richie thinks for a minute, soaking in everything his uncle has said. "You right. I got a solution to handle the additional product, but I need H2H for the connections in New York and Jersey."

"I would hate for you to have to deal with Handley. I knew his dad, Melvin, and he was a muthafucka. Just a slimy, untrustworthy cancer to the working people."

"Well, his son is a chip off the ole block," says Richie. "I got something I can use to help shut them down after I get the connects. Just remove that problem altogether. His muscle Kolax is being investigated for those Chatham murders over the last few years. Once his muscle gone, he'll be vulnerable and easier to remove."

Marble Head takes a toke from his blunt. "I hear you, nephew. You have to battle between going against the code of the streets and what new enemies will pop up after he's dead or in jail—"

Richie cuts him off. "Or I can use it to my advantage. Hmm, I have some ideas." Richie stands up. "Thanks, old man. You need anything, Marble Head?"

"Nah. Just stay safe, think three steps ahead, and always consider different scenarios that could possibly hurt you from your moves."

"Got you, unc." They shake hands, and Richie goes downstairs into the kitchen. "Mom, going to have to take what you cooked—"

"To go?" his mom interjects. "I know you, my son." She hugs him and hands him a plate.

"I love you, mother dearest." He kisses her on the forehead and heads out the door to his car. Once he gets inside and closes the door, he texts Brick, telling him to bring the package to the house. He backs out of the driveway and heads home.

* * *

Detective Coles returns to the precinct, and Detective Russell rushes toward him as soon as he walks in. "Coles, remember when we had that conversation in the car about the black businesses popping up all over the place?"

"I do. Why?"

"Well, I've been doing some research with a friend of mine who works with the FBI, off duty of course, to look at all these black businesses that've popped up all over Chicago in a four-year period."

"No pussy to fall into on your time off I suppose. What did you find?"

"Actually, we didn't find anything. No spike in profits for unknown reasons, irregular funding patterns, or no large cash deposits. There has to be something I'm missing."

"There is," says Detective Coles. "Have you checked any strip clubs? New ones or that have had serious upgrades in the last few years?"

"I thought about it, but it's a cliché."

Detective Coles stops walking and turns to look at Detective Russell. "Just like a black man looking into black businesses to try and find something illegal to possibly bring down the whole thing. Dun Dun Dun, it's Super Negro. Detective Russell, do us both a favor. If you want to use your off time to work on something, work on your interrogation skills. It sucks just like a female you obviously don't have."

Detective Coles walks off and whispers, "Fucktard."

* * *

Brick steps out of the elevator and walks down the short hallway to Richie's condo. When Richie hears the elevator, he walks to the door and greets Brick with a handshake and a hug. As they walk into the living room, Richie asks Brick, "What's up, family?" Brick nods as he puts the package on the living room table. It looks like a suitcase, but it's made of metal and shaped like an octagon.

"This is different," says Richie. He puts his ear to it and laughs; Brick smiles. "This shit bet not blow up, B... fuck my furniture up." Richie looks over the package and notices it has a digital lock on it. "Fuck, I want to know what's in it, but I don't want Maurice to know I know what's in it."

Brick swiftly turns his head, shocked by what Richie said.

"Yeah, I know. I'm making a trade: this package for his New York and Jersey connects."

Brick shakes his head.

"Brick, trust me. I been tossing and turning thinking about this, but Felix is giving us more product and expecting his return to be on time. We have to expand." Thinking aloud, Richie says, "I wonder if Tech can get this open." Richie grabs the package and tries to set it up to take a picture of the digital lock. "Da fuck nigga! This thing heavy as shit!" Brick sets it up, and Richie texts Tech: "Can you open this?" He takes a picture of the package and then sends it.

Tech immediately responds: "Is a pig pussy pork?"

"Come to the house ASAP." Richie puts his phone down and asks, "Brick, you hungry?"

Brick nods.

"Sheeree cooked enough for a few days. It's in the fridge." Brick goes to the kitchen and makes himself a plate while Richie continues investigating the package. Brick comes back into the living room with a mountain of food on his plate. Their eyes meet, and Richie smiles at Brick as he sits down and begins eating. Richie couldn't help but reminisce on how they first met. Richie was in Kuwait, his very first deployment in 2001. He was having serious issues with his back and needed to have it checked out. The on-site doctors diagnosed him with nerve issues and recommended he get an epidural, so he flew to Germany to have the procedure done. The German hospital had an influx of badly injured soldiers who were flown in from Iraq. One of those soldiers was Sergeant First Class Ronald "Brick" Daniels. It took six medics to bring him in. Brick was assigned to the Special Forces, and he was one of the guys who does covert operations, like assassination missions. He was on an assassination mission when his team was suddenly surrounded, and he was captured. Since he was the biggest of the bunch, they made an example of him. His captors tortured, burned, and electrocuted him in an effort to get him to give up information on where the US bases were located or any other information they could get out of him. Before he was rescued, they cut his tongue out because it wasn't useful to them since he wouldn't talk.

Richie was in Germany for a week after his procedure, and he asked the nurses to put him in the bed next to Brick's. Although Brick couldn't talk, Richie talked to him every day, and Brick wrote down his answers to many of Richie's questions. It was something about Brick that reassured Richie that he would become his friend, his brother. When Richie left Germany, he and Brick kept in touch through letters and emails. When Brick got out of the military on a medical discharge, he went and lived with Richie for the last ten years of his military career. Richie would fly Brick to Chicago from time to time, so he could help Marble Head get people in line, putting Brick's combat skills to use to keep him sharp until Richie needed them. Brick is Richie's closest friend and most trusted confidant.

Richie's phone vibrates; he looks at his phone and says, "Tech is here." He then calls security to tell them to let Tech come up. Minutes later, Tech comes through the door. "Richie, why can't I have access like Brick and everybody else?"

"First of all, everybody else don't have access. Secondly, you had access, and when I let you use my place for one of your THOTs, I found cum stains on my leather couch. So, you're cut the fuck off. Come open this suitcase before I have Brick detach your retina." Tech side-eyes Brick as he quickly walks past him. He starts running when Brick flinches at him. When he gets over to the table with the package, he pulls out his pocket-sized electronic equipment from his bag and tends to the suitcase.

"Dude, this shit is so elementary, my dear Watson. Give me five minutes." After a few minutes, the suitcase beeps, and the lock opens. "There ya go," says Tech. Richie opens the package and takes a look. Inside are blank passports, which are worth three to five thousand a pop.

"Looks like he has about two hundred of these in here. He got driver's license shells from different states, credit cards, diamonds, and at least a half a milli in counterfeit money. The only people that deal with these are illegals and terrorists," says Richie. "I hope this dude isn't into helping terrorists. Knowing Handley, he probably don't give a fuck as long as he gets his money." Richie looks at Brick. "We don't fuck with terrorists!!" Richie then calls Spree to see when they can get this meeting to take place.

"What's up, big homie?" answers Spree.

"What's up, Spree? When do you think it's a good time to meet with your people?" asks Richie.

"I would say the sooner the better, tomorrow."

"Aight, I'm open, just give me the time and place."

"I'll let Maurice know." Spree hangs up with Richie and immediately calls Maurice.

"Spree, what you got?" asks Maurice.

"Richie wants to meet tomorrow. What's the time and place?"

"Tell them at the office, at three." Spree texts Richie and gives him the details.

Richie reads the message aloud to Brick: "It's on tomorrow at three at H2H's." Brick grabs his phone and texts KAP to let him know the business.

CHAPTER 6

The next afternoon, Richie, KAP, and Brick pull up at H2H's office exactly at 3 p.m. They get out of KAP's GMC Yukon, and Spree meets them at the door. Spree attempts to pat them down for weapons, but Richie stops him. "No need." They each lift up their jackets to show him their weapons. Spree looks, nods, and leads them upstairs. They walk into the conference room where Maurice, Elder, and Kolax are waiting. Maurice's crew stands up when Richie and his crew come through the doorway. Richie scans the room, noticing they're strapped as well. Everyone stands in front of their seats, and no one sits down until after Brick places the package on the table.

"I knew this had your name written all over it," says Maurice as he shakes his head in disbelief. Richie pushes the package toward Kolax, who then picks it up and sets it in front of Maurice. He opens it and looks inside, making sure it has everything in it. "Is there somewhere you and I can talk alone?" asks Richie. Maurice and Richie stand up simultaneously and hand their weapons to their enforcers, then they leave to go into another room. Maurice leads Richie into a new room, which is nearly empty with just a table, two chairs, and a safe in the corner. They both sit down at the table and just stare at each other for a few seconds. "So," says Maurice, "first order of discussion: Sheldon, is he dead?"

"And gone," replies Richie. "He was pushing your counterfeit money through my LBs for months. I was getting unwanted attention from dem people. He was warned. He didn't listen. Away he went."

"From one boss to another, I couldn't get a phone call?" asks Maurice.

"We ain't talked in years before you came to the club. I don't step on your toes, but you stepped on mine regardless of the circumstance. We didn't know about the package, but ya boy reached out about it and here we are."

"Even still, you took one of mines; I need something back."

"You know the game. And you still gained something you didn't have, that package. I'm sure you got people invested in what's in there."

Maurice nods, then responds, "You bring your crew here to bring me this? You could have left this by my front door. Like you so kindly put it, What can you do for me?" Richie smiles a bit and goes in.

"I'm expanding my business, and I need your connects in New York and Jersey and wherever else you got roots. I'd like to give them an opportunity to make more money than they currently making. I'll move the product to the states, and in turn, they invest a percentage of their profits back into the communities we quietly destroying."

"Oh, you still preaching and pushing this black power shit, huh?" asks Maurice. "Ole miniature Farrakhan ass nigga."

Although he's irritated by Maurice's reply, Richie couldn't help but smile and reply, "That's funny."

"Yeah, I got jokes too," says Maurice. "Here's the most important question I got: what's in it for me?"

"All you have to do is oversee the operations of your people. That's moving the product, making sure your people happy, and when they ain't, that's on you. I'll provide guidance and the foundation for their businesses, if they ain't got the knowledge. You'll get a percentage of every business they start and a percentage of each package, and all you gotta do is babysit. Together, we'll have the streets, the businesses, and the coverage. The streets stay the streets."

Maurice nods his head, thinking. "We been enemies for a long time, since the eighth grade. How I know you not gone cross me now and try to pull some slick shit and have me fucked up?"

Richie reaches into his jacket pocket, pulls out Kolax's file given to him by Detective Coles, and tosses it on the table. Maurice picks it up and looks it over. "He's a target for the murders of Jamal Thomas, Courtney, and about ten others."

"This ain't shit. They probably got twenty-five other muthafuckas they looking at too," says Maurice.

"Ion think so, Maurice. See, once they connect the dots to Mr. Telephone Man, he's done. They calling ya man the Dispatch Calling Killer." Maurice looks at Richie shocked that he even knows this information. "That's right. Mr. Telephone man. Ronnie, Bobby, Ricky, Mike, Ralph aaaaand Kolax. Doesn't even have a ring to it, but I know what will ring: his ears from that popcorn love he'll be getting from one of them well-hung homies in the bing. Then, it'll trickle down to you. So, I could've let this shit ride and have all eyes on you. Get your boy outta town until this shit calms down. I can't promise you it'll go away, but I can give you some time. So, another gift from me to you. Merry Belated Christmas, if that's a thing."

Richie and Maurice stand up, ready to gather their people and get to the rest of the day. Richie tells Maurice one more thing: "If you currently doing anything that involves high-level crimes with high visibility, like fucking with terrorists like I been hearing in these streets, either break from it or we can't move forward. I need an answer within seven days on your decision." Richie walks toward the door, then turns around and says, "Oh, and we've been enemies since the sixth grade, not eighth."

Richie and his crew jump into KAP's SUV and start talking about the meeting as KAP pulls off.

"What do you think?" asks KAP.

"I think he'll get onboard. It's enough money for everybody to prosper, especially the community. But Maurice is so unpredictable. Who knows what the deal is. Hopefully next month, if and when Felix gives us more than agreed, we can handle it."

"What if Maurice doesn't get onboard?"

"Then we'll have no choice but to take the keys we agreed on and the rest… Felix will have to deal with em." The car goes quiet because they know there could be dire consequences that come with doing that.

Maurice goes back into the conference room where Elder, Spree, and Kolax are sitting. Irritated, Maurice looks at Kolax and says, "I need you to pack a bag and get ready to get out of town. Call yo cousin and tell her to be ready to replace you. Cause of your phone calls, your name is circulating with them peoples."

"What?" asks Kolax. "That pretty nigga told you that shit? Ion believe it. He just want you to be vulnerable cause he knows how I gets down."

"Nah. Cause they calling you the fucking Dispatch Calling Killer, nigga. You got a title like one of these serial killing ass crackers out here killing bitches and leaving a trail of toe nail shavings behind cause they wanna get caught n shit. Fucking my shit up. In fact, pack ya shit today, nigga!" Maurice leaves out the room with Elder trailing behind. Kolax and Spree remain in the conference room quietly until Spree chuckles and says, "Dat nigga said toe nail shavings," then he starts laughing uncontrollably.

Angered, Kolax replies, "Shut the fuck up, nigga!"

Later that evening, Kolax is at his house packing a bag for St. Louis, so he can lay low there for a while until things calm down and he can return. Maurice and Elder are there to make sure he actually leaves. "Man, you know I don't want to leave, fam. It got to be a way for me to just stay here and make sure you good from a distance," says Kolax.

"You ain't no good to nobody in jail, Ko," says Maurice. "It won't be too long. Just clear ya head, relax, and change the way you do business. No phone calls, toe nails, none of that shit. Do your business and get the fuck outta dodge." Kolax shakes Maurice's hand and then they bump shoulders. He's sad he has to leave because of his actions. He puts his suitcases in the back of his Cadillac Escalade, gives Elder a head nod, starts his car up, and pulls off. Maurice walks over to Elder and stands next to him. "I told that stupid ass nigga, man. I feel fucked up and naked without him, E."

"We'll be okay, Maurice. You handling shit like you suppose to. Like your old man would've. We gotta get Karimah spun up on shit when she gets here. Plus, she knows the crew from photos and conversations, but none of the crew knows her," says Elder.

"I want to keep it like that for a minute too," says Maurice. "She can check some shit out for us before we bring her in. Anyway E, get the little niggas to take every fucking thing outta Kolax house, sell it, burn it… whatever. If the cops do come looking for him, it won't be no evidence nowhere to pin him to where he going or to us."

"I'm on it."

* * *

Richie is at Josephine's talking to Damawi and her staff about the next event for Swaggazine Entertainment. "We have thirty days before the next event. It should do well. It's a brand-new play called Sweetest Temptation that's only been showcased in Baltimore. Nothing else is going on that weekend, so we should corner the market." says Richie.

"The marketing and promotion piece is done. Radio advertisement will start Monday, and the street team has already started putting up flyers on the north side. That's where we have the weakest sales so far," says Damawi.

"Cool. I think we'll have a better turnout with this play than last year's…" Richie's phone vibrates in the middle of his sentence, "...if we do it right." Richie looks at his phone and sees a text from Spree: "Hit me up." Richie looks at Damawi, and she takes over the meeting. Richie steps out of the room and calls Spree.

"Big homie, what's good?"

"Spree, what's the business?"

"Kolax is headed out of town to lay low. Not sure where but prolly with his people in St. Louis. Maurice got some chick coming up here to fill in while he gone."

"A female?" asks Richie in shock. "As his muscle?"

"She probably some bulldog ass chick or relative of Kolax."

"Really? If she looks anything like that Kolax…" Richie laughs, "she's the ugliest muthafucka in Missouri right now. And when she crosses Illinois state line…"

They speak in unison, "She the ugliest muthafucka in Illinois." They both laugh.

"Any word with Maurice taking my offer?" asks Richie.

"He said what the offer was, but he'll talk to Elder about it before he make a move. Believe that. So, no telling." responds Spree.

"Aight, I gave him a week to let me know. His move will determine our next move."

"I'm still down regardless. If I hear something on who this bitch is or what Maurice gonna do, I'll hit you up."

Richie hangs up and heads back into the meeting. "Everything good?"

"Everything's good," says Damawi. "We on point. I'll call you if something comes up."

"D, can I speak to you for a minute?" asks Richie.

"Sure. Give me five minutes. Let me finish up here, and I'll meet you in my office." As Richie walks toward her office, Damawi looks at Gina, and they both smile at each other. Damawi wraps up some important details about the play, then she turns the meeting over to Gina before leaving the room to speak with Richie in her office. When she walks in, she sees Richie staring at a few of her old military photos.

"What's up, boss?" asks Damawi.

"Boss?" repeats Richie. "Well, that's something I ain't heard since our military days. So, D, is there anything going on in your life that'll cause you to lose focus on our goals?"

"Ummm... no. Is there something I'm doing wrong for you to question my focus?"

"Not at all. We're about to go through a major transition with some things, and I just need you to be laser-focused. Is there someone that might infringe on that?"

"You mean like a boyfriend or a boo thang?"

"Well, now that you mention it... yes."

"Like KAP?" asks Damawi.

"No," says Richie. "Why would you say him?" Damawi stares at Richie for a few seconds before she responds.

"I know the rules, Richie. I would never break them for him or anyone who works for you."

"Good." Richie's phone vibrates in his hand, and he looks at it. "It's KAP. He's at the airport. Let me take this." Richie answers the call, "KAP, hold on." He then covers the mouthpiece on his phone and asks Damawi, "We good, D?"

"Yeah, we good. As long as you not hanging up in my face."

Richie looks at Damawi, trying not to smile. He takes his hand off the mouthpiece, puts the phone to his ear, and asks KAP, "Everything good?" as he walks out Damawi's office.

* * *

KAP, Tech, and the crew arrive at the six-bedroom, eight-bathroom, gated mansion in New Orleans, Louisiana. The owner, who's still alive on paper, was once an adversary of Richie's cause. The bodies of him and his crew were turned into ashes at Lloyd's Funeral Home, mixed into cement, and then compounded within the structure of one of Richie's businesses. When he first took over his uncle's business, this was Richie's ritual for handling those who didn't want to rebuild the community. This was his way of forcing them to be a part of the process.

The mansion was a familiar place for KAP, Tech, and the crew because they visit it every thirty to sixty days to receive and transport the product to Midwestern customers where they turn white powder into paperbacks. In the back of the mansion is a large pool surrounded with a beautiful cement deck. It's followed by three acres of wooded area with a well-hidden paved road that stretches all the way to the back of an enclosed eighty-foot boathouse with two slots that face the Gulf of Mexico. The depth of the water was once shallow, but Richie hired a private company owned by an old Army buddy of his to dredge the waterway, so the submarines could get in and out.

While everyone else goes into the mansion, Tech goes into the boathouse to set up his computer and equipment to receive the submarines. Soon after, KAP walks into the boathouse with Larry, Roger, Jeff, and William to move the boats out of the boathouse to make room for the submarines. "Tech, how much longer do we have before they get here?" asks KAP.

"A little less than six hours. They'll be docked at about 8:30 p.m.," responds Tech. Larry and Jeff climb aboard each boat and head to the pilot house to move them outside the boathouse. "After y'all move the boats, get the transpo in position. Then we'll eat and get some sleep. We gonna have a long night off-loading," says KAP. Elmer and Edward, the Jones brothers, back up the sixteen-wheeler, the vans, and two cars to the back of the boathouse while their wives Barbara and Evelyn cook dinner. Tech shouts, "I'm all set! I'll come back an hour before they get here. I'm gonna go watch some porn until the food is ready."

* * *

Elder returns to H2H's office to give Maurice an update on Kolax. "His house is cleared out."

"Good shit," says Maurice. "Sit down, E." Elder takes a seat next to Maurice. "What you think, E?"

"It's not what I think, youngblood; it's what you think. Have you thought about the pros and cons of working with Richie?"

"I have. I been racking my brain trying to figure out why he would want to work with me now. I mean...the money is tight, and I'll have legit businesses. But I'll have to give up what I do, and what I do best. I'll also be working for that nigga, sort of, and he'll have control over me. I can't have that, E. I just don't trust it."

"You need long-term, clean money. You can't do what you do forever. What if you separate your businesses and have Spree run that shit Richie doing. You stay in the streets and still eat off both plates. Spree, he ready. Besides, dropping what you provide for them gang lords and them Arabs, you just can't up and stop unless you dead or in jail."

"For what Richie wants, I believe Spree is ready," says Maurice. "He ain't one-hundred percent certified for this street shit no mo. There's a lil nurse I used to smash back in the day named Kim that work at the hospital Jamal's mom was in. She gave me the whole situation. Spree ain't merc her; he stayed with her until she died. I ain't even mad, really. Only me and Kolax could've done her without hesitation. If I decide to do it, Richie don't have a say on how I do it, as long as it gets done. As far as them lords and Arabs go, it ain't an easy out, but as long as them niggas can get what they need, it's a shoulder shrug in my opinion."

* * *

KAP, Tech, and the crew sit down at the table after fixing their plates from in the kitchen. "This is one of the major benefits of coming here. My old heads' wives be throwing down," says KAP. "Almost like it's Thanksgiving up in here."

"You see why we got these big ass stomachs," says Edward.

"Man, I don't get food like this very often. I love it," says Tech.

"Why not?" asks KAP.

"My mom's white, dude. She don't cook like this," responds Tech.

"But your dad is black tho," says KAP.

"True. But all he did was work fifteen-hour days at IBM, so I barely saw him, and he didn't cook. My white side was only able to handle the blandness. My half-brother, whose mom is black, I felt sorry for him. He lived with us for about six months. He tried to hang in there with the way my mom cooked, but when he seen her put raisins in her potato salad, he was fucking outta there, dude." The table erupts in laughter, which lasts for about a minute.

"Your dad worked at IBM, huh?" asks KAP. "Is that where you get your skills from."

"Yup," Tech says proudly. "It's natural talent. I built a replica of Simon Says when I was six and a cell phone when I was like eleven. So, yeah."

"What?!" asks KAP, surprised. "Da fuq you join the military for with those skills?"

"I was accepted into MIT, but I fucking hate Massachusetts. Plus, my dad was sick…so I needed to get away after he died."

"Aww, baby," says Mrs. Barbara as she enters the dining room from the kitchen. She puts her plate down on the table, then goes over and hugs Tech, putting her huge breasts on the side of his face.

"I mean, like, so dead," says Tech. "I was so sad," he elaborates as he presses his face into Mrs. Barbara's chest.

"Son," says Edward, "if you don't back up, you gone see that nigga again come soon."

* * *

Richie calls Detective Coles while he drives to Josephine's to meet up with Brick to chill. "Richie, what's going on? You got some news for me?" asks Detective Coles.

"A little something. Not sure who you tracking, but the five you showed me came up clean. But I been hearing that Sheldon Bradley is someone you should be talking to."

"Really? Interesting," says Detective Coles. "I didn't even give you his file. He is someone of interest. Do you know his whereabouts?"

"No one knows. My people say he disappeared as if he just turned into ash and blew away." Richie smiles big as hell and puts the side of his right fist up to his mouth to muffle his laughter.

"Well, wherever he is, we'll find him," says Detective Coles. Richie thinks to himself, *Sheeeiiittt!* Richie then responds to Detective Coles aloud, "I'm sure you will, Brian. If I hear anything, I'll let you know." Moments later, Richie pulls into Josephine's parking lot and sees that Brick's car is already there.

Brick is sitting inside in the lounge area, watching Damawi conduct business while he's sipping his Grey Goose and Sprite mixed drink. He flashes back to when Richie introduced her to the crew. She was so excited to have the opportunity to follow her dreams, but she had no idea what she had to do to be in the crew. Although Richie handpicked her to be the administrator for the organization, no one got a pass in his immediate circle. Brick smiles a bit while reminiscing. The organization was in the process of eliminating the other drug organizations that wouldn't follow along with the plan. The Big Tyme Crew's demise was next, and of course, they annihilated them. One of the easiest battles they'd ever had, and there were several.

Richie, T.K., and KAP were upstairs walking through the building looking for stragglers when they heard single gunshots sounding off from the muffled weapons throughout the building; they never left anyone alive. Damawi stayed with Brick on the first floor. She hadn't fired any shots up until that point. They found someone hiding behind the couch. Brick snatched the couch away, and the guy lay on the ground, begging for his life. "Please let me go! I won't say shit!" Brick stepped aside so that Damawi could initiate herself into the organization. She snatched her gun out quick and pointed it at the guy's head as if she was about that life. The guy covered his face with his hands. "Please! I'm begging you!" She held the gun up with her arm fully extended while the man pleaded repeatedly for his life. "I have a daughter," he cried out. Brick stepped behind her; he could see her arm shaking.

"Brick! D! Anyone else down there?" yelled Richie from the second floor. "We coming down." Damawi wasn't going to shoot the guy, so Brick grabbed her hand and took her finger off the trigger. He then covered her hand with his and pulled the trigger. She jumped from the muffled sound of the suppressed weapon. Brick then pushed her arm down as soon as he saw Richie peeking around the corner. "We good, B?" Brick nodded. Richie looked at Damawi and her victim and smiled. "Aight. Good deal! Let's get these bodies over to Lloyd's. D, pull the truck around back and bring in the gasoline." T.K. went to the refrigerator and opened it. "Who wants a beer?"

"What kind?" asked KAP.

"Stella Artois."

"Oh shit! Throw me one," said KAP.

"Only three in here though. You want one, Richie?" Richie shook his head no as Damawi returned with two gasoline-filled jugs and set them down. Richie took one of the jugs and headed upstairs as T.K. offered Damawi a beer. She just stared at him in silence; he shrugged his shoulders and gulped down the entire bottle. Damawi handed the other jug of gasoline to KAP as he walked into the kitchen with T.K. Damawi then looked at Brick, disappointed in herself. "Brick, I..." Brick put his finger over his mouth, signaling for her to be quiet. He then slowly walked over to her, bent down, and whispered into her ear the best way that he could, "You good." When he backed away from her, Damawi looked shocked because no one had ever heard Brick speak, except for Richie. He just wanted her to know that what happened was their secret. One clear thing Brick learned that day was if they ever need Damawi to be a killer, they're pretty much fucked.

Brick headed upstairs as Richie was throwing bodies down the steps. "Brick, beat that! He ain't touch a step. Dude gotta weigh a buck fifty, buck seventy-five easy." Brick just smiled at Richie, the kid in him always competing. T.K., KAP, and Damawi took the bodies to the van while Richie poured gasoline all over the second floor before throwing the jug in one of the rooms. "All the bodies in the van?" asked Richie.

"Yeah, we good!" called out T.K. Everyone loaded into the van except for KAP, who lit a rag and threw it into the building. He watched the fire immediately spread throughout the first floor and make its way up the stairs to the second floor. KAP then hopped into the van, and Brick slowly drove away. "Let's drop these bodies off, take the van to Smitty's, and get some food," said Richie as they drove away from the burning building.

Richie walks into Josephine's and sits next to Brick, who gives him a fist bump. He waves the waitress over to the table, and she comes over quickly and says, "Hi, Richie! What you having?"

"Whatever Brick has and make mine a double." Damawi walks over and sits down, and for the first time in a long time, they talk the night away, not worrying about the decisions that need to be made or the directions the organization might be headed in.

* * *

Tech brings the submarines to the surface and guides them into the boathouse perfectly. The crew is standing by ready to off-load the product, and KAP walks in just as Tech is finishing. "Captain KAP!" yells Tech. "All three subs are docked and ready for unloading."

"Three subs? Da fuq you talking bout?" asks KAP.

"Those two ocean blue subs right there and the one right here in my fucking pants," says Tech as he starts humping the air.

"Dude, you stupid. Let's get this shit unloaded, so we can get the hell outta here." The crew immediately starts off-loading the product, kilo after kilo. Tech stops and sniffs the packaging of one of the kilos. "Man, you can't even smell anything."

"The smell is undetectable because the packaging is made of a thin synthetic rubber cured in a chemical that desensitizes our sense of smell. It works on humans and animals," replies KAP.

"Amazing what money can buy," says Tech. It takes them nearly six hours to off-load both submarines and load the product for transportation. Once everything is off-loaded, Tech climbs inside each submarine to inspect the integrity of the hulls, ensure they are sealed watertight, and remove all the drones except for the ones in the front. He then submerges them inside the boathouse, and Larry and Jeff move the boats back into the boathouse on top of the submarines, hidden in plain sight.

Now that everything is loaded into the transportation vehicles, all vehicles head out the gate to their destinations. Larry and Jeff are the drivers of the vans. Larry delivers to Indiana and Michigan while Jeff delivers to Illinois and Ohio. Edward and Barbara drive the sixteen-wheeler to deliver the product to Kansas, Missouri,

Iowa, Nebraska, Minnesota, and Wisconsin. The trailer of the sixteen-wheeler is filled with medical supplies and equipment that are hauled routinely to those states, regardless if the product is being moved or not. The product is concealed and separated within the walls of the custom-made trailer. The medical products are arranged in the trailer so that nothing has to be moved for the organizations to access the panels. When the truck reaches each drop-off location, KAP watches the transactions via a camera in the trailer. Each organization deposits their remaining balance for the product in a panel on the floor in the very back of the trailer, which weighs the deposited cash. If the correct amount is deposited, then the panels for that organization open automatically, and they can retrieve their share of the product.

Elmer and Evelyn drive the cars as scouts for the sixteen-wheeler. Elmer travels an hour ahead, and Evelyn follows an hour behind, giving warnings and reports on the flow of traffic and any law enforcement they may encounter. The scouts remain with the truck until all transactions are complete. Then all the vehicles get serviced and returned to Louisiana for further use. KAP and Tech remain in Louisiana to monitor everything from the cameras set up in each of the vehicles until the product reaches each destination and is distributed. If the authorities disrupt the passage of any of the vehicles holding product, unbeknownst to any of the drivers, all vehicles are filled with explosives to remove any connection to the organization.

* * *

Detective Coles walks over to Detectives Neeley and Russell's desks. "Good morning, Neeley."

"Good morning, boss," replies Detective Neeley.

"How was your vacation?"

"It was good; much needed. Thanks for asking."

"Where's your girlfriend?"

"She's home with my daughter; she's sick."

"Not her," says Detective Coles sharply. "The one who sits next to you with the pretty mouth and ass of a seventeen-year-old Asian boy?"

"Umm, he said he was going to be late because there was something he wanted to check out."

"Oh, really? Well, I have someone I need you two to run down: Sheldon Bradley. I got an anonymous tip that we need to question him. He's still missing, and he could be one out of two viable suspects. My instincts are telling me to find the other mope, Kolax Imanu, as well." Detective Coles then throws Sheldon's file on Detective Neeley's desk. "There's been very little movement with this case, so have your girlfriend bring you up to speed when he returns. And tell him to come find me when he gets back."

"Okay, boss," says Detective Neeley as he looks through Sheldon's file.

* * *

Detective Russell is on the South Side of Chicago when he stops in front of a well-known cannabis business called Up In Smoke. He parks his car, grabs his badge off the front seat, and exits the vehicle. When he walks into the store, he hears the sound of a person smoking weed, which plays every time someone opens the door.

"Welcome to Up In Smoke! May I help you?" calls out a woman's voice.

"Yes, you caaaan..." says Detective Russell as he reads the name tag on the female employee's shirt. "...Ryan. I'm Detective Russell, and I'm looking for the owner."

"Sure, he's in the back." As she picks up the phone, Randall, the owner, comes from the back office toward the front desk.

"You the owner?" asks Detective Russell."

"I am. I'm Randall. How may I help you?"

"Hi, I'm Detective Russell, and I've got a few questions for you."

"Sure, detective. Shoot." Ryan rolls her eyes at Randall's corny cop reference.

"How long have you owned this business?"

"Nearly three years now. I have three of these. One here, one on the north side, and one on the west side. Is there something that—"

"No, I just noticed that there are a lot of black businesses popping up, and I just wanted to meet the people face-to-face who are responsible for such great things that are happening in our community."

"Oh, okay, detective. I appreciate that. Yeah, we've made great strides to create jobs, give to the community—"

"So what exactly did you do in your previous life in order to afford a business like this? The resources aren't really available for the inner-city folks to start businesses." Ryan walks away from the front desk and heads to the back as she senses there's something more to Detective Russell's questions.

"Ryan, you can stay," says Randall. "The resources are there, just not in plain sight. And any of us can find them with enough education, drive, and motivation to break the systemic roadblocks that are placed before us, or to help us remove that slave mentality that's chained around our minds to make us believe that we can't find and utilize those resources."

"So, how much money would you say you make per month in this business?"

Shocked that the detective would ask him this question, Randall just pretended like he didn't hear it. "Anymore questions, detective?"

"No, but if I do, I know who to find."

"Have a great day."

Detective Russell scans around the shop, then walks toward the door and opens it. The sound of someone smoking weed plays again. "Detective," calls out Randall. Detective Russell turns around and looks at Randall, who then points to his neck and says, "Your chain is showing." Ryan gasps and puts her hand over her mouth, and Detective Russell angrily turns around and heads out the door to his car.

* * *

Richie is relaxing at home when his phone rings. He looks at the screen and sees that it's General Chris Warrington, who Richie hopes to replace him after he retires. "What's up, brother?" asks Richie, answering the call. "You good?"

"I'm great!" says Chris. "Ready to transition from this job to yours. I'm free for the next few days or so. Do I still need to head to Mexico?"

"Yeah, I just need to give him the heads up. Can you leave within twenty-four hours, if need be?"

"Really, Richie? After all the quick reaction deployments we been on, you ask me this?"

"Chris, I'm just making sure, man; you know your wife don't let that rope around your ankle reach further than your backyard." They both laugh.

"That's a sad but true story," says Chris, laughing again. "You'll be married one day, and you'll see."

"I'll be ready. Okay, I'll send him a text and then I'll let you know his availability."

"Sounds good, Richie. Other than business, how's life?"

"Good. It'll be better when you finally retire."

"You coming to my retirement ceremony next week?"

"I will, but on one condition: don't have my name all up in your retirement speech. It's your day."

"Shit, then I'll have to revise it, but it's a deal. Let me know."

"Will do," says Richie. He hangs up the call, then texts Felix: "Are you available to meet Chris within the next four days?" His phone rings again. It's his brother. "Randall, what's good bro?"

"Nothing much. You got a minute?"

"Yeah. The family okay? How's mom?"

"Everyone's good. You know I got that. Listen, there was a Detective Russell that came to Up In Smoke on the south side a little bit ago asking all these questions on how many stores we got and how much money the store makes a month. It was weird."

"Really?" asks Richie. "You ever seen him before today?"

"Never."

"What's your gut telling you from your interaction with him?"

"He trying to peel back the onion on the come up."

"Aight, we already know what our play is. Lemme reach out to some people. Be cool."

"Aight, love ya, bro," says Randall as he hangs up. Richie's phone vibrates, and he sees a reply from Felix: "I'll see him in two." Richie then texts Chris: "He'll see you two days from now. Call D. She'll square you away. Safe travels."

Richie sits there a moment and wonders aloud, "Why the fuck is this detective coming around asking questions about my businesses?" Anxiously, he calls Detective Coles. "Richie, what's going on? You got something for me?"

"No, but I'm hoping you got something for me. One of your detectives went to one of my businesses asking questions. Is something brewing in that precinct I need to know about?" Detective Coles closes his eyes and takes a deep breath. "What was the detective's name?"

"Last name Russell. Ring any bells?"

"Unfortunately, it does. Right in my fucking ears. I'll take care of it." Richie hangs up and shakes his head, wondering why now. He's sure his brother handled the detective well, probably even put him in his place. Randall has always been the protector of the family, like what Brick is for Richie. He's sacrificed many opportunities in his life just to ensure the family was good, especially for their Uncle Marble Head, who was exposed to Agent Orange, along with their Uncle Swift, during the Vietnam War. It left Marble Head with peripheral neuropathy that severely damaged his nerves many years later. Uncle Swift suffers from painful skin rashes that appear on different parts of his body from time to time. Randall has always been more than a big brother to Richie. In their younger years, Randall was his protector and confidant, and Richie has always given Randall the respect he deserves, regardless of how much success he achieves in his lifetime.

* * *

Detective Russell gets to his desk and places his coat on the back of his chair. He sits down and shuffles through some files as Detective Neeley comes into their cubicle.

"Hey, girlfriend!" says Detective Neeley. "Someone stopped by looking for you."

"Who?" asks Detective Russell.

"Coles. He wanted me to tell you to come see him when you got here." Detective Russell puts the files down and heads to Detective Coles's office. Detective Coles is talking on the phone, so Detective Russell leans against the wall and watches him from a few yards away. When Detective Coles sees him, he waves him in, and Detective Russell walks over and sits in one of the chairs in front of the desk. "Yes sir, we have two suspects we're currently looking for, and when we find them, we'll bring them in for questioning. Okay, Chief." Detective Coles wraps up the call, then hangs up the phone. "Russell, how are you?"

"I'm good, Coles. You wanted me?"

"I did. Two things: One, I'm adding Kolax Imanu back as a suspect. From the work you and Fred did on this case, my gut is telling me he's our guy. Let's find out where he lives, known addresses, and next of kin. We have to bring him in, question him, and move forward."

"Okay, boss. Got it."

"Two, what the fuck are you doing going to Up In Smoke asking stupid ass questions about their profits. I got a complaint from the owner about an hour ago. Are you working a case I'm unaware of?"

"No, boss."

"Tell me what the fuck you was doing there?"

"Boss, I'm convinced these businesses were started behind illegal activities. Nearly one hundred businesses were started over the last three years. We need to follow the money."

"Russell, you follow the cases I give you. Your witch hunt is over. I hope this is crystal clear?" Detective Russell looks disappointed that Detective Coles doesn't want to investigate his hunch, but he agrees.

"Yes, boss, crystal clear."

"Good. I need information concerning the whereabouts of Mr. Imanu within the next forty-eight hours. And bring Neeley up to speed."

* * *

Richie, who's eating breakfast and chilling at home, receives a text from Spree: "Call me."

"Spree, what's up?" asks Richie.

"Just chillin, big homie. Maurice came to his decision last night. Let's meet somewhere and chop it up. Where do you want to meet?"

"Let's meet at Up In Smoke on the south side. I can be there in an hour, hour and a half, tops."

"Aight cool. I'll be there a little after you get there. I gotta make a stop." Richie gets up from the couch excited to hear what Spree has to say. He takes a quick shower, gets dressed, and heads to the meet-up spot. An hour and fifteen minutes later, Richie walks into Up In Smoke and is met by his brother. "What's up, lil bro?" says Randall as he greets Richie with a handshake and a hug.

"I'm good, big bro. That cop come back through here?" asks Richie.

"Nah, ain't heard from him."

"I took care of it, so we should be good. Is the office free and clear? Spree coming through to discuss some things."

"Spree? Man, I haven't seen or heard from that dude in years. It'll be good to see him."

"Yeah," says Richie as he heads to the back to check out the office. The door opens and the sound of someone smoking weed plays. A customer pushes through the door and laughs at the sound. Randall looks at the front door and sees a six-foot tall, beautiful brown-skinned sista. The right side of her hair is cut into a low fade that stops at the top next to some mini locs that drape over the left side of her head. She's curvy with hazel eyes and a walk that would attract any man's attention. "Damn," Randall says to himself as he watches the woman dressed in a red business-like dress with black Louboutin shoes and red lipstick walk into the store.

"Welcome to Up In Smoke! May I help you?" asks Randall.

"Hello! No, I was just stopping by to see what was in here. Are you the owner?"

"I am. Feel free to look around, and if you have any questions, Ryan will be here to answer them."

"Thank you," says the customer as she walks off to look at the merchandise. Randall goes to the office where he sees Richie sitting behind the desk with his feet propped up. "Man, you see that female?" asks Randall.

"Yeah. She even looks fine as hell on these dusty ass cameras. You can't see anybody take shit and roll the fuck out."

"Man, can you just shut the hell up for a second and admire the beauty before you start trippin? We ain't got to be all business all the damn time," says Randall as he and Richie start wrestling and laughing.

"Did you get her number?" asks Richie.

"I was about to, but you called me back here."

"Man, ain't nobody call yo ass! Go get that number!" Randall walks back to the front with some pep in his step, but she had already left the store. "Man, damn!" says Randall. Richie yells from the back, "Fail!" Randall opens the front door to see Spree hollering at the customer in the parking lot. "So, let me get your number," says Spree.

"I don't usually give my number to guys I just met but..."

Spree finishes her sentence, "If you give me yours, I'll call you, riiiight?"

"No, I will. I think you're cute and rough around the edges." She goes into her purse, pulls out a pen and a piece of paper, and gives them to Spree. Randall looks at the whole exchange and says quietly to himself, "This nigga... damn!!" Spree writes his name and number on the slip of paper and gives it to her. Richie comes and looks over Randall's shoulder out the door. When he sees what Randall's looking at, he pats his brother on the shoulder and says, "Man, you gotta be quicker than that," and walks back to the office. Spree tells the woman bye and walks into the store. "Randall, what's up, man? I ain't seen you in years, boi! What's good with you?"

"All is well, man. Just trying to maintain, ya know? Good to see you. And you still pulling numbers I see."

"Yeah, man, but I know her type. She won't call me, dude."

"She probably will. You neva know. Anyway, Richie in the back. Gone on back there." Spree walks to the back office and greets Richie. "Big homie, what's good?"

"You, bro," says Richie. "Have a seat. So, what can you do for me?"

"Maurice gonna go forward with you and connect you to his people in New York. He didn't discuss what y'all talked about, but I do know he wants a few more things before it's one hunnit tho."

"Well, we'll see what it is he wants."

"Nothing too crazy."

"It's a go then."

"He gone call you in a day or so to confirm a meeting place for the final discussion before he starts making calls to bridge everything."

"Okay, I'll be waiting. I'm sure he made his people aware already."

"So, do you think we need to move forward with our plans with Maurice?" asks Spree.

"Eventually, yes," replies Richie. "Maurice is so grimy; he'll find a way to sabotage his own come up. In the meantime, in-between time, I'm going to build relationships with the connects and with the gang lords I don't already know, and merc Maurice soon after. Did you ever find out where Kolax is?"

"Yeah, he in St. Louis with his peoples."

"Aight cool. Any word on his replacement?"

"Not a word. She'll be here early next week is what I'm hearing. Maurice made Kolax leave the night of that meeting."

"Smart move. He should be safe for the time being. Aight, player. I'll let you get on with your day. If you hear anything, let me know."

"Aight, big homie." They both stand up, fist bump, and bump shoulders, then Spree heads to the front door, and Richie leaves out the back door to go home.

* * *

General Chris Warrington's flight has just landed at Puerto Vallarta International Airport. He grabs his cell phone and texts Richie: "Richie, I just landed in Mexico. They're going to meet me just outside of customs."

"Good," replies Richie.

"Any advice?"

"If he asks you anything about giving us more real estate, tell him you can't make that promise until you better understand the current situation. We are in the process of expanding our landscape and will let him know how much property we can maintain. He isn't a long-winded person when it comes to conversation. You'll probably be there a couple hours tops, then you'll be flying out of there soon after."

"Well, that'll make my wife happy. I'll call you when I'm at the airport if this is the case. If not, I'll send you a text if my itinerary changes."

"Okay, Chris. Good luck and talk with you soon."

Richie puts down his phone and starts thinking about how he can finally start the next stage of the organization's mission: spreading the movement beyond the Midwest to all the major cities, creating jobs and other opportunities for his people, then minimizing the influx of drugs, making it less impactful to families because opportunities will be available for all. He envisions black communities just like Black Wall Street in Tulsa, Oklahoma, as it once was before some White people burned it to the ground, destroying the lives and economic momentum of the Black community. Richie knows the meeting with Maurice and his New York and New Jersey connections is pivotal for the future.

* * *

"Free at last, free at last, thank God almighty, we are free at last!" yells Tech as he watches the sixteen-wheeler drop off its last package. KAP exhales as he leans back in his chair. "Tech, when are you going to be finished with the cars, so we don't have to be here babysitting?"

"Actually, when I get back, I'll be conducting test trials next week. My team of geniuses and I want to make sure it's perfect before we show it to the crew. What's the hurry? Are you saying you don't like spending intimate time with me, KAP?" Tech looks at KAP and bats his eyelashes. KAP smiles and shakes his head while grabbing his phone to text Richie: "Done."

"Let's head downtown tonight and listen to some jazz and get a taste of New Orleans before we fly back tomorrow," says KAP.

"I'm down," says Tech. Richie texts KAP back: "Good shit! You flying tomorrow, right?"

"Yep."

"Cool, we'll chop it up tomorrow. We'll be having another meeting with H2H shortly after you get back to see what the future holds."

"Word? Cool," responds KAP. Tech and KAP start packing up Tech's computer equipment and bags as they look forward to getting some fresh air tonight and returning home in the morning.

* * *

Richie is at home looking over business proposals for Bam-Bamm, Timmy, and Sean, sent to him by one of his business partners for the youth centers. Talking to himself, "Man, this would be pretty dope if we can get other entertainers to follow suit behind this effort. One in Richmond, Baltimore, and Detroit." He then sends everything over to them in an email and adds a note for them to have a call next week to discuss the proposals. He slides back from his desk and stretches when he hears his phone vibrating. He picks it up and sees that it's Detective Coles calling. "Brian, what's going on?"

"Richie, just calling to let you know that problem is no more. I'll keep an eye on him just in case he has the inclination to pop up at one of your businesses again."

"Thanks, Brian. I appreciate that. Any luck finding Sheldon?"

"No, we still haven't located him as of yet. But we did decide to put one of the five suspects I gave you back as someone we would like to find and question."

"Really? I bet I know which one: Keith Price?"

"No, Kolax Imanu. I have a hunch about that guy."

"Well, you're the man, so your hunches are probably better than someone's best guess. You'll find him. If I hear anything, I got you."

"Thanks. I'll be in touch," says Detective Coles just before he disconnects the call. Richie sits back at his desk and ponders aloud on the situation. "If they find Kolax before we have this meeting and they connect him to Maurice, that could delay everything. But if they find him after the meeting and it goes well, then we can move forward. It may take them days or weeks to find Kolax since he in St. Louis. But if they find him after we start doing business together, this could bring attention to my front door that Brian won't be able to close. I have to put a hurdle in Brian's path somehow to throw him off Kolax."

* * *

Chris arrives at Felix's mansion, and Felix greets him at the front door. "The General has arrived. Hello, my friend! Welcome to my home. Come. Enter. We will talk on the back patio."

"Thank you for welcoming into your home, Felix," says Chris. As they walk through Felix's home, Chris is amazed at the beauty of it. They walk side by side as Felix's guards follow a few feet behind. When Chris takes a seat on the patio, Felix waves at two waitresses who walk over with a tray full of refreshments.

"Anything to drink? You choose," says Felix. Chris picks a glass of water and a shot of liquor. "Christopher, I'm not going to waste your time or mine. Richie has spoken highly of you, and I have two, maybe three questions for you and then we are done."

"Okay, shoot," says Chris.

"That is an interesting choice of words. Because based on your answers, that's exactly what I might do." Felix's lack of emotion surprises Chris, as he sits frozen for a second before he gathers his composure.

"Well, I guess I better answer these questions correctly."

"One: let's say Richie is no longer in the picture because of unforeseen circumstances, and I need you to handle more product than we initially agreed to. What would be your response to me?" Chris looks over Felix's left shoulder and sees his guards grip their machine guns. He pauses, then answers, "Well, without Richie and not knowing the current landscape of how much we have agreed on, I would do my best to move the product without disrupting the logistics, and I would probably look to pay for the extra product you send upfront, so you won't experience issues from your boss."

"I see," says Felix. "Two: is there anyone I need to eliminate to further our business that you yourself could not do?"

Chris confidently responds, "I wouldn't eliminate someone personally, but I could give the order to do so. If I get caught, then that wouldn't be good for business. I wouldn't recommend it." Felix stares at Chris for nearly ten seconds without blinking or moving a muscle.

"You wouldn't recommend it?" Felix laughs uncontrollably for a few seconds and stands up. "I like you, Christopher. I will let Richie know my answer. Good luck, my friend. My jet will take you back to the US. You have much work to do." Chris stands up as they shake hands, then the guards walk Chris to the plane in the back of the mansion. When he boards the plane, he's greeted by a beautiful Mexican flight attendant. She shows him to his seat as the guards step away from the plane.

"Hello, sir. Will you be drinking?"

Chris wipes the sweat from his forehead and replies, "Fuck yes! Keep'em coming!" As the plane turns around and takes off for the US, he texts Richie and says, "It's a go. We good."

Richie looks at his phone and smiles at Chris's text. He sees the light at the end of the tunnel Marble Head said would never come. He walks over to his liquor cabinet and pours himself a shot. His phone rings, and he sees an unsaved number he doesn't recognize.

"Hello?"

"Yeah, this Maurice."

"What's up, Handley?"

"Let's meet tomorrow. I'm on board with what you offering, but I have a few more requests."

"Okay, we can meet. I'll give you the time and place in the morning." They both hang up, and Richie takes a sip from his drink and smiles.

* * *

KAP and Tech are heading back to the mansion in a limousine after spending some much-needed time away from working. They spent a few days checking out some of the best black-owned restaurants in New Orleans and then they hit up the jazz clubs in the area.

"Man, Dooky Chase's never lets me down," says KAP. "I love the food there."

"Café du Monde is my favorite," says Tech. "Followed by the one with the waitress with the big ole butt."

"You talking about Li'l Dizzy's?"

"Li'l fucking Dizzy's! Yeah. I always look forward to eating when I get here, and the jazz clubs stay lit." When the limousine pulls up to the front of the mansion, they exit and see a truck parked inside the gate. "Why is there a fucking truck outside the fucking house?" asks Tech. They stand outside the gate staring for a moment, then KAP walks through the slightly open gate, and Tech follows closely behind him. He walks up to the truck, hops up on the side steps, and looks inside. The door is unlocked, so KAP slowly opens it to see keys laying on the driver's seat. The key ring had two keys on it, one of which was for the truck. KAP picks up the keys, and he and Tech walk to the back of the truck where they see a padlock on the trailer door. Tech turns on his flashlight on his phone so KAP can open the lock, but before he can open it, they see headlights coming down the road. They both run and hide on the other side of the truck.

A black car with dark tinted windows pulls up to the gate, and two people step out the back of the vehicle and walk to the trunk. One of the men hands the other man his carry-on luggage from the trunk and his phone from the guy's pocket. One of the guys hops back into the car, and they leave the other man standing outside the gate as they make a U-turn and drive away. "Tech, stay here," says KAP. He then grabs his phone and turns on the flashlight. Pointing his flashlight at the guy as he walks up, KAP shouts, "Stop right there! Who are you?" The guy stops, and KAP continues to walk closer, panning the light over the guy's feet up to his face until he is able to identify him. KAP recognizes the man and calls out, "General Warrington? What the fuck you doing here?"

"I just flew in from Mexico. They took my phone once we landed, and that car was waiting for me on the side of the plane. Then we came straight here."

"Why were you in Mexico?" asks KAP.

"I just met with Felix." KAP puts two and two together and becomes highly disappointed. They all walk back over to the back of the truck, and Chris asks, "Whose truck is this?"

"Apparently, it's ours," replies KAP. "We'd just pulled up before you did, and it was just sitting here." Tech puts his phone flashlight back on the padlock, and KAP opens the lock, turns the lever, and pushes the sliding door open. Tech shines the light inside the truck, and they see four pallets of product wrapped in thick plastic. They all climb inside the truck and walk to the back. "This is about five-hundred kilos," says KAP.

"Well, I'm sure this has something to do with someone who just left Mexico," says Tech, who then locks eyes with KAP, looks over at Chris, looks back at KAP, and then stares at Chris. Suddenly, Chris's phone rings, and he answers, "Hello."

"Chris, my friend, how was your flight?" asks Felix.

"It was good."

"Muy bueno, muy bueno. Well, my friend, you said you could handle more than agreed. I trust you will do your very best as you said. I must tell you, the consequences won't be good if you don't. We'll talk soon, my friend."

KAP then calls Richie to let him know what's going on. "Yo, what's up?" asks Richie.

"We got a problem," replies KAP. "We just got back and there's a truck full of cleaning supplies we don't need." There's a long gap of silence from Richie on the other end. "Richie?" calls out KAP.

"I hear you. How many items?"

"Maybe five hundred or so."

"Where'd it come from?"

"You'll probably have to ask the General; he's here."

"Wait, what?! Put me on speaker."

"You're on."

"I know we have a lot to discuss between us three, but right now we have an issue we have to deal with," starts Richie. "Having those cleaning supplies without a company to move them to, just sitting there…that's no good. We're going to have to store them there for the time being until we figure out what these new companies can take. Agreed?" Everyone agrees with Richie. "Chris, I need you in Chicago when you guys finish up there. You, me, and KAP have to have a face-to-face. KAP, take me off speaker."

"What's up, Richie?" asks KAP.

"KAP, I hate that you had to find out like this. I had every intention of telling you once Chris was blessed. Just know, if he wasn't the one, nothing would've changed in leadership. I'm sorry, man. We'll talk later."

KAP pauses for a few seconds, then responds, "We'll chop it up later," and hangs up.

Richie sits on the side of his bed wondering what happened in Mexico. He's not concerned about Felix finding his rally point because the more money you have, the better your eyesight. His concerns lie more so with Felix's desire to move product he knows they can't handle and can't store, along with the impact the extra has on logistics, which enhances their vulnerability. Thinking aloud, Richie says, "This meeting with Maurice has to go extremely fucking well." If he really knew how much Richie needed him at this point and time, Maurice's partnership demands would be completely unreasonable. Richie calls Maurice and schedules the meeting for 2 p.m. at the Chicago South Loop Hotel. "No need to squad up; I'm just bringing Brick with me." says Richie.

Maurice replies, "See you there."

The next morning, KAP pulls the truck around to the back of the mansion, then he, Tech, and Chris spend the morning moving the product into the house. They place the kilos into the crawl space under the spare bedroom, lock the floor panel, and then gather their things to head to the airport and travel back to Chicago. As Tech heads to his room to grab his equipment, KAP asks, "So Chris, what happened in Mexico?"

"He asked me two questions: One was if I could handle extra product, and two was basically asking if I had to get rid of someone close to me, could I do it."

"You think he was talking about Richie?"

"I do. Apparently, he's unaware that Richie will be moving to more of a liaison role to push the product further along the South and the East Coast, which would demand more from him and make him a shitload of money. Just from the few moments I spoke with him, I get the feeling that he knows everything about everyone in this organization and would kill any one of us just to prove a point, regardless if it hurts him in the end. We need some kind of insurance to hold him at bay, or we'll get flushed away."

"I think you one hundred on that. But what could we do to secure that?"

"If I know Richie, he's always been one to two steps ahead of any situation." Tech comes back downstairs with his bags. "You guys ready? D just sent us our itinerary, and we have to be at the airport in an hour to make our flight."

* * *

Richie and Brick arrive at the Chicago South Loop Hotel fifteen minutes early. They walk in and speak to the receptionist who gives Richie the key to one of the meeting rooms. Brick walks ahead of Richie and checks out the room before Richie walks in and takes a seat. Five minutes later, Maurice and Spree walk in, and Richie and Brick stand up to greet them. They all sit down, then Richie opens up the floor to Maurice. "Let's get right to it. What are your demands?"

Maurice leans back in his chair and speaks, "In order for me to make this connection, I need a hundred grand and ownership of four of your businesses right here in Chicago. I already contacted my people about your movement."

"What they say?" asks Richie.

"Actually, they were tripping. Drug niggas usually be bout themselves. They definitely interested in the details and seeing what this is. Regardless of how good it may sound, they won't move until I say move. So, once the money is in my hands, I'll make the connection and everything we agreed on will be pushed through Spree. He'll be your point man, but he still works for me. I still have things going on that I just can't let go right now, so to keep it separate, that's where I'm at."

Richie pauses, then responds, "See, that's why giving up ownership of my businesses won't work for me. I have no idea what you into or who you into it with. I can't risk that, and I can't put the movement at risk. I hope you understand. So, I propose two hundred thousand, and you eat off the plates from the New York businesses and your percentages off the keys. Just from that alone, you'll be able to do what you need."

"Two hundred grand?" Maurice thinks for a second, looks at Spree, and then responds, "We can do that."

"I also need Spree to be totally disconnected from your other business and work as an independent contractor—"

"Done."

"How many keys can your people handle at one time and how often?"

"Spree will have that answer for you tonight. When will you have the two hunnit large?"

"After the meeting date and time is confirmed. I'll contact Spree when it's ready." Richie and Maurice stand up and shake hands. Richie reaches across the table and shakes Spree's hand. "Congratulations, Spree."

"Thanks, Richie! I'll reach out as soon as I get the word."

Maurice and Spree leave the meeting room while Richie and Brick stay back. Walking to the car, Maurice says to Spree, "That was easier than I thought. If he would've given up some of his businesses, I would've thought differently about his honesty. Has Richie reached out to you in any way beside me telling you to reach out?" asks Maurice.

"Not at all," says Spree. "I think in his position and what he is trying to do, honesty has to be upfront. We got enough back stabbing niggas in the game."

"That's truer than a muthafucka."

"When is Kolax people coming to replace him?"

"Karimah here, getting settled in. I'll introduce her to the crew in a few days or so."

"Oh okay. I wonder what she looks like."

"Ion look at her like that cause she fucks women, but she's a straight up killer fa sho."

Richie waits a little after Maurice and Spree walk out, then he turns to Brick and says, "That was easier than I thought. I haven't shaken his hand since Ms. Paul made us make up after our fight in the sixth grade. Something is off. Just too easy. He's been fighting with me his whole life for it to be so simple." Richie starts playing with the hair on his chin as he continues talking, "Fuck! Well, my grandfather said it'll all come out in the wash." Brick nods his head in agreement. "Come on, B." They stand up and head out of the meeting room. "Let's go eat and wait for Spree to call. I'm happy for him." Brick takes his fist and taps it on his chest in agreement as they walk out of the hotel.

Spree pulls into the parking lot at H2H's building. He drops Maurice off, then turns left onto the main road. He drives two blocks away from H2H and pulls into an empty parking lot. He parks the car and then rests his forehead against the steering wheel, feeling relieved that he can finally become the man he's always known he could be. A man who his daughter can look up to; a man who his mom, family, and even his newfound mother Ms. Thomas can all be proud of. This is his moment to seize.

* * *

Chris, KAP, and Tech's flight lands in Chicago O'Hare International Airport that evening. Tired from the day's activities, they shuffle through the airport to baggage claim, grab their bags, and then head to KAP's SUV, so they can meet up at Richie's condo to discuss what happened and the way ahead. When the elevator opens, the three tired souls walk into Richie's place and collapse onto his couch. "What's up?" asks Richie. "I know you guys are tired. After we talk, feel free to stay over and rest your heads for a few hours. Whatever suits you."

"Those keys were already on the way long before I met Felix," says Chris. "He asked me if I could handle the extra keys, and I said I would have to look at the landscape first. The way his guards grabbed their weapons after he asked me that question, I'm convinced I wouldn't have made it home."

"You right," says Richie. "He needed you to give him confirmation."

"Why?"

"I'm guessing he's having problems with his connect, or his other dealers are no longer available to push product. I'm thinking that's why we getting all the extra. Tech, when you get a chance, go online and see if you can find any major drug busts in the last thirty to sixty days."

"Bet," responds Tech.

"KAP, we need a no-bullshit number on the amount our people can handle. Keep the transpo in New Orleans until we find that number, and then they can head to New York to drop it. We need to know about any other organizations that's not in competition that need a better connect. Tell them bonuses are available to them if they can get us more customers."

"I'm on it," says KAP. "What are we going to do with the keys that's just sitting at the house? That's not how we roll."

"I know," says Richie, "and it's bothering me that it's there. Depending on how much Maurice's people can push, plus a little extra, we can get rid of what's left over and pay for the remaining balance out of pocket. Felix is putting us in a position to have to push back against his demands. I'm not putting anyone at risk because of his arrogance. Chris, after we pay Felix, break contact. As long as you're on post, you're safe until we figure out how to control and mitigate his actions. I'll deal with him."

Chris says to Richie, "He asked me if I would eliminate someone close to me, if he asked."

"Don't worry. He won't eliminate me until he's comfortable with you in the position."

* * *

The next morning, Detectives Russell and Neeley stop by Detective Coles's office. "Boss, we have two addresses for Kolax. One on the west side and one in Chatham on the south side," says Detective Russell.

"Great! Send a squad to the west side to check it out, and we can head south to see what we find." Detective Coles stands up and grabs his suit coat from the back of his chair, and they all leave the precinct together. When they arrive at Kolax's house, they see all the blinds are up, and it's evident the home is empty. The detectives exit the car, and walk to the front door. Detective Coles knocks, then checks to see if it's open, and it is. The detectives remove their weapons from the holsters and enter the house slowly and carefully. Detective Coles enters first and signals to his two detectives to look around and check out the basement as he heads upstairs. He slowly walks up the steps and cautiously peeps around the corner of the banister into one of the bedrooms. He finds a homeless family sitting on a mattress, scared of what could come next. He puts his weapon back in his holster and stares at the family.

"Boss, everything has been cleaned out down here. Any luck up there?" calls out Detective Neeley.

"Nothing here," responds Detective Coles, as he turns around to head downstairs. As soon as they leave the house, Detective Coles receives a phone call from some detectives assigned to the west district.

"Detective Coles, this is Detective Smith. The address you gave us has another family that lives there now. No relation to the suspect."

"Thank you," says Detective Coles. Turning to Detectives Neeley and Russell, he says, "Mighty funny how he just ups and leaves. Let's look for any addresses for next of kin in and out of state."

* * *

Richie's phone rings, and he eagerly answers it. "Spree, what's up, brother?"

"What's up, big homie? Just letting you know that meeting will be two days from now at 7 p.m. I'll let you know where later on."

"That's cool. We can host the meeting at Josephine's if you'd like."

"Yeah, let's do it there. I'll let Maurice know."

"How many people we expecting?"

Spree pauses for a minute and catches on to what Richie is asking him. "I was told two hunnit and fifty for now."

"I'll prepare for three. Go ahead and stop by Josephine's. D got something for you."

"Aight, I'll swing by there now, but Richie, you saved my life and my family's life. Thank you for the opportunity. I won't let you down."

"I know you won't. Glad I can help. Peace unto you." Spree hears the phone hang up and can't help but smile, knowing he's on the road to success.

Richie calls Damawi and gives her the heads up on Spree's visit. "I won't be there for that meeting. I have to pick up my nephew at six, and I won't make it back in time. Gina will be there. He's spending time with auntie for a few days since he hurt his foot and can't play. Yeah, he such a big baby, but he'll be here for a week."

"Make sure you send out emails saying you'll be closed, so we won't have any civilians stopping by. We just need the party room, very little refreshments. Meeting shouldn't last no longer than an hour or two."

"Okay, I'll let Gina and Octavio handle that. I'll stop by with Javari after it's over."

"Okay, D. See you then."

* * *

After Spree picks up the money from Josephine's, he heads directly to H2H's office to drop it off to Maurice. When he arrives, he meets with Maurice and Elder in one of the conference rooms. "Is it all there?" asks Maurice as he looks inside the bag and takes out a ten-thousand-dollar bundle, tossing it over to Elder.

"Easy money," says Elder.

"You ready for tomorrow?" asks Maurice.

"I been ready," says Spree. "I'm ready to put in this work for you."

"I hear you. You deserve everything that's coming to you. For your loyalty and patience. So, this is your send-off to be your own man, so to speak. So, since you starting your journey, I want you to wear a suit tomorrow to signify where you're going. The skies ain't the limit for you. I see you going much higher than that. I want you to show that nigga Richie that what's going down tomorrow will put me in a better position to stick around here for a long time." Maurice tosses a bundle of money to Spree. "So, go shopping, get you a nice suit, and I'll see you tomorrow. Tell your family congratulations for me."

"Thanks, big bro." They shake hands and hug for a brief second. "I wish Kolax was here to see this man. I kinda miss that dude," says Spree.

"You have no idea what Kolax would give to see you off," responds Maurice. Spree leaves out and shuts the door behind him.

"Speaking of Kolax, the lil homies in the neighborhood said some cops went by his crib yesterday looking for him," says Elder.

"Good thing you cleared his house out," says Maurice. "We need to contact him and tell him to lay low and stay low. I'm not sure what they know, but this is the wrong time for this shit to be happening."

"We may need to start restructuring," says Elder.

"Kolax is a soldier. If he gets caught up with the cops, he'd never talk. But if Richie feels he's a threat, he'll come after him without a doubt."

* * *

Richie and Brick arrive at Josephine's for the meeting with Maurice and his crew. KAP is already there sitting in his car waiting for them to show up. Richie parks his BMW and asks Brick to stay in the car, so he can speak with KAP alone. He walks over to KAP's vehicle and enters on the passenger side. They bump fists as Richie gets comfortable in his seat.

"So Larry and Jeff left this morning. They're on the way to New York. Just waiting for an address to drop the three hunnit," says KAP.

"Good, good," says Richie. "Listen, brother, I owe you an explanation on why I chose Chris."

"Nah, you don't owe me nothing, man. I was pissed at first. But the more I thought about it, you made the right choice. I could've really put us in a predicament with the Courtney shit. You right. I need to switch up if I want to be the man."

"You are the man, my dude. Don't get it twisted. Let's go handle this business, so we can keep pushing the movement."

They exit KAP's vehicle, and Brick turns off Richie's car and locks it before throwing Richie the keys as they enter Josephine's. Gina meets them as they walk in the door. "Hey guys! Gone head upstairs. Refreshments are there, and I'll stay here and greet the rest of our guests when they arrive and send them up." They head upstairs and sit and wait for everyone to arrive. Right before 7 p.m., cars start to fill up the parking lot. Spree pulls into the parking lot and parks next to Maurice and Elder, who are getting out of Elder's car. Spree gets out of his vehicle wearing a charcoal Tom Ford three-piece suit. Maurice and Elder see Spree and immediately start telling jokes. "Man, you look like you just graduated from a juvenile detention center," starts Elder.

"Nah, this nigga look casket ready, E," says Maurice as he brushes imaginary lint off of Spree's shoulder. "You looking clean though for real."

"Thanks, man!" says Spree as he pulls and straightens his suit jacket.

They see the East Coast connects hop out of their vehicles, and they walk over and shake hands with H2H. Everyone walks into Josephine's together and heads upstairs to the party room. As they start filing into the room, Richie and the crew stand up and shake everyone's hands. The New York and New Jersey crew sit on the left and right sides of the large conference table while H2H sits at the head of the table facing the door. Elder and Spree sit on the ends of the table with Maurice in the middle. Richie sat between Brick and KAP on the opposite end across from H2H.

Richie looks at Spree, and they share a smile before Richie starts the meeting. "I'm glad everyone is here. This is big. What we're about to embark on will be beneficial for everyone here, our families, and our communities. Before we start, I want to introduce my crew and have everyone introduce themselves. So, to my left is Brick and on my right is KAP."

"I'm John Champ from New York. This is my right-hand man Justice, my distro Roman, and my muscle Herc. I have about fifteen soldiers in my organization, and we looking forward to pushing the initiative."

The New Jersey connect stands up. "My name is Levi. My right-hand man is Luke, and my muscle is Nate. He not here today, but you'll see him at some point when you come our way. I have twenty-two people in my organization. I'm already familiar with John and of course Maurice. I'm looking forward to working with everyone and see how far we can take this thing."

Richie takes the floor again to explain the business structure, the plan moving forward, and to offer assistance to those who want to set up legit businesses. After about thirty minutes of discussion, they take a break to stretch their legs and mingle. KAP walks over to Justice and Luke to get drop-off addresses and let them know the product is on the way. While everyone is mingling or taking a break, Maurice remains seated, texting back and forth with someone on his phone. Once everyone returns, the meeting continues for another thirty-five minutes. When there's a break in the discussion, Richie asks if anyone has anything to say before the meeting ends.

"I'm not sure if you're all aware, but there have been some changes within H2H. Kolax couldn't be with us for obvious reasons, so this caused me to have to make some additions and a change," says Maurice. "Spree won't be the connection between Richie and the East Coast crew anymore due to some shit that just caught my attention. My new number two will be taking that responsibility from here on out." Spree looks confused and looks at Richie. Before Richie can speak, Maurice continues, "Let me introduce my number two, Karimah, to everyone." Maurice waves her in. As the door opens, Richie looks at Spree and sees the disappointment in his face, wondering why the change. Like Spree, Richie's also wondering why the sudden change. Spree was so close to ensuring his family would benefit significantly from the financial gains that come with the new position. As Richie continues to study Spree's face, he notices his facial expression change from disappointment to shock, then to fear.

Richie turns around and sees this six-foot tall, beautiful, brown-skinned woman enter the room. He stares at the woman with a half head of mini locs dressed in tan Timberland boots, baggy blue jeans, and a polo shirt, and wonders where he's seen her before. Then it hits him. Up In Smoke. When Richie turns back around to look at Spree, he looks as nervous as an antelope trying to drink from a pond surrounded by hungry lions. Richie then looks up from Spree and notices Maurice standing with his gun extended close to the side of Spree's head with a menacing look on his face. A waterfall of sweat runs down the sides of Spree's face. *Oh shit!* thinks Richie as he stares at Maurice, shocked by the turn of events. Everyone in the room is frozen, confused by what's taking place.

Richie and Spree lock eyes, and everything seems to move in slow motion for Richie. He blinks and has a flashback to when he first met Spree as a kid playing basketball at Pirie Park, laughing, talking, and walking to the neighborhood store with the rest of the crew. Just young kids doing what kids do. The sound of the gun interrupts Richie's thoughts, and he stares in horror as the bullet rips through Spree's head, splattering blood, brains, and skull all over the right side of the room. Spree's head falls lifeless onto the table as everyone in the room jumps up; their chairs flying back as they look around shocked and in disbelief. "I apologize if this put a bad taste in everyone's mouth, but I don't tolerate disloyalty that could jeopardize the movement. Richie, I appreciate the tip. You won't have to worry about him spending counterfeit money in your legit businesses anymore."

Richie just stares in disbelief at what just happened. Karimah walks over to him and shakes his hand, passing off a piece of paper from her palm to his. He opens his hand slowly and then opens the note to see Spree's name and cellphone number written in his handwriting. Richie stands up and gathers himself mentally. "No problem, Maurice. We got it from here." Everyone but Richie and his crew exit the room. Gina weaves through people exiting to get inside and see what's just happened. She stops suddenly when she sees Spree slumped onto the table with blood everywhere. Richie walks over and stands over Spree's lifeless body; his eyes are still open as his blood drains from the hole in his head. Richie looks at KAP and says, "Call the cleaning crew. Get them here ASAP." He then turns and calls Gina's name, who doesn't respond as she stands frozen, staring at Spree's body. "Gina!!" shouts Richie. She jumps and turns her attention to Richie. "Go downstairs, make sure all our guests are gone, then lock the doors and wait for the cleaning crew!" He then looks at Brick. "I knew something was off. Fuck!!"

An hour later, the cleaning crew arrives. Raymond Johnson, who owns the majority of the cleaning business, is one of Richie's childhood friends. He wasn't the smartest guy in school, but he was extremely loyal and hardworking. Richie helped him start his cleaning business knowing that he needed to launder money along with the possibilities of needing a crew for situations like this. "Hey, Ray," says Richie. "My apologies for the short notice, but we had no other options."

"It's okay, Richie. Where he at?"

"In the party room upstairs." Ray starts toward the steps when Richie grabs his arm. "Ray, I must warn you…"

"Come on, Richie. We been through this before. I have the body bag right here. I'll clear out as much as I can and have the crew finish up afterwards to make it look like something small."

"Ray..." Richie pauses, saddened by what he's about to tell Ray. "It's Spree." Ray looks dazed for a second, then gathers his composure and heads upstairs to do the job. Richie heads upstairs after him, and he sees that KAP and Brick have already moved Spree's body onto the floor, laying on top of some garbage bags. Ray puts his gloves on and starts removing Spree's clothes, placing them into garbage bags. He then strategically places the body inside the body bag. "I need someone to help me put his body and clothes in the back of my van. Put these gloves on." Brick and KAP put on the gloves and carry Spree's body out of the room. Ray places his cleaning supplies on the table and follows KAP and Brick out to his van. Shortly afterward, Richie sees Damawi and Javari walk into her office, and he walks over and shuts the door.

"Javari, what's up, brother?" asks Richie, shaking his hand. "I didn't think you could get any bigger. They must have you living in the weight room at V State, huh?"

"Hey, Mr. Richie. Yeah, I grew too. I'm six-foot-eight now, two hunnit and fifty."

"I see, and a good-looking young man. Javari, have a seat. I need to talk to D for a minute." Richie and Damawi walk out of the office and into the hallway far enough away, so Javari doesn't hear them.

"D, I need you to get Javari out of here."

"Why? What's wrong? How did the meeting go?"

"The meeting went well until the last two minutes when Maurice killed Spree. He shot him point blank in the side of his head. Blood, brains, and skull is all over the place. The cleaner is here, but I need you to take Gina and Javari and get gone until we get this place back to normal."

"Oh my God!!! But I thought Spree was going to—"

"Me too. I'll let you know when we're done."

KAP, Brick, and Ray return to the room from the van. "Okay, fellas," says Ray, "I need to be alone in here for about an hour. When my guys get here, just let them up. We'll be out of your hair in no time." Richie, KAP, and Brick head downstairs and sit at one of the tables. KAP slouches back in the chair and says, "Man, that was a power move. That nigga kept himself alive."

"For the time being," says Richie. "Perfectly played fa sho. We still have the connects tho. And Maurice made sure he didn't fuck up our relationships with the new connects with that counterfeit money bullshit."

"We taking Spree's body down to Lloyd's?" asks KAP.

"No, I have to make a play with his body that is going to be just as fucked up as that shit upstairs," says Richie.

* * *

The cleaners finish cleaning the party room, which now looks as if nothing had ever happened. Richie texts Damawi to let her know things are somewhat back to normal. Richie and KAP then walk outside to the van and wait for Brick. When Brick comes out, KAP and Richie hop inside the van, and Brick follows them in Richie's car to the south side. They arrive at Pirie Park a few hours after midnight. Richie opens the back of the van as Ray opens the body bag and positions Spree's body to be carried away. Brick walks over, picks up Spree's naked body, and carries him over to the middle of the basketball court as Richie follows. Brick lays Spree's body down and places his driver's license on his chest. Richie stands over Spree's body and says, "So long, lil homie. You left way too soon. Don't worry about your family; I got em. Your lil girl won't have a need for anything."

They walk back over to Ray's van, and Ray puts Spree's belongings and the garbage bags from the club into the body bag, rolls it up, and hands it to KAP. Brick hands Ray a cell phone, and Ray dials a short number and puts the phone on speaker.

"911, what's your emergency?"

Ray replies in his deepest voice, "He's at Pirie Park. Come get this nigga," and hangs up. Brick takes the phone, turns it off, and gives it to KAP to place in the bag. Richie hands Ray $20,000, and Ray hops in his van and drives away.

Richie, KAP, and Brick get into Richie's car, and Brick drives them over to Lloyd's. Richie thinks over what happened at Josephine's and now understands that Maurice must have figured out his long-term plan to remove him. *I should've known he'd have someone following me*, Richie thinks to himself. He smiled briefly thinking about Maurice's counterfeit money jab. Although a lie, that would've been something Richie would've said. *But to kill someone who we've both known for over thirty years without hesitation... Maybe I underestimated Maurice. Never again. Tighten up, Richie. You're a god!* Richie reclines his seat and closes his eyes for a quick meditation session.

Twenty minutes later, Brick pulls up at Lloyd's, and they all walk inside the funeral home and head directly to the cremation chamber. They hand the bag with Spree's belongings to Lloyd, and he places it inside the chamber and pushes the button. As the door slowly closes, it symbolizes the final chapter in Nathaniel "Spree" Green's life.

CHAPTER 7

Elder is up early the next morning surfing through channels on the TV and stops at the Channel 5 News. They are live at Pirie Park, showing all the police cars and ambulances on scene. Elder turns up the volume and leans forward in his recliner to hear what's going on. "At this moment, detectives from the 6th district precinct are on scene where a murder victim is lying naked on the basketball court here at Pirie Park. The victim's name has not yet been released by police. As you can see behind me, Chief of Detectives Ronnie Watkins has arrived on scene. This murder is identical to an ongoing murder investigation involving victim Jamal Thomas about a month ago. His body was found at Pirie Park in the exact same way, naked for all to see. Could this be a serial killer on the loose in Chicago? We will have more information throughout the day. Stay locked in to Channel 5 News for updates."

Elder finishes watching the news segment, then turns the TV off. "Damn, Chief of Detectives, huh?" He grabs an old photo with himself, Michael, and Maurice when he was a kid at a Chicago White Sox game. He reminisces on his last moments with Michael as they headed to meet up with a connect. It was the summer of 1986, they had arrived at their regular spot: an empty and dark parking lot on the south side off Cottage Grove across from the Rothschild Liquor Mart. "Man, these muthafuckas always late," said Michael.

"Be patient, brother. They'll be here." Just as Elder spoke, headlights from a vehicle blinded them as they tried to identify who entered the parking lot through the rearview mirror. "Got dammit!" said Elder as he moved his eyes away from the side-view mirror. The vehicle stopped, and the headlights turned off, showing a dark-colored Lincoln Continental directly behind Michael's car. "Who the fuck is that?" asked Michael. He pulled out his gun from his waistband, grabbed his flashlight from his glove box, and exited the car. Elder grabbed his gun from under his seat and followed Michael out of the vehicle. They both stood outside the car by their doors for nearly a minute.

"They gonna get out the car or what?" asked Michael. One of the men in the Lincoln Continental stepped out of the car and walked toward Michael and Elder. Michael shined the flashlight on the man, but he didn't recognize who it was. They both point their weapons at the man. "Fucking stop right there. Who the fuck is you?" asked Michael. The man walked closer with his hands up.

"Relax. Dominic is no longer available to make the runs. I'm the guy now. Nick. My partner Jay is in the car." He waved at Jay, and he stepped out of his car with a duffle bag full of product. Both men walked toward Michael and Elder. Michael pointed his gun at Nick's head. "You ain't my fucking guy. Stay the fuck back." Michael then looked at Elder, and they got back in the car and left. After driving a couple blocks, Elder noticed two cop cars driving behind them.

"Michael, look behind us."

"How long dem pigs been on us?"

"I have no idea. Make a left to see if they follow." They made a left at the light, and the cop car followed behind them.

"What you think?" asked Michael.

"I think we just got set up." Michael sped up and then turned the corner and made a complete stop. He then put the car in reverse and rammed it into the first police car, disabling it. Michael then sped off, and the second cop car followed in pursuit. "Michael, what the fuck?!" asked Elder.

"Dem two crackers in the parking lot was cops, Elder!"

"Aw shit! What's the play?"

"We gonna get back to the projects and ditch the car and leave it. Burn it up if we can." While they drove down 87th street, more cop cars converged on Michael as he turned onto Martin Luther King Jr. Boulevard. Cops were coming from behind him and in front of him from blocks away. He quickly turned onto 85th street and then he stopped the car and told Elder to get out.

"What?! I ain't leaving you!" said Elder.

"We ditching the car!" yelled Michael. Elder jumped out the car, leaving the door open. Michael drove off, and the passenger door closed from the momentum. Elder screamed at the car, "Michael!" Michael stopped briefly and yelled out the window, "Take care of my boy!" Then he drove off. Elder dipped behind some bushes; seconds later, cop cars sped past him in pursuit of Michael, who took them on a high-speed chase through the south side of Chicago.

* * *

Inside the tent at Pirie Park, Detectives Coles and Neeley are looking over Spree's body for any evidence. "It's way too early in the morning for this bullshit," says Detective Coles.

"This body is identical to Jamal Thomas: naked with the driver's license on the body. But this one has a Gangster Disciples tattoo drawn on his chest with a magic marker."

"No footprints or anything leading from the sidewalk to where the victim is," says Detective Russell as he enters the tent.

"Feels like we are being fucked with," says Detective Coles.

"The person who called dispatch voice is different," says Detective Neeley.

"What does that mean? Why imitate another killer's ritual?" Detective Coles thinks for a second. A patrolman sticks his head into the tent to let Detective Coles know that Chief Watkins has just arrived. A few seconds later, the tent's curtain slowly opens up and Chief Watkins ducks and steps inside.

"Hey, Chief," says Detective Coles.

"Brian, detectives. We have to stop meeting like this. It's getting old."

"I know," says Detective Coles. The chief walks over and examines the victim's body, paying extra attention to his face. "He looks familiar to me." He grabs a pair of tweezers from Detective Russell, picks up the victim's driver's license, and studies it. "Nathaniel Demarcus Green." He shakes his head and thinks to himself: *I know him but from where.* "Looks like a gang initiation," says Chief Watkins. "We had similar cases years back. Whenever a new gang lord comes into power, they immediately get rid of their enemies. This is the second murder like this in a month. Any luck on that mope you guys were tracking down?"

"No luck, Chief," says Detective Coles. "We went to his house, but it was empty. He has a few relatives here, Atlanta, and St. Louis. We've been patrolling here but got nothing."

"I'll chop this up as gang violence," says Chief Watkins. "I'll talk to the First Deputy Superintendent about upping the patrols in this area, look at the recent change of powers among the leaders, and then put the word out to them that we'll start kicking in doors if this bullshit doesn't stop."

"Okay, Chief," says Detective Coles. "What do you want us to do with Kolax Imanu?"

"Fall back for right now. Let's locate him and watch him. Contact Atlanta and St. Louis and let them know he's a person of interest and to let us know if he pops up on their radar."

"Okay, Chief," says Detective Coles. Chief Watkins leaves the tent to go talk with the waiting press outside.

* * *

Richie, at home, wakes up the next morning with a lot on his mind. He needs counsel to clear his thoughts about Spree, so he can continue to push the movement. He hops in his car and heads to Buffalo Grove, IL, to his mother's house to check on Marble Head and reset his mind. While driving, his mom calls and tells him that his uncle isn't having one of his better days. He's about five minutes away when he gets a call from Tech. "What up, Tech? What you got for me?"

"What up, Richie? I heard what happened. You good?"

"Yeah, I'm good, Tech. Thanks for asking."

"Well, I did that research for you, even dug into the DEA's database, and there's been three major drug busts in the last two months. One in Atlanta and two big ones in L.A. All three were getting their drugs imported from Mexico. And get this, they all had the same exact packaging as we do."

"I knew it. The pressure is on him, so he's pushing it on us. Thanks, Tech. Where are we with the autonomous vehicles?"

"Really? It's always business with you. How about how's your love life, Tech? Did you fist that chick last night?"

"Tech?"

"Less than two weeks, boss."

"Awesome. So…did you?"

"Actually, I did. Wanna smell my hand?"

"Bye, Tech."

Richie pulls up to his mom's house and immediately goes into his uncle's room. When he enters, he sees two nurses in scrubs, massaging and moving Marble Head's legs to help with his blood circulation.

"You good, unc?"

"Hey, nephew. I'm good." He then turns to the nurses and asks, "Ladies, can you please give me and my nephew a moment to talk?" The nurses finish up what they're doing and leave, both giving Richie a smile as they pass by. Richie shuts the door behind them.

"They looking at you, boy. Come lay beside me, so you can get a sponge bath too." They both smile.

"I'm good, unc," says Richie as he sits in the recliner next to the bed. Richie begins to tell Marble Head about what happened with Spree. "I get it; you wanted to put someone in there you can trust and remove Maurice. I would've done the same thing, but you wouldn't have never known if you were being followed or who he put on you to do it. He made a power move, so what are you going to do about it?"

"Right now, I just want to ensure this new connect is taken care of and build a relationship with them, expand, then handle Maurice."

"Let me tell you a story, so you understand what you may be up against." Richie leans in and listens. "Maurice's dad, Michael, was a grimy ass muthafucka in his day. We had run-ins that almost provoked a war between us, but at the time, I wasn't strong enough to win. He went to pick up some product, and it was undercover cops he was dealing with; he knew it, and he left. They were gonna stop him and search his vehicle and see if he had the money to purchase on him. Going to jail again wasn't an option for him because if he'd gotten arrested with his rap sheet, he was gone for good. He took them on a high-speed chase through your grandmother's neighborhood until he lost control of the car, crashed it, and took off on foot with the money and his gun.

"He was running, made it to a wooded area, and almost got away until your uncle got behind his ass. They exchanged shots, but your uncle put him down hard. He was new to the police force and killing Michael catapulted his career, and he never looked back. Bout time the other police cars and ambulances made it to the scene, Elder was there looking from a distance. So the mayor decided that the wooded area needed to be leveled. A couple of women was sexually assaulted there before your uncle's shooting, so the mayor decided to turn it into Pirie Park. Where Michael died is exactly where the basketball court is."

"Get the fuck outta here! Uncle Swift killed Maurice's dad? Does Elder know this for sure?"

"I'm not sure, but the streets talked. Even if he knew, I doubt he would say anything. Your uncle may be the Chief of Detectives today, but Swift was a different muthafucka before Vietnam." Richie stands up and walks over to the window. "You can't make this shit up. I have no idea what this means. My thought is Elder ain't said shit cause he knows Maurice would risk it all trying to seek revenge."

"So, since we going back in the past: why haven't y'all talked in four years?" asks Richie, turning to look at Marble Head. "Don't say it's cause you cussed out Aunt B. Everyone in the family has felt your wrath at some point. Why?"

"The business. He wanted me out once word got back to him that I was in the game. I wouldn't leave, and he told me he would do what he has to do if it comes to that."

"So, do I have to worry about him too?"

"No, but once he gets word, he'll come knocking."

"You need anything?"

"Nah, I'm good. You can call those nurses back in when you leave. They're my only joy for the day."

Richie heads downstairs to see his mom waiting for him at the bottom of the stairwell. "Son, I just got off the phone with Swift, and he asked me if I knew who Nathaniel was. I'm so sorry about your friend; he was a good kid."

"He was mom. It's unfortunate."

"Swift said he would reach out to you later. He said he wants to talk with you." Richie thinks to himself, *Here we go*. "I'm sure he does, mom. You need anything?"

"No, son. Please be careful out there, please." Richie hugs and kisses his mom and heads out the door.

* * *

Richie arrives home, thinking about his uncle's health and wondering how life in the drug game will be without his Uncle Marble Head. He has been there to guide Richie through some of the most difficult times, especially when he was a kid. His uncle was a man who was so feared but is now weakened. He hates that he gave his life to the game and his health isn't where it needs to be so he can enjoy the fruits of his labor. Richie wonders if he'd be so lucky to live as long as his uncle or be in his exact same shoes, ailing from something caused by his military service. He walks over to the wall leading to his second bedroom and looks at all his family pictures, paying close attention to those that include his uncle. He pauses at the picture with his uncle when he was sporting a medium-sized afro that was perfectly round. Sometimes he would leave his pick with the metal teeth inside of his afro and use the pick as a weapon, if necessary. He was wearing a white wing tip dress shirt with an orange and olive green paisley print and olive green bell bottoms. His belt buckle, which he also used as a weapon, was large but not big enough to believe he was a lightweight boxing champion. He was leaning on his burnt orange, 1979 Ford Thunderbird with a matching interior. He used to spray pimp oil over the seats and dashboard, which smelled like dial soap. Even with the windows up, you could still smell it outside the car from five feet away. Standing there looking at the photo, Richie reflects on the day it was taken.

At thirteen, Richie had just started running drugs to his uncle's customers. He would walk through the neighborhood with his baseball glove, tossing up a tennis ball that had a small slice in it, so the drugs could fit inside. One day, he walked up to this two-story, red and brown brick house with a five-foot metal fence around it. The cement steps leading to the front door were riddled with cracks. He paused before he opened the gate to check around the front yard for any signs of a dog that could possibly live there. When he was confident he wouldn't be attacked, he opened the gate and mentally calculated how far he was standing from the door and how much physical power it would take to make the ball reach the front door. Richie then took a step back, wound up for the pitch, and threw the ball against the wooden front door. The ball knocked on the door and then bounced back directly into Richie's glove. Richie stood outside the house looking at cars passing by and people walking down the street as he waited for the customer to respond.

After a few minutes, a black man about 5'10" with an athletic build, a thick, full afro, and navy coveralls came to the door and held up one of his large hands. Richie threw the ball to the guy, and the man took the ball inside the house. A few seconds later, the man returned outside and tossed the ball back to Richie. When Richie squeezed the sides of the tennis ball to check the inside, he saw that there was no money inside and threw the ball back to the man. The guy immediately tossed the ball back to Richie and said, "Get the fuck away from my house!" before going inside and slamming the door behind him. Richie, shocked and frustrated, threw the ball against the front window with everything he had, hoping to smash it. The ball banged against the window as it ricocheted off into the bushes. Richie waited to see if anyone would come outside. Nothing. He briefly searched through the bushes for his ball, and when he found it, he angrily pushed through the gate and headed toward a pay phone two blocks up the street.

When he made it to the graffiti-covered pay phone, he dropped a quarter into the coin slot and dialed his uncle's number. Marble Head picked up on the third ring. "Hello?" said Marble Head. "Unc, I got an issue with the dude at—" The phone went dead, and Richie pulled the handset away from his ear briefly to look at it. "Hello? Unc?" Perplexed, Richie hung up the phone and then walked over to the next street to use another pay phone. He dropped another quarter into the coin slot and dialed his uncle again. "Hello? Unc, mom didn't pick me up from practice. Can you come pick me up? I'm on 84th and Paulina."

"Do you have your baseball equipment with you?"

"No, I lost the ball."

"Okay, give me fifteen minutes. Be out front." Richie hung up the phone and quickly walked back to the two-story house. Five minutes later, he saw the burnt orange Ford Thunderbird rolling up the street. The car stopped in front of the house, and Marble Head's girlfriend stepped out of the driver's side, walked over to the passenger's side, and opened the car door to let Marble Head out of the vehicle. He stepped out of the car and walked past her directly up to Richie. Marble Head then knelt down to Richie's height, removed Richie's baseball cap from his head, and looked him dead in his eyes. "What did you do wrong?" asked Marble Head calmly.

"I didn't have phone discipline," said Richie, looking down at his tennis shoes. Marble Head put his thumb under Richie's chin and lifted his head up, so he could see his eyes. "How much phone discipline do you need to survive in this business?"

"One hundred percent."

"Is ninety-five percent good enough?"

"No."

"Why not?" Richie started slowly tilting his chin down toward his chest, but his uncle raised it up again, using a little more force. "Say it!"

"Cause five percent can get you fucked up. Fucked all the way up." Marble Head rubbed the back of Richie's head, then placed his hat back on his head, making sure it was adjusted perfectly.

"Where's your ball?" Richie opened his glove and presented the ball to his uncle. Marble head grabbed the ball out of the glove and walked through the metal gate and up to the wooden door. He didn't knock on the door or anything. He just turned the knob and walked right into the house like he owned it. Still standing outside, Richie heard the man in the house call out in a trembling voice, "Oh shit, Marble Head. This you?! Man, I didn't—" A woman's screaming from inside the house is heard as the background sounds to Marble Head smacking the man around. "Harold! Where is the money?! Where is the money?!" the woman screamed repeatedly. Richie turned around to look at Marble Head's girlfriend to see if she was as shocked as he was, but she was just leaning against the Thunderbird filing her nails, unbothered by the ruckus inside the house. While it was normal to her, Richie had never seen his uncle react so violently in any situation. As soon as he turned back around toward the house, Richie saw Harold come flying out the front door and tumble down the concrete stairs as his uncle looked on. Richie and Marble Head met eyes, and from the calm look on his uncle's face, Richie knew this was a normal occurrence for him. Part of the game that couldn't be avoided. Once Harold came to a complete stop, Marble Head grabbed Harold by his thick black afro and drug him over to Richie right outside the gate. Harold's girlfriend ran out of the house behind Marble Head, holding a fist full of dollars. "Here, here, here! Take it please!"

"Nah, we gonna do this how it should've been done in the first place. Give that shit to yo man." She bent down and shoved the money into Harold's hands. Marble Head pulled the tennis ball out of his pocket and dropped it onto the grass next to Harold. "Put the money in there." With his hand shaking, Harold stuffed the money into the tennis ball as fast as he could. "Now give it to my nephew," commanded Marble Head. Harold reached out to hand the tennis ball to Richie when Marble Head kicked him in the stomach. "Not like that! Richie, step back. Throw it to him." Harold sat up on his knees, blood trickling from his afro down the center of his face, and weakly threw the ball to Richie. The ball landed at Richie's feet. "Richie, throw it back to him," commanded Marble Head. He throws it back to Harold. "Again!" Richie and Harold went back and forth a few times, tossing the ball to each other like a father teaching his son how to catch.

"Stand up, nigga! See how easy that is? Next time my nephew comes by here, huh…"

"There won't be no problem, Marble Head."

"Okay, good," he said nonchalantly. Marble Head then punched Harold in the side of the face, and Harold stumbled and fell down right in front of Richie's feet. "Richie, kick him in the face," directed Marble Head. Richie looked at his uncle for a second or two and then he cocked his leg back, ready to send Harold's head back up on the porch from which it came. As soon as his foot moved forward to connect with Harold's head, Marble Head blocked Richie's foot with his. He then grabbed Richie and laughed out loud. "You see that?" he asked his girlfriend. Marble Head knelt down and grabbed the brim of Richie's hat, moving it back and forth with his right hand with a fist full of Richie's shirt in his left. "You gonna be terrible on these niggas. Let's go, boy." Richie and Marble Head turned away from Harold as his girlfriend knelt down to help lift him up and support him as they walked back into the house. Marble Head's girlfriend opened the driver's side door for Marble Head and then went to the passenger side of the car. They all hopped inside the Thunderbird, and as they drove off, Richie was mesmerized by his uncle's dominance. His desire for power was conceived, and his innocence was left right where Harold and his woman were picking up the pieces from Marble Head's wrath.

Richie smiles at the memory of that day, then he walks toward the kitchen to grab a snack. As he's walking down the hallway, he feels his phone vibrate in his pocket, and he pulls it out to look at the screen. He sees an unknown caller on the screen and thinks, *This can't be.* "Hello?"

"Richie, my friend! How do you do?"

"I'm good, Felix. What can I do for you?"

"I have a shipment that I need you to pick up, Richie."

"A shipment? It's too soon. We don't have the storage space for the medical equipment. We won't have it for at least another two months. I apologize, but we need to stick to our..."

"You don't understand. This is a conversation that goes from me to you. Again, I need you to pick up equipment quickly, Richie. When can you have your transportation available?"

"Felix, I won't have equipment just sitting without a place to move it. I'm doing us a favor by not putting us at risk. I hope you understand."

"So, you're saying you will not do as I ask?" Richie could tell by his voice that Felix was getting irritated with him pushing back on his wishes. Richie wasn't willing to put his people or the vision at risk, even though he knew that Felix's troubles were pushing his initiative.

"I'm not saying no," replies Richie. "I'm just saying not right now. We are still moving the extra you gave us last time. You'll see I'm doing this to protect us."

"I will call Chris."

"Felix, this is still my organization. I call the shots." Richie's phone vibrates, he sees a video notification that he has a visitor trying to access his elevator.

"Richie, are you sure this is the route you are taking with me?"

"Felix, this is the route I'm taking for the both of us. Trust me on this. We'll be in touch." Richie hangs up the phone and authorizes access to his private elevator.

"Uncle Swift! What's going on?" says Richie as he greets his uncle with a hug.

"Hey, Rich! How's the entertainment business?"

"Good."

"I got word from a couple of my officers who went to your show. They said it was great. I'm proud of you."

"Thanks."

"Let me know when your next show is. I'll bring Babs."

"Whatever, unc. You're a workaholic. Aunt B will be there, not you." They both smile because he knows it's true. "You need anything? A drink?" asks Richie.

"No, I still have some work to do. I just came by to talk about your friend Nathaniel. Sorry that happened to him. How long did you know him for?"

"Well, we had a break in friendship because I left for the military, of course, but since I wasssss... twelve."

"Do you know if he was into anything that might help us find who may have killed him or is connected to or involved in his murder?"

"No, I wish I did. He was a good dude. You guys don't have any leads?"

"We have a few. Looks like it's gang related. If I hear something, I'll let you know. I'm headed back to the office. I just was checking on you to see how you was holding up."

"I'm fine, unc. Thanks for stopping by." Walking toward the elevator, Richie couldn't help but say to his Uncle Swift: "Unc, you and Marble Head really need to sit down and squash whatever beef you two may have. I was over mom's, and he isn't looking his best these days. I mean, what would it take? One of you in your final minutes before you speak? You know more than anyone, life is too short."

"That's true. Thanks for that. Keep doing what you doing, nephew. The family is proud of you." They shake hands and hug, then Uncle Swift steps inside the elevator, and Richie watches the doors close before he walks back into his condo.

* * *

Elder walks into the H2H building to find Maurice already in his office counting stacks of money while listening to some ole school hip-hop. "Maurice, you see the news?"

"I did," says Maurice. "I heard they talking about a possible serial killer and later confirmed a gang initiation."

"I didn't hear anything bout a gang initiation, but that's good. Richie kept his word and took Kolax out the spotlight."

"He did, and I'm shocked. If that was me, Spree would've been laying on that nigga's front door. This is what fucks with me, E: I thought what I did would have shook that nigga. He ain't even blink. He took that shit like a G, and that got me trippin. Like I suppose to be in this position." Maurice thinks silently to himself and shakes his head in disbelief.

"You think we can bring Kolax back now?" asks Elder.

"Nah, I'm thinking bout splitting ways with Kolax. Now that we making this doe, we can't be careless. That nigga careless."

"As careless as you were with Spree? That should've been handled a different way."

"True, but I had to make a statement. So Karimah will hold it down until I say otherwise."

"Have Spree's peoples got with you yet?"

"Yeah, blowing my muthafucking phone up about that nigga. I told dem ion know shit, and I'll look into it."

"You know his people gonna want some answers, and they won't leave it alone until they get some." Maurice sits and thinks about what he could possibly tell them. After a second or two passes, he decides, "Fuck em."

* * *

Chris is in his office on the Fort Lee, VA, military base with his wife Janine, packing up all his awards and gifts he's received throughout his military career. As Janine is removing some photos from the bookshelf and walls, she comes across a photo of them at a bar in Washington D.C. She walks over to Chris with the photo and hands it to him. Chris looks at it, wipes some dust from it, and smiles. "I remember this day." It was a picture from over twenty years ago with Chris, Janine, and a young lady he met while in

D.C. "Not sure if I would be a General Officer today if it wasn't for Chief."

"I don't think you would be married if it wasn't for Chief," says Janine with a little snap in her voice.

"This is true." Staring at the photo, he remembers being a young captain with two kids and a wife who was home supporting his military career while putting hers on hold. Back then, he was a serial cheater, and Janine knew it. She was hoping he would come to his senses, grow up, and be the man she thought she married. She grew tired of acting like a wingman for her husband, helping him come up with lies and excuses for his infidelities just to keep the family together.

The weekend the photo was taken, Chris and his team had traveled to the Pentagon for a conference. Janine asked her mom to watch the kids, and she traveled to D.C. without his knowledge in hopes of catching him in the act and finally closing the chapter on their marriage. After that day at the conference, the team went to a bar, as they often did when away from home. Richie was new to the team, but he was Chris's right-hand man. Whenever Chris started drinking, he started being extra flirtatious with every woman within arm's reach. Chris is a very handsome man, standing at 6'1" with smooth deep chocolate skin, a pearly white smile, and almond-shaped eyes. Plus, he's educated, confident, and charismatic, which made infidelity too easy for him.

Janine followed them into the bar from the hotel they always stayed at when in D.C., and she sat across the room out of Chris's sight for several hours. As Chris narrowed his prey down to one, Janine sat in a corner of the bar watching her husband woo this woman, watching him prepare to leave the bar with her. Each time he leaned in close to whisper into the woman's ear, Janine became more and more enraged. She was furious watching him be so reckless and uncaring about her feelings, their family, or their future. She wondered, *Where is this kind of love and affection for me? I've sacrificed everything for this fucking asshole! My identity, my career, my body... my body has been dismembered because of his children!* Her eyes flooded with tears. "I'm about to snatch his fucking soul in this bar!" she whispered angrily through clenched teeth.

When Richie looked up and saw Chris headed for the door with the woman he just met, he quickly walked up behind Chris and grabbed his elbow. "Whoa, sir, where you going?" Richie asked, knowing Chris was married with children.

"I'm out, Chief! I got something to handle."

"Excuse us for a minute, ma'am. He'll be right back." said Richie to the young woman as he forced Chris over to the hallway leading toward the restrooms. Chris brushed Richie off of him and followed Richie around the corner. They got halfway down the hallway leading to the restrooms when Richie stopped and turned to talk to Chris. "Captain Warrington, da fuck you doing?"

"What you mean, Chief?" Before Richie could answer, he saw Janine come flying around the corner, headed straight for Chris. Although Richie had never met her before, he knew from her pace and the look on her face that she was Chris's wife. Without Chris knowing, Richie raised his palm in her direction, signaling her to stop. She stopped a few feet away and leaned against the wall to listen to their conversation. "Let me ask you something, sir. You love your wife? I mean, really love her?"

"Of course, I do."

"Then show her that by walking away from this chick tonight and the ones tomorrow. Focus on your career and take better care of your family. She put her whole life on hold for you, my dude! She stuck in the house wiping your babies' asses and shit. You're smart; you'll probably be a General Officer one day. Be different than those other officers who throw it all away for some pussy. You're better than what you showing the team. We need you on the hill. You have a picture of your family in your wallet?"

"I do."

"Let me see it," demanded Richie. Chris grabbed his wallet out of his back pocket, pulled out a photo from last Christmas, and handed it to Richie. "Great looking family," said Richie, smiling at the photo.

"Thanks, Chief."

"You're welcome." Richie then ripped the photo in half, cutting off their heads, and handed Chris the piece of the photo with only their bodies.

"Chief, what the fuck!" yelled Chris. He reached for the other half of the photo, but Richie smacked his hand away. Chris aggressively tried again to get the other piece, but Richie blocked Chris and pressed his left forearm against Chris's chest while holding the other half of the photo away from Chris in his right hand, fully extended behind him. Richie smiled at Chris's attempt and taunted him while still keeping the torn photo out of Chris's grasp. "Down boy, down!" After a few seconds of pushing him back, Chris stopped and stood there staring at Richie with a face filled with anger.

"Are you done? Good," said Richie. "Now, I'm going to keep this half. And every time you feel the urge to step out, look at this photo of your wife and kids decapitated. This basically signifies what you're doing to your family for some pussy. So, she's over there still waiting for you to fuck your whole life up for a one-night stand. What you gone do?" Janine, who had been watching the whole exchange, sneaked away from the hallway before Chris noticed her. Chris stared down at his half of the picture for a few moments, thinking about his family and what they mean to him. Once he calmed down, he put the torn photo into his wallet and turned around to disappoint the woman by the door, but she was gone. So he headed straight to the bar and ordered a beer.

When he got his drink, he took out the photo again and nearly wept at the bar. He then grabbed his phone to look at more photos of his family. After he scrolled through a few photos, he texted his wife: "Baby, I love you so much. There's a lot of things I've done I wish I could take back. I know you know about those things. I promise to be the man I told you I was."

Janine quickly replied: "This would sound much better in person, don't you think?" Then she walked up and sat on the stool next to him. Shocked, Chris immediately started weeping and hugged her. She wrapped her arms around him and consoled him as he apologized repeatedly. Looking over Chris's shoulder, Janine looked Richie in the eyes and mouthed, "Thank you." He smiled and then headed out of the bar with the rest of the team.

As Chris is placing the picture in the box, his cell phone rings. He looks at it and sees an unknown caller on the screen. He has an idea of who it is but is uneasy about answering the call after Janine handed him the photo from the bar. Chris quickly whispered to Janine that he had to take the call, reassuring her that it wasn't a woman, and then he answered the call while stepping out into the hallway.

"Hello," says Chris.

"General, how do you do my friend?" asks Felix.

"I'm well, Felix. How may I help you?"

"I'm calling because you promised me you would do what you needed to do to move this equipment. Can you deliver on your promise, General?"

"Felix, this is still Richie's lane. I haven't taken over, so you're going to have to talk to Richie. My hands are tied."

"Are you telling me no, General?"

"I'm not telling you no, just not right now. I'll talk to Richie after my retirement ceremony."

"That's right! Bueno, Bueno. When do you retire?"

"In two days."

"Okay. My patience has met its limit. I assure you, you will not be bothered by me again." Felix hangs up. Chris, feeling relieved that he was able to avoid any issues, walks back into his office to finish packing.

* * *

Damawi is entertaining Gina, Octavio, and two waitresses from Josephine's, Kelly and Tammy, at her home in Hyde Park. She cooked barbeque ribs, her Aunt Josephine's baked macaroni & cheese, and baked asparagus with toasted almonds and garlic. "D, I didn't know you could cook like this," says Gina. "You been holding out."

"I can cook, but it's just me, and I hate cooking just for myself. Since Javari's here, I cook when I'm not busy at the club."

"Where's he at?" asks Octavio.

"He has a lil friend he hangs out with when he comes here. He think he slick talking about coming to spend time with me. Whatever!" Kelly and Tammy are heading out, so they thank Damawi for the dinner as she walks them to the door. After she sees the waitresses out, Damawi walks through the kitchen gathering Coca-Cola and rum to make drinks for her guests. She notices that she's almost out of soda and doesn't have enough to make everyone's drinks, so she calls Javari and asks him to pick up some since he's already heading back to her place with his friend. Damawi walks back into the dining room with the drinks that she has, and her, Octavio, and Gina discuss what happened at the club a few days ago. "So, tell me everything that happened in detail," says Damawi.

"Girl," starts Gina, "I was downstairs making sure the guests knew where the meeting was taking place. Everything was cool, but then after about an hour, I hear a loud noise coming from the party room. So I went upstairs to see what the hell was going on. When I got up there, people were walking out calmly like it was nothing, and when I weaved through the crowd, I see the light-skinned dude laid across the table. Girl... and his brains was blown all over the wall!"

"Oh my goodness!" says Octavio. "Why you ain't tell me, bitch?!"

"I told her to keep it low, Octavio," replies Damawi.

"I was shook, you hear me?" says Gina.

"I would've been too. Ion know, girl. That scares me. D, I know you all military and shit, but that don't bother you?" asks Octavio

"It probably would've if I'd seen it go down, but Richie said he'll handle it." Gina and Octavio look at each other in disbelief.

"Hold up," says Octavio as he looks at Damawi, "A nigga gets his head blown to bits in your club, and you talking bout Richie got it. Chile, that pussy is soooo gone!" Octavio and Gina laugh, then slap hands while Damawi looks on, smiling uncomfortably.

* * *

Javari pulls over to stop at a corner store on the south side to pick up some Coca-Cola before heading back to his Aunt D's house. "Javari, you sure you want to stop here?" asks India.

"Girl, we good. You better check my street cred."

"You don't have street cred, college boy." Javari sticks his tongue out at India, then smiles as he gets out of the car and heads into the store. He goes to the aisle in the back and grabs a liter of Coca-Cola, but then he puts it back down and heads back out to the car. He opens the door to the store, and he moves to the side to avoid contact with the three men walking into the store wearing black hoodies. He walks to the passenger side of the car, and India rolls down the window.

"I forgot to ask you. You need anything outta here?"

"I was wondering if you were going to ask me with your rude self. Could you grab some gum please?"

"For what? You ain't getting no kiss talking about my street cred."

"Boy, grab my gum." He smiles and heads back into the corner store. He opens the door and steps in to see the cashier's hands raised high. Two of the men are pointing guns at the cashier while another one is emptying out the cash register.

"Fuck you doing back in here, nigga?" Javari raises his hands and freezes. "Get yo shit, nigga. It's free now." Javari didn't move a muscle. One of the assailants points his gun at Javari and says, "Go get yo shit, ole bitch ass nigga." Javari heads to the back, grabs the liter of Coca-Cola and some gum, and then stands in the back. "Go ahead and leave," says the assailant. Javari starts to head out the store when the cashier says, "I wouldn't do that. I've already alerted the police, and they're on their way here." The assailant behind the register puts the last bit of money from the register into his bag. "You think calling the police gone save you, muthafucka?" He pulls out a revolver from the back of his pants, puts it to the cashier's head, and pulls the trigger. The cashier flies back from the force of the bullet, hits the wall filled with merchandise, then plunges toward the floor. Javari falls to the floor and covers his head at the same time as the cashier hits the floor. The bottle of Coca-Cola rolls toward the front door, and one of the assailants violently kicks it back in Javari's direction.

In the distance, Javari hears the sirens from the cop cars nearing the store as the assailants quickly flee the scene on foot. After all the assailants leave the store, Javari waits a few seconds before he uncovers his head. When he looks up, he sees a pool of blood traveling across the floor to one of the aisles. "Javari, Javari!" screams India in a panic. Javari gets to his feet, grabs the Coca-Cola, and heads toward the door. He hears the cop cars screeching into the parking lot, and he stops right in the puddle of blood and slips, crashing to the floor. He rolls onto his side and gets back up. His light blue coat is stained with blood along the back, down his left sleeve, and across his chest. He forcefully pushes open the door and is met with the flashing red and blue lights of the police vehicles. He immediately freezes as numerous officers shout various commands at him.

"This is the Chicago PD!"

"Stop!"

"Put your hands up!"

"Get down on the ground or I'll shoot!"

In an effort to follow the commands, Javari quickly raises his hands, dropping the two liter of soda. The bottle falls to the ground and explodes when it hits the corner of the curb. A single gunshot is fired, followed by a chorus of gunshots, sounding off like fireworks. Multiple bullets forcefully penetrate Javari's six-foot-five, two-hundred-and-fifty-pound body, piercing his face, chest, and legs. The officers continue shooting as Javari's lifeless body falls to the ground. India's screams from inside the car are the only sounds heard over the gunfire. As soon as the shooting stops, India opens the door to get out and run to Javari, but a police officer quickly shoves her to the ground and places his knee into her back. He holds her securely on the ground while the other officers slowly advance toward Javari's body.

After the police are assured the scene is secure, the officer holding India down takes his knee off of her back and helps her to her feet. She's crying and screaming uncontrollably as the police officer then places her in handcuffs and escorts her to one the cop cars, where she remains until after other units, detectives, an ambulance, and the coroners arrive.

* * *

"Shut up!" says Damawi. "You two are so dramatic."

"Whatever, bitch!" says Octavio. "We know who keeps them panties wet at night." They all laugh, but their laughter is interrupted by a phone call. "It's Javari's lil friend. Why she calling me? Hello."

"Ms. D!" India screams into the phone. The sound of India's voice makes Damawi's heart drop.

"What's wrong, baby?!" asks Damawi, panicked as she stands up.

"They shot him!!"

"Who shot who?!"

"The police! They shot Javari!!"

"What do you mean they shot him?!" screams Damawi into the phone. Gina and Octavio look at each other worried, trying to piece together the conversation.

"Where are you?!" asks Damawi.

"We're at the corner store on 66th and Morgan."

"66th...why are...I'm on my way!!" Damawi immediately runs out the house with Gina and Octavio following closely behind her. They all get into Octavio's car, and he quickly drives to see what has happened to Javari. Damawi texts the crew: "911 Javari 66th and Morgan." Richie, KAP, and Brick all immediately reply: "On my way."

After twenty-five minutes, Octavio parks as close as he can to the corner store, and Damawi immediately jumps out of the car and runs toward the front of the store. She quickly ducks under the yellow police tape, but a police officer blocks her path. Octavio and Gina remain frozen in the car, looking at the scene in disbelief. "Where's my nephew?!" screams Damawi frantically. The officer continues to hold her back as she looks past the cop's shoulder to see a stretcher pushed toward the ambulance. When she sees a body covered by a white sheet, her heart drops, and she loudly asks, "Who's under there?! Who the fuck is under there?!" She eventually wrestles past the cop and runs toward the stretcher. Two cops walking near the stretcher see her coming, and one of them tries to intercept her but accidently brushes the body and removes a corner of the sheet. Damawi instantly spots the shoes she bought Javari for his twenty-first birthday just months ago. The cop in front of her smacks into her while the officer she broke away from comes running up behind her. They each grab an arm, pick her up, and carry her back over to the other side of the yellow tape. "NO! NO! NO! NO! You muthafuckas killed my baby!" Damawi is kicking and screaming hysterically, trying to overpower the officers and make her way toward the stretcher.

Richie pulls up on scene first, followed by Brick directly after him. They both hop out of their cars and weave through bystanders as they make their way toward the yellow tape. When Richie sees Damawi going crazy, he swiftly ducks under the yellow tape to get to her. A police officer grabs his wrist, but Richie easily breaks free, reverses the hold, and quickly takes the police officer to the ground. Other nearby officers witness the take down and quickly converge on Richie. "Brick, make me a hole," shouts Richie. Brick steps in front of Richie and shoves anyone in Richie's path, so he can have an opening to Damawi. With Brick holding the officers back, Richie walks past them and frees Damawi from the officers' hold. When she realizes it's him, Damawi hugs Richie tightly, and he picks her up and carries her away from the scene. "My sister is gonna hate me so bad. She's gonna hate me! I KILLED HER BABY!!" cries out Damawi. She then tries to break free from Richie's grasp, but her attempt fails as she is physically and emotionally drained. Richie just holds her tighter as he has no words to comfort her. He's enraged that someone he cares for so deeply is going through this much pain.

Detective Coles arrives on scene, and Richie hands Damawi off to Brick as she continues to sob over the loss of her nephew. Richie advances toward Detective Coles, but a few officers attempt to block his path. Richie removes his coat, throws it onto the ground, and moves forward. The cops close in, prepared to take Richie down to the ground. "Hey!! At ease! Let him through," calls out Detective Coles.

"Brian, what the fuck?!" shouts Richie.

"Richie, walk this way." They walk over to Detective Coles's car. "Do you know the cashier or the shooter?" asks Detective Coles.

"Shooter?!" says Richie with a sharp tongue.

"Alright, the officers on scene are saying he came out the store, shirt full of the cashier's blood, brandishing a weapon, and they shot him."

"Brian, that's D's nephew. A senior at Virginia State University, a defensive end football player driving a fucking Mercedes. Your boys are dirty, Brian. Who were the officers?"

"I can't give you that, Richie."

"Brian…"

"Richie, let me do my job, and I'll reach out when I get things together. I know this is a fucked-up situation, but let me get to the bottom of this." Richie points at Brian, frustrated, then he walks away and heads toward KAP and Brick, who is carrying Damawi over to Octavio and Gina. As Brick sets Damawi down in the back seat of the car, Richie tells her, "D, we got it," trying to reassure her that the situation will be handled. Richie, KAP, and Brick watch as Octavio drives off, shaking their heads at another senseless murder by the Chicago Police Department.

Richie turns and walks back over to the border of the yellow tape. Detective Coles is walking over with India, whose face was swollen from crying. "We're going to need her to come to the station tomorrow for questioning and to fill out a statement. We can't get anything from her right now." Richie helps India cross to the other side of the tape, then hands her off to KAP and says, "Take her to the crib." KAP puts his arm around her and leads her to his truck.

"Richie, I'll be in contact with you." Richie looks at Detective Coles, shakes his head in disgust, and walks off toward Brick. "You good, big dawg?" asks Richie.

Brick nods.

Richie pats him on the chest and says, "I'm headed to the morgue where they're taking Javari, then to D's. Call Lloyd and let him know to be ready." They both get into their vehicles and go their separate ways. Detective Coles walks over to the store and stands in the spot where Javari was shot, examining the remnants of the earlier events. He bends down, dips his finger into a wet spot and smells it right before he tastes it. He then walks into the store to look around and see what he can find. He sees blood seeping from behind the register and smeared across the floor, heading toward the door. He inspects the smear pattern. He notices the floor is uneven and looks behind the counter where the store clerk once laid. Finally, he looks at where the soda is located in the store, putting things together in his mind. He then walks over to the first detective on the scene, Detective Russell, to ask him a few questions. "Hey Russell, so there was no video recording of the incident?"

"No, detective. The robber must've taken the recorder."

"What makes you believe it was just one person?"

"Well, that's what Officer Carlson is claiming. It very well could've been more."

"I would think that it was more than one. Who found the weapon on the kid?"

"Detective Morris found the weapon. It's been bagged and is with forensics."

"Good work, detective. Your first lead. You're not a virgin anymore."

"No, I'm not. The patrolmen made it easy for me. They're good cops."

"Are you familiar with them?" asks Detective Coles.

"Yes sir, I been knowing them for quite a while," replies Detective Russell.

"Well, good for you." Detective Coles walks around the store once more and then he slowly walks to his car.

Richie parks outside the city morgue and sits in his car as he repeatedly replays Damawi's reaction to her nephew's death in his mind. He has never seen her like that before. Unfortunately, he knows that trauma well. He reclines his seat and takes a deep breath, preparing to meditate. As he focuses on his breathing, his mind flashes memories of when he was standing on a corner waiting for the final bus to take him to school for his basketball game at Kennedy-King College. He then thinks about the night when a revolver was pressed hard against his forehead, hearing the sound of the hammer being cocked back. Click, click, click, click… He's pulled out of his memories by the sound of Detective Coles tapping on his passenger-side window with his key fob. Richie rolls the window down. "Follow me," says Detective Coles. Richie steps out of his vehicle and follows Detective Coles into the morgue. They walk past the front desk toward the elevators and take one down to the basement. They step out of the elevator and walk into the room where all the victims of senseless murders, the homeless who've succumbed to Chicago's weather, and the John and Jane Does are stored.

"Do you still have the body of the Pirie Park victim here?" asks Richie.

"Actually, we do," replies Detective Coles. "He's right over there. We're waiting for the family to tell us what funeral home they want us to release the body to."

"Release him to Lloyd's. I'll handle it. Keep it anonymous tho."

"Really?" asks Detective Coles. "Cool, will do."

They walk over to the medical examiner, Dr. Jose Medina, who is preparing Javari's body for an autopsy. "Will this bother you?" asks Detective Coles while they're walking over. Richie looks at Detective Coles but doesn't answer.

"Brian, you're right on time. I was just about to examine the body. Are you ready?"

"Proceed, Jose." Dr. Medina pulls the sheet back to reveal Javari's body riddled with bullet wounds. "Jesus!" says Detective Coles, shocked at the state of Javari's body.

"My best guess is this one here," says the medical examiner as he points to the bullet wound under Javari's right eye, "is the first one to hit him. He was dead before he even hit the ground. You see how the hole here goes in straight? The others go in at an angle as if his body was twisting or headed to the ground when they penetrated." Richie looks over Javari's body from head to toe and then walks away to search for Spree's body. Detective Coles studies the body and asks the medical examiner more detailed questions on Javari's wounds.

After a thorough inspection of Javari's body, Detective Coles signals to Richie that it's time to leave, and they leave as the medical examiner returns to removing the bullet fragments from Javari's body. "Give me a day or two, and I'll be able to put things together. I need you to be cool, Richie," says Detective Coles as he walks Richie over to his car.

"I trust you, Brian. You know this is close to me. I'll be in touch." Richie opens his car door and is about to sit in the driver's seat when Detective Coles says, "Hey Richie, don't do anything reckless. We don't want anymore bodies showing up at Pirie Park." Richie stops and stands straight up. "Not my style. I'm more personable. I'd leave em in your living room with a sign on their chest that would read 'Fuck you, Brian' in all caps."

"You know I had to check, Richie." Richie sits in the car, closes the door, and then reverses out of the parking spot, giving Brian the middle finger as he drives away. About twenty minutes later, Richie arrives at Damawi's house and is met at the door by Octavio and Gina. "Hey, Richie," says Gina.

"Is she sleep?" asks Richie.

"No, she's in her room."

"You guys can bounce. I appreciate you guys so much." He hugs Gina and gives Octavio a head nod as they head out. Richie then walks upstairs to Damawi's room and peeks around the door. She's sitting on the end of her bed with her phone in her hand.

Without looking up, Damawi says, "I can't do it. I can't call my sister. Richie, what have I done?" Still standing by the door, Richie attempts to reaffirm her. "You've done everything a good auntie does. Your sister knows you loved that boy, and you wouldn't have let anything happen to him that you could've controlled. This is a shitty deal for you and her. But you gotta call her. Don't let the news tell her before you do." Richie walks over to the bed and sits behind Damawi. He runs his right hand slowly down her right arm to her wrist, turns her hand over with her phone in her palm facing upward, and taps the call button on her phone. It rings. Damawi closes her eyes, and tears start to fall down her face. Richie places his arm around her and squeezes. The counter on the phones starts. 0:00, 0:01, 0:02…

"Hey sis, it's late. What's wrong? Is everything okay?" Damawi's body starts to shake like the last autumn leaf on a branch with a steady wind blowing. She lowers her head and inhales deeply.

"D, you there? What's going on?"

CHAPTER 8

Detective Brian Coles walks into his home, and he's greeted by his wife Sandra, who is holding their sleeping son against her shoulder. Brian kisses his wife, then takes his son, kisses him, and rests his son's head on his shoulder.

"I know you're tired, baby. Get some sleep," says Sandra.

"No, baby, I have a few things to do before I lay it down. You go ahead and get some rest." He kisses her and pops her on the butt as she heads upstairs. He turns on the hallway light leading to the family room. While walking down the hallway, he looks at his family pictures on the wall thinking of how blessed he is to be able to hold his son. He turns on the family room light to see his high school photos, football trophies, and pictures when he was in the police academy. Brian heads for the black leather sofa in front of his sixty-five-inch flat screen television. "Come on, Byron. Let's put you down, so daddy can do some work." He lays his son comfortably on the sofa next to him, grabs his laptop, and begins doing some research. "Hmm, it would be nice to know his last name. Lemme see…" He opens Google in his browser and enters, "Javari, Virginia State, Defensive End," into the search bar. The results return information for Javari Lewis. Brian spends the bulk of the night looking at highlight films, interviews, and articles about Javari, trying to get a feel for who he was. After a few hours of research, he closes his laptop, grabs his son, and then heads upstairs to get some sleep.

Early the next morning, Detective Coles kisses his wife goodbye, then leaves to go take another look at the corner store. He arrives at the store just after sunrise, and the owner, who Detective Coles spoke with the day before, is waiting outside the store in his car. The owner opens the door to the store and then returns to sitting in his car until Detective Coles is ready to leave. Detective Coles walks around the outside of the building, and he sees a trail of dirt that leads to an empty lot in the alley. He pauses to inspect the deeply smeared footprints that lead to the alley, and he mentally compares them to those going into the front of the store. "Looks like whoever left these were in a hurry to get away." He continues walking around the store until he's made it back to the front. He scans the outside of the building, painting a mental picture of what could've taken place outside the store, and then heads inside. Once inside, he slowly walks around the store before stopping next to the aisle where the soda is located. He closes his eyes and then takes a deep breath.

He starts to put the events of last night together. He pictures two assailants at first, then he flashes to the footprints in the empty lot and remembers that there were three sets. So he places one assailant behind the register, and the other two in the front with weapons. He starts to talk aloud as he continues piecing everything together: "So Javari stood right where I am now. The clerk triggered the alarm, and that irritated the assailant behind the counter. Why else would he kill the clerk so brutally?" He walks over and looks down at the blood streaks left on the floor. "Javari's shoes. He most likely dropped to the floor after the clerk was shot. The uneven floor caused the blood to run over here from behind the counter."

Detective Coles imagines Javari getting up after the assailants leave the store, and he slips on the blood as he's trying to run out too. He recalls looking at Javari's coat the night before at the morgue and seeing the pattern the blood stains left on the coat. "So Javari fell and rolled over this way." Standing, Detective Coles twists his body to reenact Javari's movements. "He gets up and then runs out the door still carrying a soda, but when he gets outside, he drops it..." Detective Coles continues to talk through the events as he walks outside, "And it explodes right here. That's when the cops fire." Detective Coles looks around. No soda bottle in sight. He walks over to the dumpster on the side of the store and looks inside. One empty liter of Coca-Cola. He reaches into his coat pocket and grabs some tweezers, then pulls the bottle out of the dumpster using the tweezers. He walks back inside the store, places the bottle inside a plastic bag, and walks back outside. Based on what he read and watched last night about Javari, he's confident there was no gun. Unfortunately, this young man is a victim of horrible policing and a cover up.

"Them dirty motherfuckers!"

* * *

Richie returned home from Damawi's early that morning to pack for his trip to Virginia to attend General Chris Warrington's retirement ceremony. He asked KAP to take him to the airport and to chop it up about last night's events. Richie, who was waiting outside his condo for KAP, places his bags in the back of KAP's SUV, then hops in the passenger seat. Once Richie is inside, KAP drives off toward the airport. After riding in silence for a few blocks, KAP asks, "How's D doing?"

"She's a wreck," says Richie. "This will leave a mark on her for a lifetime. Her sister had to be taken to the emergency room after D told her what happened."

"Damn. Javari's girlfriend had to be taken to the hospital too. She watched him get gunned down like an animal. She cried all the way home, B."

"Hey, let's make a stop before we hit the airport."

"You sure? You'll miss your flight."

"I know, but this is a priority." Richie pulls out his phone, scrolls through his contacts, then sends a text: "We need to talk. You available?" After a few seconds, he receives a response: "Yea,

I'm available. Come through." Richie shows the messages to KAP, who then says, "I see where you going. Let's do it."

"So when will we be ready for a re-up? Felix is stressing me," says Richie.

"About another three weeks, and we'll be good to go. They been working hard trying to move the extra keys. We don't want to overload them."

"No doubt. That's why I been pushing back, but he won't hold off for long." KAP pulls into the parking lot of H2H. Maurice and Karimah are standing outside waiting for them to pull up. KAP parks right in the front of the building, and he and Richie step out of the car and walk over to them. Karimah steps in front of Maurice, blocking Richie and KAP from getting too close. KAP looks at her from head to toe, checking out her polo shirt and low sagging jeans. "Look at her, Richie. She wanna be us so bad," says KAP.

"Give me some slow music, a condom, and an hour with her, and I guarantee I'll bring the bitch out this boy like Bruce Jenner!" Angered by his remark, Karimah stares fiercely at KAP, and they go into a staring contest as Richie chuckles and walks past her, letting them continue their pissing match. "Maurice, I need some information from you," says Richie.

"What's up?" asks Maurice.

"Last night there was a robbery at a corner store on 66th and Morgan. You know of it?"

"Of course. You know these streets is mine."

"I need the names of the dudes that hit the spot."

"That football kid that got murdered one of yours?"

"Family of family, so yeah."

Maurice thinks for a second and starts to slowly back away from KAP and Karimah. Richie follows. After they get out of ear-hustling range, Maurice says, "I can get you all three of their names, but I need something in return."

"How much?" asks Richie.

"Nah, no money involved. I need you to merc Kolax for me."

"Merc Kolax?!" Richie was thrown by Maurice's request. Kolax was his number one. "What's the reasoning?" asks Richie.

"He's a loose end. I'm making a turn with my organization, and his way of doing business is risky."

"You mean like blowing off one of your people's head in my club? That's acceptable?"

"You know as well as I do he was your people, and we both know your play. Plus, I got Karimah."

Richie turns and looks at her. "Yeah, I'm sure she's everything you looking for in a man."

Maurice, irritated by the comment, asks, "Is it a deal, or do you need a mic and a stage?"

Richie thinks for a second. "Okay, I'll do it. I'll feed him to Brick. Nice little snack for him. When can I expect these names?"

"Let me clear it through the lord, and I'll get back to you. As far as Kolax goes, I need it done quietly, and I need proof of death."

Richie nods at Maurice's request. "I got business to handle, so when I return, we'll exchange whereabouts," says Richie, walking back toward KAP and Karimah. KAP breaks away from staring down Karimah and walks next to Richie as they head back to his SUV. When they get inside, KAP asks, "We good?"

"We good. We'll have the names in a few days."

"I know that wasn't free. What it cost?"

Richie looks at KAP and says slowly, "Kolax's head."

"You bullshitting! I thought that was his man?" KAP shakes his head in disbelief.

"Bruh, it's a dirty game." They both sit in silence as KAP takes the ramp for the highway. Richie looks at KAP and recalls, "You said like Bruce Jenner!" They both laugh as KAP picks up speed and merges into traffic.

* * *

Richie's flight has arrived at the Richmond International Airport. After he gets off the plane and collects his bags, he picks up his rental car, a 2022 Cadillac XTS, and heads to Chris's house in Fort Lee. Richie hadn't been on a military base since he retired nearly four years ago. Seeing the soldiers running by in their physical training uniforms as the First Sergeant calls cadence brought back great memories of his time in the military. He remembers working at the sustainment command as a young officer, putting in work to make rank. He arrives at Chris's house and pulls into the driveway. The general housing looks like mini mansions compared to the enlisted quarters. The red brick home with pearly white window frames, a three-car garage, and the well manicured grass is pretty impressive.

When Richie steps out of his rental car, he sees Chris and Janine waiting to meet him at the door. "Richie, how was your flight?" asks Janine. Richie hugs and kisses Janine on the cheek and then hugs Chris. "It was good. I slept the whole way here." Chris grabs Richie's bags as they head into the house. "Life of a General Officer, huh?"

"Yeah, they take care of you pretty good at this level, but this is nothing compared to your place, so let's just stop it." Richie looks at Janine and shrugs his shoulders while cracking a smile. "Vaulted ceilings, multiple bathrooms, windows in the ceilings, and you have a golf course in your backyard. You stop it."

"I'll put your bag in your room," says Chris. Richie watches Chris as he goes upstairs.

"Richie, I'm so glad you could come," says Janine. "You've done so much for Chris and this family…"

"Come on, Janine." Richie puts his arm around her as she wipes a tear from her eye. "Let's save the snot bubbles and the tears for tomorrow." She laughs, closes her eyes, and rests her head on the side of his chest.

After Chris heads back downstairs, he and Richie walk through the kitchen to the patio. A bottle of Wild Turkey Bourbon and two glasses are sitting on a table near two comfortable chairs overlooking a golf course.

"You still drink this?" asks Richie.

"I sure do," says Chris. He fills up two glasses half way, and they both take their seats. Chris hands Richie a glass, and they tap their glasses together.

"Here's to the second chapter of life after Uncle Sam," says Chris.

"Second life," repeats Richie. They both take a sip as they stare out over the golf course. After a few hours, they've drunk half the bottle of Wild Turkey, and they're still sharing old stories and laughs. "Chris, I just want to say that I'm proud of your accomplishments, man. You were a young punk ass captain who's achieved the final rank of major general." Richie reaches in his back pocket and hands Chris an envelope. Chris opens it and pulls out the other half of the photo Richie ripped in half over twenty years ago. "You done good, my brother," says Richie.

"Look at this," says Chris as he pulls out his wallet from his back pocket and rejoins the two pieces.

"You ever think of the female and what would've happened if you took her to your room?" asks Richie. Chris turns around to see if Janine is within listening distance.

"Every Wednesday and twice on Sunday."

"Ha!"

"Honestly, I never looked back. Plus, Janine took my balls and never gave them back to me." Richie chuckles. "No, I'm serious. Watch this." Chris yells toward the house, "Baby, where are my balls?"

Janine yells back, "Downstairs! In the drawer on my side of the bed!"

"See," says Chris, turning back to Richie. Richie laughs and shakes his head. "So, Richie, back to business. Felix called me the other day asking about picking up a load. I told him that you were still running the show, and he needed to contact you."

"Good," says Richie. "I spoke with him too."

"Is this going to be a problem?"

"No. With the information I got from Tech, it looks like he needs us more than ever. I won't turn things completely over to you until our loads normalize, and Felix settles down. KAP said we will be ready for more product in a couple of weeks."

"Great, I can't wait to get started."

"Tell me this: what did you tell Janine you'll be doing?"

"She thinks I'll be taking over your entertainment business."

"That's perfect. Cause I don't want my balls in the drawer next to yours."

With a wide grin and a head nod, Chris replies, "Amen to that brother. Amen to that."

The next afternoon, Richie is jogging back to Chris's house after a six-mile run, and he waves at Chris's Chrysler 300 as it passes him on the road. When he reaches the house, he stops running and paces the length of the house until he catches his breath before he heads inside. In the living room, he sees Chris packing his bag as he's getting ready to depart for his ceremony. "Old man, you made it back alive I see."

"Barely," says Richie. "Where's Janine going? I seen her pass me on the way here."

"Nah, she's upstairs. I had my staffer Sergeant Perkins take the car to the Kabana Rooftop downtown for the after party. It'll be there waiting for us. The van's going to pick us up from here in a few minutes to take us over to the Performing Arts Theater."

"Okay, I'll get ready and meet you guys over there." The van pulls up in the driveway as Janine is coming downstairs. "You ready, baby? The van is here," says Janine.

"Yes, babe. Let me grab my ASU jacket, and we are out of here. See you in a few hours, Richie." Richie follows behind them and shuts the door as they head down the driveway.

Heading upstairs to shower, Richie looks at all the family photos all over the house. He remembers when they were at their worst, but he's happy to see that they stuck it out and made it through the rough times. Seeing Chris's family grow through their pictures over the years was an accomplishment in itself. So many black families are ripped apart for things that can be worked out by simply communicating. In every picture he looked at, he could track Chris's achievements as he progressed higher and higher through the military ranks. It was clear that his achievements were linked to the health of his family. Janine had always been the one to sacrifice her solo accomplishments for the family. Although Chris is an intelligent person, it is Janine who has made their household a home. Looking at all the family photos made Richie think about Nicole, his Janine, who was snatched from his life by her bout with cancer. Dead at twenty eight years old and a week before their two-year relationship anniversary.

Two hours later, Richie arrives at the Performing Arts Theater. He texts Damawi to check on her before he heads inside. The theater is packed with soldiers, family, friends, and old associates of General Chris Warrington. Richie walks in and hands one of the ushers his VIP badge, and the usher escorts him to the front row of the theater where he takes his reserved seat as a distinguished guest a few seats from Janine. The Master of Ceremony guides the proceedings of the night's event until Chris takes the podium near the end of the event to give his retirement speech. He gives an emotional but inspiring speech. He spoke highly of Janine, and what she has meant to his career, his accomplishments, and their family. Richie looks at Janine and sees her trying not to cry, but she can't stop the tears from flowing or the snot bubbles from forming. Richie turns his attention back to Chris, and he's filled with excitement to know that he's chosen the right person to help his team of quiet professionals move the ball down the road to black excellence. Chris is a great leader of men and women, and his abilities will help narrow that four-hundred-year head start, in which his ancestors were handed concrete sneakers to compete in a foot race with no chance of victory.

After the ceremony, a large convoy of guests head to Kabana Rooftop & Bar. As Richie pulls into the James Center parking garage, he receives a text from Damawi. She says that she's doing okay and has been working to keep her mind off of things. He tells her he will reach out to her later. Richie walks into The Kabana and sees that it's packed full of people. As he scans the room, he notices a lot of familiar faces that he hasn't seen since his retirement. While he's enjoying catching up with old friends, Richie's mind is steadily on Damawi, finding the people responsible for Javari's murder, Kolax, Spree's family, Felix... After a while, he just fades off into the background to have a drink alone in a corner of the bar.

Being at Chris's retirement party made Richie look back over his journey thus far after his retirement, and he realizes that he has a far greater responsibility now than he did while in the military. Now, he can't believe that he was willing to die for a country that hates him and implemented systemic oppression to keep his people pinned down. Martin Luther King Jr., Malcolm X, and many other black leaders were assassinated trying to change the conditions of Black people. Richie has become extremely dedicated to surpassing their accomplishments. Now if it meant ordering the murders of people who look like him to get there, so be it.

"Richie, why are you all the way over here by yourself," asks Chris. "Come have this last drink with us." There's about fifteen people who attended the ceremony and who are closing the club down. The waitresses are putting chairs on the tables and taking empty glasses back to the kitchen as the rest of Chris's party is leaving. As they enter the parking garage to head home, Chris says,

"Is everyone good to drive? If not, let's pool up and get folks home safely." Everyone piles into the elevator. On the second floor stop, Chris, Janine, and two of his staffers get off the elevator. Before the elevator doors close, Richie notices two well-dressed Latino men just hanging out by the elevators. He glances down and notices that they're wearing the same type of custom-made shoes that he owns, and he wants to know where they purchased them. Before he could react, the elevator doors close, and the elevator proceeds to the next floor. Richie and the other six people get off the elevator on the third floor.

On the second floor, Chris is saying his goodbyes and waiting for his staffers to get in their vehicles. "Okay, guys! Thank you for coming out," says Chris.

"No problem," says Major Hills. "I appreciate you, sir, and thank you for everything." Major Hills hugs Janine and then Chris.

"Stephanie, you were the best aide I ever had. If you need anything, you won't know where to find me, but you have my number," says Chris, laughing. "And when you find Sergeant Perkins, tell him thank you for dropping my car off, but kick him in the ass for not coming to the party."

* * *

Richie gets into his car and watches the other soldiers get into their vehicles and drive off. Before he leaves, Richie sits for a moment and thinks to himself, *Where did I get those shoes from?* He leans his elbow on the driver side window sill and strokes his beard as he thinks. The answer flashes across his mind like lightning.

* * *

Chris gets to his car and opens the passenger door for Janine. She sits down inside the car, kicks off her high heels, and puts her seat belt on. Chris walks around to the driver's side door and opens it when Janine asks, "Baby, can you get my flats out the trunk please? My feet are killing me."

* * *

Richie remembers the day Felix handed him a box with those same custom-made shoes from Mexico as a gift. "NO, NO, NO!" shouts Richie as he jumps out of his car and races down the stairs to the second floor.

* * *

Chris presses the trunk button on his key fob, but it doesn't open. "Here we go," says Chris.

"What's wrong, baby?" asks Janine.

"This freaking trunk or the key fob is broken." He presses the button again. Nothing. He places his hand beneath the Chrysler emblem and presses the button to manually lift the trunk. When the trunk doesn't immediately open, he puts some force behind it, and it opens. As he lifts the trunk…

* * *

Richie gets to the second floor and looks through the small door window to see if the two Latino men were still in the area. He didn't see anyone, so he opened the door slowly. He peeks his head through the slightly opened door and sees Chris about to open his trunk.

* * *

Chris looks inside the trunk and shouts, "What the fuck!" at the sight of Sergeant Perkins's body stuffed inside.

"Chris! Chris!" calls out Richie, running across the garage. Chris looks to his left to see Richie running toward him. Janine, concerned, gets out of the car and walks around to the back to see what the commotion is all about. Still running, Richie screams across the garage, "Chris, get away from the—" A huge explosion shoots out from the trunk of the car, covering the whole area with flames. The pressure from the explosion knocks Richie back ten feet. When he hits the pavement, he slides another three feet on his back until he's stopped by a cement wall. Car alarms echo throughout the parking garage as the water sprinklers rain down over the cars and bodies remaining on the second floor.

His ears were ringing. His Kevlar helmet suddenly felt heavy on his head. The blinding sun blurred his vision as sand and dust fell back to the earth. Shouts of "Medic! Medic! We need a medic over here now!" rang out all around him. He watched disoriented as soldiers rushed to gain control of the situation. Richie looked down at his legs to ensure everything was still intact, but he got easily distracted by the bodies of soldiers and civilians scattered around him.

"Chief! Chief! Are you okay, Chief?! Can you hear me?! Oh my God! Where is the General? Chief, where is the General?"

As Richie's faculties slowly return, he swings his arms as if he's fighting people off of him, then he realizes he's not in the Middle East, but inside a parking garage. Soldiers from the ceremony are kneeling over him, tending to possible injuries. His clothes are tattered from sliding across the ground. His face was covered in debri from the explosion. "I'm fine, I'm fine." Richie stands up and stumbles toward the area where his longtime friends were standing just moments ago.

Richie falls to his knees as he's trying to gain his composure and make sense of what has just happened. The vibration of his phone draws at his attention. He reaches inside his pocket and pulls out his phone. The caller ID reads: "Unknown Caller." Richie looks up to the ceiling and sighs before answering the call.

"Richie, my friend."

"Felix, what the fuck?! Why would you do that?!"

"Your friend Chris made promises he could not keep. There are consequences to breaking promises to me."

"We would've been ready for more in two weeks!!"

"That's two weeks too long, my friend. You are only alive because you're more valuable than the general. You have talents he does not have. Besides, there can only be one general. Although you are alive, I do not take your disobedience lightly."

"Disobedience!"

"I have to rearrange our agreement, Richie. I hope you understand." Felix hangs up.

"Felix, Felix! Hello, Felix! Muthafucka!" Richie slams his phone against the concrete ground, shattering the screen. "Fuck!!"

The police, EMTs, and firefighters have all arrived to tend to the people who may have been injured or witnessed what took place. Richie is cleared by the EMTs while the firefighters put out fires that the sprinklers didn't extinguish. The police question Richie and all the other witnesses. Richie admits to being a long time acquaintance of the general, but he lies and says that he didn't know why the car exploded or who could've done such a heinous crime.

Once Richie feels fully aware, he takes the stairs up to the third floor of the garage, taking his time as he walks up each step. He gets into his rental car and takes it back to Chris's house. He pulls up to the dark house and sits in his car for a moment before going inside. He stares at the house through his windshield, regretting ever introducing Chris to Felix. Richie takes a deep breath, exits the vehicle, and walks inside the house. He opens the door and then immediately pauses in the doorway. He stares briefly into the quiet, dark house before he takes another deep breath and closes the door. He rushes upstairs, avoiding looking at any of the family photos he stared at so lovingly earlier that day, and silently gathers all his belongings from the guest bedroom. After he's stuffed everything into his suitcase, he runs back downstairs. On his way out of the house, a family photo of Chris, Janine, and the kids catches his eye. He pauses and takes the framed picture off the shelf, looks at it for a few seconds, shakes his head in disappointment, and tucks the photo under his right arm. He then heads out the door, jumps into his car, and heads for a hotel by the airport.

After he checks into his hotel, Richie goes up to his room and lies across the bed, thinking about the events that took place just hours ago. He pulls out his phone and sees that he has numerous missed calls and text messages from family, friends, and the crew, all wondering about his health and whereabouts. He isn't ready to talk to anyone yet, so he turns on the TV and sees the night's events being reported on every local news channel. The news anchors haven't said what caused the explosion, but Richie was sure they'd soon be talking about a possible terrorist attack. If there was any trace of Chris going to Mexico, the investigators will start figuring out why he was there and why he didn't have a return flight. *Felix has no fucking idea how this may come back to bite us in the ass*, thinks Richie. *Killing a fucking general on the day he retires. That nonthinking, barbaric, stupid ass muthafucka.*

Richie finally picks up the phone and texts the crew: "Keep your heads on a swivel. We'll meet up as soon as I land tomorrow."

* * *

The next morning at 8 a.m, as soon as she arrives at her office, Arielle calls Richie to ask him what his text was about. "Richie, are you safe? What's going on?"

"I'm good. Headed to the airport. I need you to check out the news from Richmond, VA. That'll tell you everything. I also need you to send Phil to the port to ensure everything's okay. Have him get some of his goons to stay in the area for a few days until I get us back to normal. Felix is showing his ass right now, and he's very unpredictable. Have Phil with you at all times until I tell you otherwise."

"I don't think Felix is worried about me."

"He's not, but he knows that I do. Please, do what I ask and call me if something out the normal is going on."

Arielle sighs, "Okay, Richie. I'll text Phil and tell him." She hangs up with Richie and immediately texts Phillip to run by the warehouse to check on things. Moments later, Ren and Kay enter Arielle's office to see if she wants to go to lunch. "Hey girl, you hungry?" asks Ren.

"Yes, I'm starving, but I have a few more students I need to see before I eat," says Arielle. "You two should take Chantel with you. She's the new girl, and you two should be welcoming her with open arms."

Ren rolls her eyes. "She is so annoying. I'm not sure what you said or did to her, but she actually thinks she's you. She wears her hair like you now, dresses like you…"

"Well, my mini me is going to have to do because I'm busy." Arielle calls Chantel into the office and asks her if she's hungry.

"I could eat," says Chantel.

"Where do you want to eat?" asks Ren.

"I was thinking Celebrity," says Chantel.

"We were thinking…no," says Ren.

Arielle cuts in. "I'll tell you what…" She reaches in her desk drawer and pulls out the academy's business expense credit card. "Go to Riverside Tavern. But, in order to legally use this card, you have to make this a work-related lunch. Brainstorm about the curriculum for the new art class or something to that nature." The ladies all look at each other then at Arielle and nod. "Bring me back something unhealthy to eat, please. Have a great lunch, ladies," says Arielle as she waves them out of her office. As the three ladies exit the academy toward Kay's car, three men sit and watch the ladies from inside a black sedan parked about fifty feet from the parking lot. The driver says, "There she goes." The front seat passenger looks at the photo and says, "Yep. That's her. Dark-skinned, nice braids, nice round ass." The guy in the backseat passes the passenger a semi-automatic weapon over the seat. The driver pulls away from the curb and follows Kay's car as they head toward the restaurant.

Phillip texts Arielle: "I'll check it out before I pick you up after work. Give me an hour or so."

"Pick me up?" replies Arielle.

"I talked to Richie bruh. So yeah, picking your ass up." Arielle responds with a sad face emoji.

Kay turns down Main Street, trying to avoid lunch hour traffic, and gets caught by the traffic light. "Whatever, Ren! Mr. Bovell got a wife and three kids; he ain't checking fo yo ass," says Kay.

"Whatever, bitch! Mr. Bovell be all up in my face. He wants it, and he can get it," says Ren, as she throws her hands up in the air and thrusts her hips in her seat."

"Don't be corrupting Arielle's pride and joy in the back seat," says Kay.

"Get down, get down!" commands the driver in the black sedan as he maneuvers the car into the lane with oncoming traffic. The girls are all laughing when the black sedan side swipes Kay's car on the driver's side. Startled, Kay's proper English is quickly replaced with her Belizean dialect. "Dis fuckin asshole jus scrape my whip right suh? Well mada rass. Oh… and he nuh stop."

"Dis nuh gwen suh mek we guh ketch fi he rass!" shouts Ren. Kay safely runs the red light and speeds up behind the black sedan. The driver puts his hand out the window, signaling for Kay to follow him. He then turns down a side street, stops in the middle of the road, and cuts his car off. Kay pulls up a few feet behind them, then turns her car off. "I don't think it's a good idea to stop here," says Chantel.

"He guh explain weh dis alla bout!" shouts Kay as she opens her car door. She steps out of the car and stands on her left leg, leaving her right leg planted on the floor inside the car. The right-side and left-side passenger doors open slowly, and two men step out of the black sedan holding semi-automatic rifles and point them at Kay's car. Ren screams, "What the fuck!" Kay tries to jump back inside and start the car. Chantel ducks behind the front seat. Bullets shatter the windows and penetrate the side of the vehicle. The screams from the women quickly stop as blood paints the inside of the car.

When the gunmen are out of bullets, they walk over to the car and look inside. Ren and Kay's faces and bodies are riddled with bullets. One of the gunmen opens the back passenger door and sees Chantel crouched on the floor, shaking but still alive. He calls over the other gunman, who walks over and bends down outside the opened door. "Chica, it's okay. Look at me." Aside from the uncontrollable shaking, Chantel doesn't move. The gunman strokes her hair and whispers, "Shh, shhh, it's okay. I know you're scared. Look at me." She raises her head slowly and shows him her face. "No es ella," says the gunman as he raises his weapon. Chantel puts her head down and screams as he fires one bullet into the back of her head.

Nearly two hours after texting with Arielle, Phillip arrives at the locked gate leading to the warehouse. He gets out of his car, enters the security code into the keypad, and then hops back in his car to drive through the opened gate down the long road to the warehouse. He parks his car directly in front of the warehouse doors, then gets out and goes inside. He takes a look around, checking for anything suspicious, and then he texts Arielle to let her know that all is well, and he's on the way to pick her up. While driving to the academy, Phillip runs into traffic on Main Street, so he makes a U-turn to take another route to the school. He drives past a side street and sees the Belize Police and people blocking the view of why traffic is so backed up. He looks at his phone and realizes he has a few minutes to spare, so he pulls over, gets out of his car, and lights a cigarette as he walks over to join the crowd. When he gets close, he sees a car that mirrors Kay's and thinks, *Da fuq!* He scans the car for confirmation, noting the damage to the driver side bumper, and lands on the license plate, which confirms his concern.

Phillip throws his cigarette down and quickly walks to his car. He speeds to Those to Inspire Academy and parks in the first available spot. He scans the cars in the parking lot and around the facility as he walks toward the doors of the academy. Before he opens the door, he stops and scans the area again. He feels his phone vibrate, and he removes it from his pocket. He reads a text from Arielle: "I see you. I'm on the way down." He continues to look around the area and sees a black sedan with three men parked a few feet from the academy. He notices the large scrape on the passenger side front bumper that matches the one on Kay's car.

Phillip heads inside and sees Arielle walking toward the front door. She smiles when she first sees him, but, looking at Phillip's face, her smile instantly turns to worry. "What's wrong, Phil? You and Randy fighting again?" He hugs her and whispers in her ear, "Follow me." She follows him into a corner to the right side of the main entrance away from the windows. "Listen, I need you to do exactly what I say and don't deviate from what the fuck I'm telling you. Understand?"

"Phil, what the fuck is going on?"

"Do you understand?!"

"Yes!"

"There's a black sedan outside. I'm pretty sure they were sent here by Felix." Arielle's eyes widen with fear. "When you get to your car, get in it and go home. There are a lot of cops in the area, so they will probably wait until you get home to come for you. When you get home, go in and walk out the back door. I'll be waiting for you. Get in my car and head to Randy's."

"Okay. I can't believe this is happening." Arielle takes a deep breath and walks out the door with some of her teachers.

"Hey Arielle, see you tomorrow."

"See you tomorrow, ladies." She gets into her car and starts it up. She waits until Phillip gets into his car before she pulls out of the parking lot. The black sedan starts to follow her, but Phillip blocks their path and drives in between them and Arielle. She drives nervously through the busy traffic, checking her rear-view mirror every few seconds to ensure Phillip is still behind her. Her phone vibrates, and it startles her. "Phil, what's wrong?"

"I'm going to keep straight. I don't want them to think we together. If they pick up speed and try to get close, lose them." She makes a right, then looks in the rear-view mirror and sees Phillip's car continue straight. The black sedan turns right and is following directly behind her. "Be cool. Be normal. Breathe," recites Arielle as she tries to focus on the road. "Home is just two blocks up the road." She pulls in front of her house and looks in the rear-view mirror, checking for the black sedan, which has parked a few houses down the road. She grabs her things, gets out the car, and heads to her front door. She walks in her home and nearly faints. She drops her stuff at the front door, then walks through the house straight out of the back door. When she gets outside, she sees Phillip walking up to the back door. "The car is running. Get to Randy's."

"Come on, Phil! Let's go!"

"No, I have to handle this. If I don't, they will keep at you until you're dead. Go!" Arielle starts to walk off but then stops and turns to ask, "How did you know?"

He walks over to her and places his hands on her shoulders. "Ren and Kay are dead. They must've thought you were with them."

"Oh my God! Chantel!" Her knees weaken, and she collapses to the ground, knowing her childhood friends and her protégé are gone because of her. Phillip grabs her under her arm and helps her stand up.

"They're gone," says Phillip as his eyes fill with tears, "but we're still here. Now go. I'll text you in a little while." Arielle gets in his car and takes off to Randy's house. Phillip heads inside Arielle's house and locks the back door. He runs to the front door and looks out. He sees two men casually walking toward the house. He unlocks the door and runs to the bathroom to turn on the shower. He then closes the bathroom door and hides behind the living room couch.

Crouched behind the couch, Phillip quietly takes out his knife when he hears the front door open. The two men enter the house, close the door, and pull out their Glock 17s from their waistbands. They both pause in the living room, listening for any commotion. The only sound they hear is the running shower, so one of the gunmen proceeds toward the bathroom as the other one stays near the front door. Phillip stands and creeps up behind the gunman near the door. As the other gunman opens the bathroom door, Phillip covers the first gunman's mouth from behind, slices his throat, and then eases him onto the living room floor. He grabs the deceased gunman's weapon and quietly walks toward the bathroom. He hears the gunman snatch the shower curtain open and knows he's taken the bait. Phillip, standing against the wall next to the bathroom, extends his arm toward the bathroom door and waits for the gunman to exit. As soon as the gunman walks past the doorway, Phillip squeezes the trigger and puts a bullet in the side of the gunman's head, spraying blood inside and outside of the bathroom. When the gunman's body hits the floor, Phillip stands over him and puts two more bullets in his head.

The driver in the black sedan outside hears the gunshots and says through clenched teeth, "En silencio, en silencio, imbeciles." Phillip picks up the gunman he knifed and carries his lifeless body to the front door. He props the gunman's body up by the door, opens it, and waves the gunman's hand out the door, signaling to the driver to come inside. "¿Que putas pasando?" asks the driver as he gets out of his vehicle and heads toward the house. Phillip pulls the gunman back away from the door and drops his body in the middle of the living room. He then takes the gun out of his waistband and hides behind the front door. The driver opens the door and immediately sees the gunman lying on the floor. When he turns around, he's met with the barrel of a gun. Phillip squeezes the trigger and puts a bullet in the middle of the driver's forehead. Blood sprays across the couch and the wall as the driver goes crashing to the floor.

* * *

Richie's plane arrives at Chicago O'Hare International Airport early that afternoon. When he turns on his phone, he receives a text from Tech: "Boss, I'll be picking you up." Richie replies: "Pick me up outside of ticketing." He walks outside and looks for Tech's car. When he doesn't see him, he calls. "Where you at?"

"I just pulled up. Red sedan." Richie hangs up the phone. The car parks along the curb, and the trunk opens. Richie places his luggage in the trunk and closes it. He opens the front passenger door and sees that the car is missing a driver. He then looks at the backseat to see Tech with a computer in his lap. Richie smiles as he gets into the car and closes the door. "Tech, you're making me smile."

"Well that's nice," says Tech. "Where to?"

"Josephine's. We have a meeting."

"Put your seat belt on and let's roll." The car pulls out into traffic after yielding to other cars driving by.

"This is incredible," says Richie.

"Thanks! Me and my team of geniuses have been working nonstop. We're working on the vans now, and we're saving the truck for last."

* * *

Phillip calls Arielle and tells her to come back to her house. She drives over with Randy, and she notices that the black sedan is still parked down the street from her house but with the trunk open. As a precaution, they park behind the house and enter through the back door. When Arielle walks into her home, she screams at the sight of pools and trails of blood in her living room. Phillip has wrapped the bodies in garbage bags and stacked them on top of each other near the back door. "I need help getting these bodies in the car, so I can dispose of them. Have you told Richie?"

"No, I was waiting until I heard from you," says Arielle.

"Call Richie and tell him what's up and find out what the next move is. Randy, grab his feet." Randy grabs the bottom of the plastic-wrapped body, and they take the bodies to the car as Arielle goes into her bedroom to call Richie.

"A, what's going on? You good?"

"No, Richie, I am not. Ren, Kay, and Chantel are dead, and Felix sent some guys to my house to kill me." Richie pauses, takes his phone from his ear, and holds it against his chest. "What's wrong, boss?" asks Tech. Richie takes a deep breath and then puts the phone back to his ear. "Where's Phil?"

"He's putting them in the trunk now."

"Do you have a place where you can stay and lay low for a day or two?"

"I do."

"Get there and stay there. I'll call you tomorrow with our next move. Okay?" Arielle nods but says nothing. "Who was Chantel?" asks Richie.

"She was my protégé, Richie." Arielle starts to weep.

"I'm sorry this happened, A. I have no words to express—"

"Richie, I would be gone if you didn't text Phil."

"Everything in me told me to double down. You're alive for a reason. Now it's time for you to serve your life's purpose. It's so vivid to me. We'll talk more when you arrive at your safe place. Rest well, my queen."

CHAPTER 9

I t's 10 a.m., and it's a cold and overcast day as Lloyd's Funeral Home opens its doors for Nathaniel "Spree" Green's service. The funeral home was once an abandoned building that was converted into what it is now when Lloyd, Richie's cousin, was ready to run his own business. The white building is well-known in the neighborhood with its burgundy doors and windows matching the awning over the front door that reads, "Lloyd's." Inside, the lobby has beautiful dark hardwood floors with a burgundy rug in the center of the room. Lining the lobby are four chapels with wall-to-wall burgundy carpet and dark wooden pews. Pictures of the deceased are hanging on the walls next to each room where the service is being held. A large framed photo of a youthful Spree hangs on the wall to the right of the chapel that holds his casket.

Music is playing from an old organ as family and friends, dressed in all white, walk into the building in a single line to see Spree one last time. Before taking their seats, close family and friends pass by the casket to say their final farewells. Some are sobbing while most are shaking their heads, frustrated with the senseless murders. Spree's immediate family is sitting on the front row, hugging and consoling one another. His sister, Natasha, is devastated. Her only sibling is now gone, and now she must raise his daughter without him. Spirit, Spree's ten-year-old daughter, stands up first to give a sentimental speech about her father. "You were doing everything you could for me to be proud of you. I wish you knew how proud I was to be your daughter. Although you're not here with me anymore, I will make sure I do my best as you watch over me from heaven. I love you, dad." She holds back tears as she rushes to her seat and buries her face into the side of her Aunt Natasha's arm. Her auntie wraps her other arm around Spirit and holds her tightly while crying and rocking back and forth. Other than the music playing and a few scattered sobs, the room is quiet until Bishop Murtaugh takes the podium. He gives a thoughtful sermon on the beautiful relationship Spree had with his family, and he speaks on the urgency for the community to take back the streets from the gangsters and the drug dealers. Everyone sits silently reflecting on Spree's life and their own. Looking at someone you know in a casket makes you think about your own demise, wondering when your number will be pulled for you to come home.

Suddenly, the chapel doors open. A few people sitting in the back turn around to see who has entered. Karimah walks in first, followed by Elder and then Maurice. Karimah casually walks to the front of the room and stands a few feet in front of the family, blocking the view of Spree. Elder stops across the aisle from Karimah, and Maurice passes between them and up to the casket to pay his respects to Spree. He stares at Spree's body for a few seconds. Maurice then slowly bends down close to Spree's face and whispers, "Yeah, you bitch ass muthafucka. You was neva built fo dis shit. Rest with dem maggots." He then spits in Spree's face, forgetting where he was. The funeral director looks on with shock and disgust. The director steps to move toward the casket, but Karimah stares at him and he freezes.

Maurice wipes the spit from Spree's face, making it seem as if he was lovingly patting Spree's cheek. He then turns to walk over to Natasha to give her his condolences. She stands and hugs Maurice, and he wipes the spit off his hand onto the back of her dress, moving it up and down as if he is consoling her. "I loved him. He was my lil brother too. Anything you need, let me know. I got you."

"I know he was, Maurice. He loved you too. Thank you so much!" Maurice kisses her on the cheek, then he, Elder, and

Karimah walk to the back of the chapel and take the empty seats on the last row.

* * *

Richie arrives at Josephine's with Tech in the autonomous vehicle. After the car parks itself, Richie and Tech get out and head inside directly to the party room where the rest of the team is waiting. "T.K., I didn't expect you to be here," says Richie.

"We in the trenches, brother. Wouldn't miss it." Richie smiles at him and then asks everyone to take a seat. "Not sure if you all know, but Chris and his wife was killed yesterday by Felix. Today, he had some dudes kill Ren, Kay, and another person who was in the car. Wrong place at the wrong time. They attempted to kill Arielle, but Phil handled that. Today, moving forward, we have to close ranks. No more going out solo; now, we move in pairs. Brick, you're with D, KAP and Tech, me and T.K." Everyone nods in agreement. "Brick, we need your security peoples available to us."

Brick nods.

"Tech, can we get the subs out to sea without you going to Louisiana?"

"Yeah, I can do it from here."

"Good. Get that done immediately. KAP, tell the organizations to slow down pushing the product if they can; we'll probably have a delay with product in the near future. Tell them we'll discuss incentives if we go beyond the re-up timeline."

"I got it, Richie," says KAP. "What will we do if we don't have the product?"

"We'll have the product. Felix needs us. He's just sending a message. Everyone from the main body within the organization is still here. I believe the costs, quantity, and logistics will be different going forward. Until then, it's still business as usual. Any questions?" The room is silent. Being hunted was unfamiliar territory for the crew, but Richie believes that this will make them stronger in the long run.

* * *

Detective Coles leaves his home and drives downtown just days after his solo corner store investigation. He's on his way to meet with Chief Watkins, so they can discuss his findings on Javari Lewis's shooting. When he arrives, he sits down in the chief's office, and over a couple cups of coffee, they discuss the possibilities of evidence being purposely removed or hidden from the case, which leads Coles to believe that the officers involved are dirty. "Really?" asks Chief Watkins. "This is unfortunate. Some people believe loyalty to the fraternity of officers is more important than doing the right thing, especially when no one is looking."

"What should we do, boss?"

"Well, the right thing. I thought it was odd that the surveillance tape mysteriously disappeared, and the backup was disabled."

"Me too. But the soda bottle being in the dumpster sealed the deal and could be a huge piece of evidence used against the officers—"

"What about his girlfriend?" asks Chief Watkins, interrupting Detective Coles.

"Mentally, she's not there, boss."

"I understand. I'll get IA on this and see what they can find. We're being pressured because of who this kid was. We need answers. Put Detective Neeley under your wing; train him up. The FBI is looking for detectives that have the capability to perform on a national level. I dropped your name in the hat."

"Really, boss? Why?"

"Well, first off, you're welcome, and secondly, the department is changing, and I'm retiring soon. I think you should go off to bigger and better things."

"Thanks, Chief."

"You deserve it, Brian. Let me know if you find anything else involving this case."

* * *

Richie is in Damawi's office conversing with her on how she's doing with everything going on, especially after the death of her nephew. She reassures him that she's doing fine. When they're done talking, he walks out of her office with a duffel bag and signals to T.K. that he's ready to go. They have a few things they need to do before the day is over, but first, they stop by the club's safe and pull out a couple of semi-automatic weapons and then head to the autonomous vehicle. Before they take off, Tech enters the address into the GPS from his laptop while sitting in the party room. The car starts up, leaves the parking lot, and merges into traffic perfectly.

"Man, this shit is crazy," says T.K. "I'm nervous and relaxing at the same time."

"It feels weird to just sit here," says Richie. "Don't ever repeat this, but Tech's a genius. Sometimes I feel like we keeping him away from the world with his talents." A voice comes through the car's speakers.

"Awwww, Richie! You have the tip of my penis all tingly and shit."

"Great to hear, Tech," Richie says smiling. "Now let's act like you're not here. Thank you."

About fifteen minutes later, the vehicle arrives safely at H2H's building and parks. Richie hops out of the car, leaving T.K. inside, and heads upstairs to Maurice's office. Maurice is there alone when Richie walks in. He walks over to Maurice's desk, and Maurice hands him the names and addresses of the guys responsible for the corner store robbery and murder along with the address to where Kolax is staying.

"Like I said, Richie: I need proof of death."

"That's no problem. I'll hit you up and tell you where to come for a visual."

"Good. Also, the East Coast connect can handle more than what you sent before. That Farrakhan shit seems to be working on that side."

"Okay. Anything else?"

"No. But I'm curious to see what you do with those names."

"The lords approved this?"

"The lords wouldn't approve this for something they ordered. This is off the books. I got this information from another source. So, what you do is what you do." Richie puts the paper in his pocket and heads back to the vehicle.

As the vehicle leaves for its next destination, Richie reads the names written on the paper Maurice handed him. "Hey Tech, I need you to research some people for me."

"What you got?" asks Tech.

"Roland Outlaw, Curtis Walker, and Jordan McVeigh." He reads off the addresses too.

"I'll get on it once you done joyriding."

"So, what's the play with Arielle?" asks T.K. "She's vulnerable in Belize. Too close to Felix. Once he finds out she's still alive, he's going to come at her until he kills her."

"I have a plan to counteract Felix's attacks, but I need her to be at full strength with a clear mind. I want you present when I speak with her because I need you involved. We'll call her when we leave Spree's people's house." Twenty minutes later, the vehicle pulls up at Spree's place. Richie and T.K. put their weapons in their coats, and T.K. grabs the duffle bag as they both exit the vehicle. They both scan the area before walking up to the apartment. Richie knocks, and Natasha opens the door almost immediately. "Oh my God! Richie!" She stands on her tiptoes to hug him, and he says, "Hey Natasha," as he wraps his arms around her waist. "You two come on in and have a seat. I haven't seen you in years. Spree talked about you being back." They sit down on the living room couch. T.K. is scanning all the family pictures as Richie and Natasha continue talking. "Yeah, sorry we had to meet under these circumstances," says Richie.

Natasha puts her head down. "I know, Richie. Do you have any idea who could've done this?"

"You know the streets. It'll come out sooner or later. How's Spirit doing?"

"She's not really saying much, but I know she's devastated."

"Do you mind if I go up and talk to her?"

"Sure, go on up." Richie heads upstairs and stands outside Spirit's ajar bedroom door. He gently knocks on the doorframe, and she sits up on her bed. "Who is it?"

"It's one of your dad's childhood friends, Richie. Can I talk to you for a moment?"

"Sure. Come in." He opens the door fully, walks in, and pushes it closed slightly before he sits on the foot of her twin-sized bed. He scans her room and looks for something to talk about to break the ice. Her all-white furniture stands out in the pink-filled room. Her fuzzy pink rug is neatly placed on the side of her bed. She has all her drawings hanging up all over her room, and nearly all of them have the color pink in them.

"You like the color pink I see."

"Yeah, it's my favorite color."

"How are you holding up, Spirit?"

"I'm okay. How you know my name?"

"Your dad talked about you all the time. He wanted nothing but the best for you."

She smiles. "How long have you known my dad?"

"Ever since I was twelve years old."

"Wow! That's forever."

"So, your dad told me if something ever happened to him that he wanted me to make sure that you have everything you need to become an awesome adult. So he gave me some money to give to Auntie Natasha for you to go to school, buy your books, clothes, everything."

"He did? Did you work for my dad?"

"I did. He was such a great boss and a better person, but sometimes bad things happen to good people. If you ever want to talk about your dad, your auntie has my number." Richie hugs her, squeezes her tightly for a few seconds, and stands up to leave. As he's heading out the door, Spirit calls out after him.

"Mr. Richie?"

"Yes, Ms. Awesome?"

"Do you know who killed my daddy?" She looks at him as her eyes fill with tears. Richie pauses for a few seconds.

"Yes, I do." She wipes her tears from her chin.

"Are you going to kill them?" Richie drops his head to his chest and takes a deep breath. He could feel tears welling up in his eyes.

"Yes, I am."

"Why?"

Richie walks over to her and kneels on one knee in front of her. "Because I want him to explain to your dad why he took him away from such a beautiful little girl." A tear drops from Richie's right eye, and Spirit wipes it away before it rolls down his face. He gently grasps the back of her head and kisses her on the forehead, then he leaves and shuts the door behind him.

He stands at the top of the stairs and gets himself together before heading downstairs. When Richie enters the living room, T.K. and Natasha stand up. He reaches into his pocket and hands her a card. Natasha reads it out loud: "Mandatory Prep Academy."

"Call Mrs. Cowart on Monday; she'll be awaiting your call. She'll assist you on getting Spirit enrolled in school." Richie then turns to walk toward the front door, and T.K. follows him.

"Are you sure, Richie? This is way on the South Side."

"He owns it," says T.K. as he hands her the duffle bag. Natasha opens it and is taken aback by the stacks of money.

"My realtor will be in touch with you in a few days," says Richie. They walk out the house, and T.K. shuts the door behind them.

Richie and T.K. get back into the vehicle, and Tech programs the car to send them back to Josephine's. Richie is quiet during the ride, reflecting on Spirit and how her life is going to be different without Spree. T.K. breaks the silence, "We should call Arielle and give her some guidance." Richie dials her number, and she picks up immediately.

"What's up, A! You good?"

"I'm good, Richie."

"I got T.K. in the car."

"Hey lady, I heard what went down. You stay strong, queen."

"I don't feel strong," says Arielle.

"Stop that nonsense," says Richie. "Where's Phil?"

"Right here," says Arielle.

"Put me on speaker."

"Go ahead, Richie," says Phillip.

"Speaking of queens, you're about to be the most valuable piece in this game of chess, but I need you to do a few things first. You still connected at the news station?"

"Yes," responds Arielle.

"Okay, I need you to get down there and make sure they don't release Ren, Kay, and the other young lady's names from that hit yesterday. Felix thinks you're dead, so let's keep it that way for as long as we can. Did those guys have cell phones on them?"

"Yeah, they're right here," says Phillip.

"Look and see if there are any messages from his people checking in with them." Phillip looks through each of the phones. The driver's phone has four missed calls. He looks through the text messages and sees one from an hour and ten minutes ago. "Yea, there's a text that says, 'Esta hecho?'" says Phillip.

"That means is it done? Text back and tell them it's done," says Richie.

Phillip responds to the text: "Si"

"A, I can't protect you there," says Richie. "Once Felix finds out you're not dead, and his people is missing, he'll be coming at you full force."

"What can I do, Richie? Come to America?" asks Arielle.

"No, you're going to do what you were born to do. You're going to run for prime minister."

T.K. smiles and says, "That's a good idea."

"Richie, I'm not prepared to do that, especially not right now. It's so much—"

"A, you run for office, and you'll be protected. He won't touch you… or any of us for that matter. The people of Belize love you, and you're all about the people. All the charity work, donations, and the three schools you've opened in such a short time. People know your face from being a news anchor. You're educated. Plus, you have money backing you. Set up an interview and announce that you're running."

Arielle remains quiet.

"I also need to know whose Felix connect is. Call me when you get those things done; we gotta move fast. A, this is your time."

Shortly after Richie gets off the phone with Arielle, they arrive at Josephine's. They head inside and upstairs to the party room where Tech is working on the items Richie requested. When they walk into the room, Tech stands and hands Richie the police files of the three assailants from the corner store murder. Richie sits down and looks through the files, reading each aloud: "Roland

Outlaw, twenty-four years old. He's had a lot of run-ins with the law since he was fourteen. Curtis Walker, thirty-one. He did some years in prison for breaking and entering." Richie pauses and wonders if he was the one who put one in the head of the cashier. "Jordan McVeigh…" Richie pulls the paper closer to his face. "Oh, she's a female. She's twenty-one and she has been in and out of juvie since she was thirteen for drug possession with the intent to distribute. One year in the bing." Richie finishes looking through the files, then tosses them on the table and releases a deep sigh as T.K. grabs the files and looks over them.

* * *

The next morning, Richie wakes up to text messages from the team reporting that they are all safe and sound. He hops out of bed, pauses at the smell of breakfast, and thinks, I thought I told Sheree she was off. He walks into the kitchen and sees T.K. making breakfast. "Really?" asks Richie. "I knew I should've married you when I first laid eyes on you."

"Man, you stupid," says T.K. Richie walks over to the cabinets and grabs some plates. They each pile food onto their plates and sit down at the table to eat breakfast.

"So, what are we going to do about those youngsters?" asks T.K.

Richie, chewing his turkey bacon, responds, "Nothing at all. I thought about leaving it up to D, but, I'm going to let this just ride out. Not even going to tell her I have the names."

"That might be a good idea concerning D, but I'm sure we can use this in the future."

"You may be right. But until then, we'll let her mourn. Her and Brick are on their way back from Pennsylvania for Javari's funeral. We should do something special for her when she gets back."

Before T.K. can respond, Richie's phone rings. He looks down at the screen and says, "This is going to be an interesting phone call." He shows T.K. the phone before answering. "Hello."

"Richie, my friend, how do you do?"

"What can I do for you, Felix?" asks Richie in a dry tone.

"You still sound sore from the events that happened over the last few days. I hope you understand that it was just business, just as this call. You have a shipment of equipment coming in within the next few days. The prices we established is no longer. You will pay American rates, which include my transportation services. Do you understand?"

"I understand, Felix. Since you changed our arrangement, I don't have the money for deposit. If you don't mind, I would like to get the equipment on consignment."

"That's fine, Richie. You do understand the penalties for being late or delinquent, right?"

"I do," says Richie.

"We will be in touch," says Felix before he hangs up.

"Really, Rich? On consignment?" asks T.K., sipping on his orange juice.

"Yep," says Richie. "If everything goes as planned, this will be our last business transaction with that fucker. Period."

"What if everything doesn't go as planned?"

"Then we all die." T.K. freezes, his glass of orange juice midway between the table and his mouth, and stares at Richie, who is just casually looking at his plate and eating.

"Is there anymore turkey bacon?" asks Richie as he looks up at T.K.'s shocked face.

* * *

Detective Coles is at the precinct early, and he stops by Detective Neeley's desk before he heads to his office. "Fred, you got a minute?"

"Sure, boss," responds Detective Neeley.

"Follow me."

"You need me, boss?" asks Detective Russell. Detective Coles just stares at Detective Russell until Detective Neeley is ready to follow him, then he turns around and walks away. Once they're both in Detective Coles's office, they both sit down, and Detective Coles gets right into the reason he wanted to talk. "Things are shifting in this department. Some people will be moved, some will have greater responsibilities even though they haven't earned it, yet. I'm splitting up you and Detective Russell. I would like to assign you as the lead on a hot case. But, before I do, Fred, what's your background?"

"What do you mean?" Detective Coles leans forward and looks Detective Neeley directly in his eyes. "Tell me about your parents, your upbringing, your beliefs, religion, race, and most importantly, why did you ask to work in this precinct as a white male. The floor is all yours."

Detective Neeley pauses for a second to gather his thoughts. "Well, I'm an only child and an Army brat. I was born in Fort Sam Houston at the Brooke Army Medical Center on January 6, 1995. My mom was a high school English teacher, and my dad was in the Army from the time I was born until I was about seven years old. My dad served over in Iraq for fifteen months after 911 and came home safely. Not a scar on him. Three days after he returned, my parents went out for dinner and a movie. My parents took me over to my dad's best friend's house, Mr. Memphis Hinton, so he could watch me while they were out. They would often do that, so they could have time for themselves. Well, my parents never made it back. They died in a car accident headed to pick me up.

"From that day forward, I never left the Hinton's household. When he retired from the military, we moved to his hometown, Chicago, on the North side. If you haven't guessed by now, Memphis and Hope, my mom and dad, are black. They raised me as their son. I went to a predominately black school, and my two sisters protected their white brother every day. I love my family. All of my parents are now deceased, but Hope and my mom instilled great values in me, and Hope was extremely strong but caring. So strong and caring that I couldn't see myself married to nothing other than a black woman. So, I married one, and I have two kids of my own.

"I understand the struggles of Black people in this country, this city, and I became a cop because of that and my dad's military service. It's the closest thing to being in the military, and I didn't want to be away from my family."

Detective Coles sits back in his chair, staring at Detective Neeley for a moment. "Wow, that's a great story. Okay, detective, let's begin. I want you to take the lead on the Javari Lewis case." He reaches in his desk and pulls out a file. "Look over everything here, and we'll talk about it later. Do not share anything in this file with Russell and don't ask why. Copy?"

"Copy, sir," responds Detective Neeley.

"Alright, enjoy your day, Fred. We'll talk soon." Detective Neeley grabs the file and heads back to his desk.

* * *

After breakfast, Richie and T.K. head over to Richie's mom's house so they can bring Marble Head up to speed on current events. While he's driving, Richie receives a call from Arielle telling him the news won't be releasing the names of the victims from Felix's hit. "And Richie," says Arielle, "I'm also going to be interviewed in a few days to announce my run for Prime Minister of Belize."

"That's great news, A! How do you feel?"

"I'm nervous, Richie, but I have a lot of politicians behind me. Their only concern is raising enough money to support the campaign."

"You know you don't have to worry about that. Just focus on the task at hand."

"Okay. By the way, we've narrowed it down to three possible drug cartels that Felix could be connected to. I just need a few more days to get the information for you."

"I need that info like I need water. Let me know as soon as you can." They hang up with one another as Richie pulls into the driveway at his mom's house. Richie and T.K. walk inside the house to an abundance of laughter. Richie's mom has a few of her friends over, sitting in the family room having drinks and talking.

"Hey, baby! Hey, Terry," says Richie's mom as she stands up and gives them both a hug.

"How's everyone doing?" asks T.K., waving at the ladies. Each of her friends greet them with a smile and a wave. Richie and T.K. pay their respects to the women, then they head upstairs to chat with Marble Head. When they walk into his room, he's laying back in his recliner watching television, as usual. "What's up, unc?"

"Hey, nephew! Hey, boy! I ain't seen you in a while! How you been?" asks Marble Head as he leans forward to hug T.K.

"I been good," responds T.K.

"Have a seat." Marble Head grabs the remote control and puts the television on mute.

"How come you not downstairs entertaining those ladies?" asks Richie.

"Man, don't nobody want them old bitches." Richie and T.K. look at each other and chuckle as Marble Head puts out his cigarette. They take a seat on Marble Head's bed, and Richie recaps everything that's transpired over the last week or so. Finally, he shares his plans on how he's going to handle Felix once he gets his connect. Marble Head sits in his recliner in disbelief and has only one word for what he's just heard: "Damn!"

"Unc, I need Felix's connect. Everything is riding on that."

"I told you ain't no getting out. Putting everything on this connect without knowing how important Felix is to him can be a death wish," says Marble Head.

"That's true, unc, but it could liberate us all." Marble Head rubs his head while he thinks for a moment.

"Let me get word out to some cats. It may not be as hard as we making it. Give me a few days. I'll have something that'll get you what you need or close to it. Since Felix is giving you another shipment, I think it's safe for your crew to loosen up a bit. He's going to send you way more product than ever before. He believes he got you right where he needs you." Richie looks at T.K. and nods in agreement.

"You may be right, unc. Thanks." Richie and T.K. stand up to leave, and Richie asks, "You need anything, unc?"

"No, I'll be in touch with some answers." They exchange handshakes, and Richie and T.K. head back to the city. Once they're in the car, T.K. asks Richie, "So, what's the next play?"

"Next order of business is to get this shipment squared away, then Kolax. It's time to feed the bear."

"Man, I don't think there isn't anyone in the crew who wouldn't want to see Brick handle that business." Richie thinks for a minute.

"We might can make that happen. That depends on when the shipment gets to Louisiana. Let's stop by Josephine's to see if Brick and D are back." They arrive at the club and see Brick's car in the parking lot. When they walk inside, Brick is lying down on one of the couches. "What's up, B?" asks Richie. Brick lifts his hat from over his eyes and sits up as T.K. and Richie sit on the couch across from him. "How did it go?" Brick shakes his head, indicating that it didn't go well. Richie looks down for a second and then gets up to go see about Damawi. He hops on the elevator, and during the ride to the third floor, Richie searches for some words of encouragement that he can share with Damawi to help her with her grief. The elevator doors open, and he steps out and heads directly to her office. He notices that the lights are off, so he assumes she's resting her eyes or having an emotional outpour. He slowly opens the door and walks through the doorway; the lights turn on automatically, revealing that her office is a mess. Damawi had thrown papers everywhere, knocked the books off her bookshelf, and turned over some furniture. She isn't in her office, so Richie must have just missed her.

He gets down on his knees to pick up items off the floor to help get her office back in order. While putting papers back on her desk, he comes across one of the folders that Tech gave him about the corner store robbers. He opens the folder and sees that the papers are missing. Richie walks to the party room to see if she's in there; it's empty. He pauses and strokes his beard as he thinks, then he quickly runs down the stairs to the first-floor office. He runs inside, goes directly to the safe, and places his thumb on the fingerprint reader. He opens the safe and immediately notices that the 9MM handgun and an extra magazine are missing. He jogs out to the lounge area and asks, "Brick, how long ago did D leave?!" Brick looks at Richie confused, which told Richie that Brick had no clue she was gone. Richie takes off running for the main entrance to the club. "Richie! What up? Where you going?!" yells T.K. Richie doesn't answer as he pushes through the doors, heading to his car.

Once he's inside his car, he starts it up and calls Tech. "You rang, master?" asks Tech.

"I need those addresses for those three youngins ASAP. Send it to my phone immediately!"

"Okay, boss. Sent."

"How far apart are these addresses?" Tech takes a few moments to calculate the distances.

"They're in the same neighborhood, so maybe three, four blocks apart."

"How's the police presence this time of night?"

"Very minimum. Hey, what's—" Richie hangs up, cutting off Tech, and heads south. About fifty minutes later, he arrives at Roland Outlaw's last known address. It's dark outside, so he drives slowly to look for Damawi's car. When he doesn't see her vehicle, he drives off thinking, *She's probably going after the person who she feels she can take out the quickest.* He heads to Jordan McVeigh's last known residence. When he turns onto her block, he slows down and almost instantly spots Damawi's car parked one house away from where Jordan lives. The car lights are off, but he notices exhaust coming from her tailpipe. He turns his headlights off and parks a few feet behind her. He grabs his weapon and puts it in his coat pocket. He quietly gets out of his car and then dips down next to the curb, scanning the area. This isn't the best neighborhood to be in at night. Crime has always been an issue since Richie was a kid. Gangs and drugs ran rampant back then, and it's gotten worse every year since because the police turn a blind eye to neighborhoods like this.

He contemplates walking up to her car, but he knows she's on edge, nervous, and hypervigilant. He didn't want to chance getting shot, so he calls her phone as he cautiously approaches her car. He looks through the back windshield and sees the light from her phone as she lifts it to see who's calling her. She looks at it for a few seconds, then answers. "Hello?"

"Unlock the door," commands Richie.

"Unlock the door?" asks Damawi.

"Yea, unlock the door." He then bangs the tip of his gun on the passenger side window. Startled, Damawi jumps and tosses her phone out of her hand. She fumbles trying to catch it, but it falls between her legs onto the floorboard. She bends down, picks up the phone, and puts it to her ear again. Richie thinks to himself, *Look at this rookie ass shit.* He puts the bottom of his phone close to his mouth and says slowly, "Opeeennn theee dooooor!" Damawi presses the unlock button, and Richie opens the car door. He sees the papers from Tech's files laying on the passenger seat. Richie puts his weapon on the dashboard, picks up the papers, then sits inside the car and closes the door. He gathers the papers together neatly and places them on the dashboard, exchanging them for his weapon.

Richie then turns to Damawi, who's looking at him with the phone still up to her ear. He smiles, then shakes his head. He puts the bottom of his phone to his mouth and says, "Hang up the fucking phone, D." She hangs up and continues to stare at Richie. He looks straight ahead, clears his throat, and takes a deep breath. "D," Richie says calmly, "what are you doing here?" She pauses. Richie looks at her. He sees her eyes start to fill up with tears. She stares out the window and doesn't answer. "D, you're a lot of things, but a killer isn't one of them. I know what happened to Javari is a terrible thing. I miss him too. But you out here trying to seek revenge won't do your family, me, the crew, or you any good when you in prison."

"Prison!" shouts Damawi.

"Yes, prison. Let's see," says Richie as he scans the neighborhood through the car windows. "It's dark, and we're in a drug-infested neighborhood. You're sitting here parked in a brand new 2023 BMW—which is nice by the way; I hope you got the extended warranty—with a personalized license plate and a weapon registered in your name. Before you make it back to the club, the cops will be sitting there waiting on your Black ass!" Damawi puts her head down and begins to sob.

"MY SISTER WON'T TALK TO ME!! I HAVE TO DO SOMETHING!" she cries out. "I have to do something."

"D, you know you're special to me, to all of us. If murdering them will make you feel better, you give me the word, and they'll all be dead and cremated before morning. But Javari will still be gone and that could've easily been you and I. They just on the wrong side of making it." As Damawi wipes her tears and then wipes her hand on her pants, their attention turns to the sound of a door closing nearby. Richie wraps his hand around his gun on his lap and grabs the paperwork from the dashboard. He shuffles to Jordan's file and looks at the photo, then the person leaving the house. It's her. The description from the file was spot on. Slim build, five-foot six, brown skin with braids. It's so quiet inside the car all you can hear is their rhythmic breathing.

Jordan looks directly at Damawi's car and starts walking over. Richie places the files back on the dashboard and grips his gun. When she gets close to the car, he rolls down the passenger side window and asks, "May I help you?" She stops about six feet from the car and responds, "Um, yeah, my people sent me out here to see if you needed that thang."

"Maybe. Come closer." Jordan looks at Damawi in the driver's seat and feels safe coming closer. As she walks closer, Richie cocks the hammer on his gun and puts his finger on the trigger. "What's the business, D? Just say the word," he whispers. Jordan walks up to the car and sticks her face in close to the passenger window. Damawi gasps when she sees that Jordan doesn't fit what she imagined. She's a beautiful girl, but her environment tainted her aura. She was a rose that bloomed from concrete. Her nearly perfect face wore a black eye, which gave a glimpse into her story: either her environment was overtaking her optimistic thoughts and dreams, or an abusive relationship was conquering her self-esteem.

Damawi then reaches over and grabs Richie's left arm, squeezing it. Richie knew Damawi's answer before Jordan ever walked over. "It's late. Why you out here all alone?" asks Richie. Jordan shrugs her shoulders. "Seems like you need a new crew, sweetie." Richie looks at Damawi and then back to Jordan. "What you got?" asks Richie.

"I got some red tops, whatever."

"I don't buy from people I don't know like that, but I won't waste your time either." Richie reaches in his pocket and hands her a one-hundred-dollar bill. "How we get in touch with you?" Her eyes widen as she examines the money, making sure it's real. "You can hit my cell." Richie grabs her file, flips it over, and hands her a pen that Damawi passed to him. "Write your number on the back of here." Jordan jots down her name and number. "You got a weapon, Jordan?" asks Richie.

"Yeah, it's in the house. Why?"

"Maybe it could've helped you against whoever gave you that shiner." Jordan drops her head to her chest. "We're done here. Now go back inside. We'll be in touch." She quickly turns around and walks back into the house. Richie hops out of Damawi's car and says, "Follow me."

"Where we going?" asks Damawi. Richie stares at her for a few seconds and shuts the door. Once Richie's car passes hers, Damawi turns on her headlights and follows him. He then calls and talks with her while he leads her on a tour of the city, reminding her of all the businesses they've started and helped people get started. They drive past the strip malls, private schools, funeral homes, youth centers, movie theaters, and many other businesses they've impacted throughout Chicago. His last stop on the tour is the Chicago Riverwalk where Richie owns two riverboat casinos. They park their cars and then walk to the pier where the boats are docked.

"D, what we're trying to do is bigger than you and me. We're trying to change the condition of our people. With that being said, we can't act on emotions, regardless of the situation. I know your emotions are going crazy. Your family is hurting, and I get it. Put in your mind that you and your sister's relationship will never be the same. But it will get better one day. Everyone in the crew is just as important as the other. But you and Tech are irreplaceable. You need to put your energy into something other than Josephine's. It's doing fine—"

"But there's so much I can do," says Damawi, finishing Richie's sentence. "But I can expand the club."

"D, the club has exceeded all competition; it's on cruise control. Give the responsibility to Gina and move on to the next."

"I don't know what else to do."

"We just met a young lady in need of mentorship. Think about it, D." Richie's phone vibrates. He pulls his phone out of his pocket and reads a text message from his Uncle Swift that says he wants to meet immediately. "I got to go and meet Uncle Swift. Get home safely and start giving Gina more responsibility. Take time for yourself." He hugs Damawi, and when he tries to let her go, she tightens her grip around his neck, and he hugs her for a few seconds more until she finally releases her hold. When they pull away, the sides of their cheeks brush against each other, and they stare into each other's eyes for a few seconds, which feels like minutes. A seagull squawks as it flies past, interrupting the moment. Richie grabs Damawi's hands, squeezes them, and then walks with her over to their vehicles. Once he's inside his car, Richie starts the car and puts it in reverse, getting ready to pull off. He can feel Damawi staring at him through her passenger side window, but he backs out of the parking spot without making eye contact. He loves her, but his rules and the vulnerability of this business makes loving her too risky. He simply isn't prepared for the responsibilities that love brings.

As Richie drives to the SUITE Lounge where his Uncle Swift texted for them to meet, he wonders about the reason for the meeting. *Could this be that conversation Marble Head warned me about? What does Swift know?* He plays a thousand scenarios in his head on how the meeting could possibly play out. Richie isn't as close to Swift as he is to Marble Head, who took on the role as Richie's father, introducing him to the game in the eighth grade. When Richie was in the seventh grade, he and Uncle Swift had a face-off at the dining room table. Swift was interrogating Richie about why his grades were so mediocre. He always wore a suit to work, and all Richie could focus on was his three-piece suit, his badge connected to his belt, and the smell of his cologne.

Marble Head was standing behind Swift crossing his eyes and sticking his tongue out at Richie, trying to make him laugh. When Richie smiled, Uncle Swift quickly asked, "Oh, this shit is funny to you, huh? Everything is a joke." Richie put his head down and pressed his chin into his chest to stifle his laughter. "We'll see what's funny when yo ass living on the streets. And every time I see yo ass wandering around out there, Imma lock yo ass up! Get outta my face!" Fortunately, Richie was never homeless, but Uncle Swift did put him in lockup when Richie was in eighth grade after he was forging his mother's signature for months on his weekly progress reports.

Richie pulls up to the SUITE Lounge and stops in front of the valet booth. Before he gets out of the car, he reads a text from Damawi letting him know that she's made it home. She also thanks him for the motivation and ends the message with a kissing emoji. The valet walks up to the car and opens the driver side door. Richie steps out and hands the attendant a one-hundred-dollar bill. "You see that spot right there? That's where she going, right?" The attendant folds the money and puts it in his pocket. "Yes, sir."

Richie enters the lounge and tells the waitress who he's looking for. She takes him to a table in the very back of the lounge where no one else is around to hear their conversation. *This isn't a good sign*, thinks Richie, walking up to the table. Swift stands up and hugs Richie, then they both sit down. "What you got there, unc?"

"My usual: rum and coke."

"I'll take a double of Redd Rose Vodka and get him a double of rum and coke," says Richie. The waitress jots down the order before leaving to retrieve the drinks. Richie and Swift exchange small talk until the waitress returns with their drinks. "Pretty lady, we'll signal you when we need you to come back," says Uncle Swift.

"Okay, Chief. I'll peek in every once in a while," she says before walking away.

"So, unc, what's going on?"

"I got an interesting call today from one of my buddies in the FBI. You knew someone who was car bombed in Virginia, and you didn't feel the need to tell me about it?" Richie thinks, *Aww shit.*

"It was way in Virginia, and I wasn't hurt, unc. I didn't want to have you, mom, and Marble Head to get all worried, and she start babying me. You know how she gets. So, when the FBI gets in contact with me for questioning, I'll tell them what I know."

"Which is?" asks Uncle Swift.

"Nothing, unc."

"You won't have to worry about the FBI interrogating you. They allowed me to question you, and I'll pass the information." Swift takes a large swig of his drink and leans forward. He was wearing a nice navy-blue single-breasted suit with his badge pinned to his suit jacket. Richie imagines Marble Head behind Swift sitting in his wheelchair, crossing his eyes with his tongue out, and he snickers.

"You think this shit is funny?!"

"No, Uncle Swift," says Richie. "Just been a long time since I was subjected to one of your interrogations." Uncle Swift thought back to all of their one-on-one conversations.

"Let's just hope this doesn't result in you back in lockup." Richie smiles then goes into great detail about what happened in Virginia. All of the events that day, the people in the bar, what he knew about General Warrington, etc. They talked for nearly two hours. Finally, Swift asks his last question: "It seems like people close to you are being taken out. Your childhood friend, now the general. Are you into something I should know about?"

"You know everything there is to know about me."

"Is that right?"

"That's right!"

"If you're into something, and it gets back to me…" says Swift, wagging his finger at Richie. That angers Richie. Maybe it was the fear of his uncle finding out what he's been doing since his retirement, but the thought of a family member being the one to take him down made his blood boil. "You know what Chief, what you should do is get back to finding out who killed Javari Lewis."

"Excuse me?"

Richie leans forward, "Javari Lewis. You know that kid? Virginia State, football player, promising future? You remember Damawi, don't you? He's her nephew."

"Ah, that makes sense. Someone else close to you murdered." They both quickly stand up and stare at each other. Eventually, Uncle Swift breaks the silence first. "Don't tell me how to do my job," says Chief Watkins.

"But I most certainly will," says Richie. "See, I pay your salary with my taxes. So, when your little Klan members dressed in blue go night-sticking us colored folk or murdering us in cold blood for a simple traffic stop or because they're intimidated or feel threatened, I'm actually financing the destruction of my own people. So, I have a say. So, don't worry about ole nephew Richie. I'm doing great. Put your efforts into stopping Tanner, Shane, and Becky the bullshitter." Richie then changes his voice to sound like the old stereotypical negro before he continues to lay into his uncle. "And weez gone be aight boss, ummm hmm." They both stare at each other for about ten seconds as the waitress, frozen still, watches in awe. Swift breaks the silence again. "How's my brother doing?"

"He's good," responds Richie. "How's Aunt B these days?"

"Excellent." They then break eye contact and turn to the table to pick up their belongings. The waitress carefully walks over and hands Richie the bill, and he gives her his credit card. She swipes the card on the card reader in her hand, prints out the receipt, and awkwardly waits for Richie to sign it. When Richie looks up from signing the receipt, he sees his Uncle Swift walking away. "We'll be in touch, Richie," calls out Swift over his shoulder as he turns the corner. Richie places a one-hundred-dollar bill under his glass and exits the lounge.

CHAPTER 10

The crew are at Richie's condo enjoying a meal prepared by his chef Sheree. They casually talk about each other's lives and random topics until they finish eating, then they start talking about business, the organization's priorities, and the plan for the next few days. Felix sent word to Richie that the next shipment will arrive in Louisiana in two to three days. After getting the notification, Richie relaxed their security measures because once the product is in hand, Felix won't disrupt the organization with violence. He explains to the team what's going on with Arielle and how he's trying to neutralize Felix. It's risky, but the crew is on board with Richie's course of action. "Our next order of business is to get KAP and Tech to Louisiana and to get the product out to the organizations," says Richie. "D will be taking some time off, and Brick and I will be headed to St. Louis for Kolax."

"Am I really needed in Louisiana?" asks Tech. "I never get to get in on any of the gangster shit. It's always, 'Tech, what's the addresses?' 'Tech, what's the deal with the autonomous cars?' 'Tech, why is your penis so wide?' Is it because I'm half white?"

"Richie, let him go. He can fly into Louisiana later," says KAP.

"See, Richie! Listen to KAP!" says Tech.

Richie ponders on the discussion and responds, "You know, it might not be a bad idea to let him drive the car to St. Louis. We need to test the battery life and see if it can hold a charge the entire time. It hasn't been tested long distance yet. We can have him meet the team at one of the drop off points and use it to deliver the New York and New Jersey packages. Okay, we can do that."

"Yes, yes, yes!! Fucking half white power man!!" shouts Tech.

"We'll leave tomorrow afternoon for Kolax," says Richie. "When will you two leave for Louisiana?"

"I'll book their flight for tomorrow afternoon," says Damawi.

* * *

Detective Coles walks into the precinct and walks directly over to Detective Russell's desk. "Russell, follow me please." Detective Russell gets up and follows Coles into one of the interrogation rooms. Inside the room are three Internal Affairs agents waiting at the table. Detective Russell pauses before he enters the room. Standing in the doorway, Detective Russell looks at Detective Coles then back at the agents before he steps into the room and closes the door behind him. He looks nervous and impatient, and he starts fidgeting with his hands. His body language tells the whole story as he takes his seat. Detective Coles sits across from Detective Russell on the same side as the agents.

"Hello, Detective Russell. I'm Special Agent Ramona Clarke. This is Special Agent Nate Broussard and Special Agent David Morrison. We would like to talk to you about the events that happened on the night of the corner store robbery and officer-involved shooting of Javari Lewis." Special Agent Clarke turns on the recorder, and each of the agents rotate through a series of questions regarding his actions when he arrived on scene that night. They ask him to recap what the responding officers told him about what happened and to describe the condition of the crime scene. They ask if he removed the tapes from the recording device in the store or knew who did; he denies knowing the tape was removed. They even question if he knew Javari was unarmed and had only soda in his possession. The agents give Detective Russell plenty of chances to tell the truth, but he continues with the narrative he included in his report, thinking that the four white officers he was protecting would stand tall and back his story.

After two hours of questioning, the agents hand Detective Russell the statements from four officers who were on scene. They all pointed to Detective Russell as the one who wanted to taint the crime scene in order to avoid a wrongful death case and to protect his fellow officers. Detective Russell is devastated. The officers did not follow the blue code of silence. He felt betrayed and left out to dry. Detective Coles remained silent during the interview and just stared at Detective Russell with a disgusted look on his face as if he was feeling sick.

The agents wrap up their investigation for the day and leave the detectives in the room together. Detective Coles stares blankly at Russell before speaking. "Detective Russell, I need your service weapon and your badge. I also need you to clean out your desk and your locker downstairs. You are suspended without pay, so stay by your phone in case the agents need some more information from you. If you want to stay out of jail, I suggest you find those fucking tapes. Those white boys killed an innocent black male and here comes your Uncle Tom ass taking the precinct down the drain with you. Get your shit and get the fuck outta here you shit bird!"

* * *

The next morning, Richie, Brick, and Tech all meet up at Josephine's for their four-hour drive to St. Louis. They load up into the van they often use for occasions like this one, and Tech programs the autonomous car to follow them. Brick is driving the van with Tech in the passenger seat, and Richie rides in the car to further build his confidence in its capabilities. Alone with his thoughts, Richie thinks about the Felix situation, the possible Columbian connect, and the shipment they will be disbursing soon. Going around Felix directly to the source is risky, but he feels this is the best move to make. Richie leans back in his seat and recites his mantra repeatedly, "I am the driver of my own destiny, a passenger to no man," until he falls asleep.

Dreaming, Richie is in Columbia at a beautiful mansion enjoying dinner with Felix's boss. The man's face is blurred out, so Richie can't make out who the man is. There are no identifying marks anywhere visible on his slim body, and his clothing is an outfit only a very wealthy and distinguished gentleman would wear. He's wearing an all-white designer silk shirt and pants set, white Gucci loafers, and black Gucci sunglasses. His hair is slick back and his curls rest just below his shoulder blades. Richie looks content and prideful sitting across from the man. While they're talking and laughing, a server brings over the main course on a stainless-steel serving tray and places it onto the table between the two men. The elegant gentleman gestures with his hand for Richie to remove the cover. Richie smiles, leans forward, and pulls the tray toward him by the handle. He slowly picks up the top cover, and he doesn't take his eyes off the cover until he rests it on the table beside the tray. Then he turns his attention to the tray, only to see KAP, T.K., and Arielle's heads laying on the platter surrounded by flowers.

Everything starts to move in slow motion as Richie pushes away from the table, shocked and horrified. Two of the elegant gentleman's guards grab Richie by his arms and force him to turn and face the pool. Out the window, he sees Damawi and Tech kneeling next to each other on the opposite side of the pool facing Richie with a look of fear in their eyes. Two guards dressed in all-black suits are standing behind them. As Richie fights to get loose from the men holding him, one of the guards standing poolside puts his gun to the back of Tech's head and pulls the trigger. Richie hears only silence as he watches Tech's blood spray onto Damawi's face and clothes. Tech's body then falls forward slowly into the pool, making a small splash that mixes pool water into the blood splattered on the tile lining the pool.

Richie fights harder against the guards holding his arms, hoping to get to Damawi before she's shot next. Suddenly, the two men turn Richie's body to the right. He sees two horses facing away from each other with Brick in the middle. His hands and feet are bound by ropes that are tied to the saddle of each horse. Two men standing alongside the horses smack each horse on the back simultaneously, causing the horses to run in opposite directions. Brick's body jerks up from the ground, and Richie is forced to watch as his close friend's arms and legs are forcefully ripped from his body. Richie's knees buckle when he sees Brick's limbless body fall to the ground.

They force Richie to stand when they turn him back toward Damawi, who is now naked on her knees with her hands bound behind her back. One of the men is holding her head close to his body, forcing her to perform fallatio. She tries to squirm away, moving her head from left to right, but the man tightly grips a handful of her hair, holding her in place. Richie is fighting like a wild man to break free when a third guard walks up and places him in a choke hold to keep him still. Richie stares on in horror, tears rolling down his face, as another man holds a gun up to the side of Damawi's head. The guard holding Damawi's head steps back and zips up his pants. Damawi turns her head and locks eyes with Richie for the last time. The force of the gunshot makes Damawi fly sideways onto the grass; her blood spilling from the side of her head.

"NOOOOOOOOOOOO!!" Richie yells, but no sound comes out of his mouth. The guards force him onto his knees, and Richie drops his head to his chin, realizing that his decision was the reason for his organization's demise. In the distance, he hears a man's dress shoes clacking against the marble floors and coming in his direction. When the man stops in front of Richie, he opens his eyes and sees a pair of black custom-made cowboy boots with gold tips. Richie brings his head up to see Felix standing over him. Felix smiles and puts his gun to Richie's forehead, placing it exactly on the indentation that was left many years ago. Bang, bang, bang, bang!! Richie, startled, wakes up and frantically scans the area to get a sense of where he is. Tech steps back from knocking on the back passenger window and says, "My bad, Richie. I didn't mean to scare you. We stopped at a rest stop to stretch our legs and use the head." Richie rubs his hands across his face, trying to get himself together, then he exits the vehicle and heads into the restroom.

Hours later, they arrive onto the street where Kolax is staying, just as night falls. They see his Cadillac Escalade parked on the street in front of the house, and Tech directs the autonomous car to park directly behind it. Brick drives the van past the house and then circles around to drop Richie off in the alley behind the houses about half way down the block. Richie, wearing all black, hops the fence and quickly ducks down while looking into the kitchen windows to see if Kolax is alone. Richie crouches in the backyard for several minutes, watching Kolax walk from the kitchen and back to the living room. Richie walks over to the side of the house and peeks into the living room windows. He sees Kolax sitting on the couch alone, looking as if he just returned from somewhere.

Brick and Tech park the van a few blocks down and walk up the alley near Richie's location. Richie walks back out to the alley and signals for Brick and Tech to follow him. Once they are all standing near the back door, Richie looks at Tech and signals for him to engage the plan. Tech taps a few items on his phone, and the autonomous car moves forward slightly and bumps into the back of Kolax's Escalade. The alarm sounds, then the car returns to its original position a few feet from the SUV. Kolax grabs his keys and runs outside to check on his vehicle. Brick quickly pulls out a towel he had tucked in his pants, covers a small section of the window with the towel, then punches the spot, breaking the window on the back door. Richie reaches his hand inside the broken window and unlocks the door.

Kolax presses the button on his key fob to turn the alarm off, opens the passenger door, and looks inside and around his vehicle. When he reactivates the alarm, music starts blasting from inside Tech's car. "Mr. Telephone man, there's something wrong with my line. When I dial my baby's number, I get a click every time, Mr. Telephone man." Kolax walks over to the car and tries to look through the tinted windows, but they're too dark. He investigates the car for a few seconds, looks down the block in each direction, then walks back into the house and throws his keys on the table by the sofa before sitting down.

Richie, Brick, and Tech are standing in the kitchen, being extremely quiet and perfectly still. The house is old, so the floor creaks with the slightest pressure. Only moving his hand, Richie signals to Tech again. The car moves forward again and hits the SUV, sounding off the alarm. This time, Tech leaves the car much closer to the bumper than before. "What the fuck is going on?" asks Kolax. "Somebody finna get fucked up out here."

Kolax grabs his weapon and his keys, then he cautiously steps outside and cuts off the alarm again. Richie and the crew quickly move to their planned positions in the house. Kolax scans the area and notices that the car behind his vehicle is a lot closer and the windows are lowered a little bit. He walks toward the car slowly with his weapon extended toward the passenger side window. The music suddenly turns on again, surprising him. "Must be a bad connection. I give her my love and affection. I just can't take this no more..." Then the music stops. As he bends down to look into the window, all the windows roll down completely. He looks dumbfounded. "What the fuck? Ain't nobody in this bitch." He walks around the back of the car and stands in the middle of the street, looking down the block in both directions. He shakes his head and walks toward his front door. As soon as he walks between his SUV and the car, the music starts up again, playing a little louder. "This situation blowing my mind. Can't get my baby on the line." Then it shuts off again.

Kolax jogs to the front door, and he walks inside. Immediately, he sees the back of Tech's head as he's sitting on the couch, with his phone in his hand, singing, "I tried calling information, Mr. Telephone man, I'll use my hand for masturbation, Mr.Telephone man. My dick is all on bone…"

"Nigga, what the fuck you doing in my crib?!" screams Kolax. Before he could raise his weapon, Richie steps from behind the front door and puts his gun to the back of Kolax's head. "Gun please," says Richie. Kolax raises his hands, and Richie takes his weapon from behind.

"Do y'all have any idea who you fucking with?"

"Hmmm let me think. Ronnie, Bobby, Ricky, Mike, Ralph… so that makes you Kolax," says Richie, walking around to face him.

"How the fuck did you know where to find me?" asks Kolax.

"Ya boy gave you up; you're a loose end," says Richie.

"Bullshit! Get the fuck outta here," says Kolax.

"I wouldn't shit you, Kolax. You're my favorite turd. But he did, and here we are." Brick walks around the corner from the other side of the living room and stands next to Richie facing Kolax.

"I knew this fucking mute wasn't far behind. We gonna get to it, straight up?" Brick nods and takes off his shirt. Kolax looks at Brick's upper body. He underestimated what was under Brick's clothes. Brick stands up tall and straight, his eyes bulging with rage. His body is rippled with lean muscle. Burn and knife wounds, gifted to him by terrorists, completely cover his chest and abdomen. Every opponent that challenges Brick transforms into the men who tortured him, beat him, and forcibly removed a vast piece of his tongue with primitive tools. Looking at Brick now, Kolax finally understands that Brick has been through some shit. However, Kolax's street cred needs no introduction. He has sent many men and women to the afterlife with his bare hands. That is all the confidence he needs in this fight. Richie and Tech step back and look on as spectators observing two gladiators ready for combat.

Brick and Kolax charge at each other. Their upper bodies clash, sending Kolax stumbling backward from the impact. Brick continues to advance as Kolax regains his footing. He throws a punch that blasts into Brick's chin. It has little effect. Brick just walks through it, grabbing Kolax by his neck and head-butting him. Kolax flies into the wall, leaving an indentation of his body in the drywall; blood gushes from his nose and mouth. Staggering, Kolax quickly stands up and wipes the blood from his face while Brick stands by awaiting his next attack. Kolax darts toward him, and Brick scrapes his head with a glancing blow. Kolax ducks and counters the near contact with an elbow upward into Brick's chin, moving him backward. Kolax then rushes at Brick, throwing a punch that barely misses. Brick grabs Kolax's arm and turns him around, his back facing Brick, who then bends his knees and launches Kolax's body over his back. The force of the move sends Kolax flying across the living room, crashing down on his television and entertainment set, smashing it to pieces. "I was fucking watching that! It's shark week," yells Tech.

Brick advances, his killer instinct blazing in his eyes. Lying on his back, Kolax kicks at Brick, but Brick grabs his foot. Kolax continues kicking at Brick until Brick grabs his other foot and drags him into the middle of the living room and lets go. Brick then steps back, allowing Kolax time and space to get back up on his feet. Kolax stands up and faces off with Brick again. Brick puts his hands behind his back to toy with his prey. Kolax throws another punch, landing it square on Brick's chin and sending his head back only slightly. Brick looks at Richie and smiles, then he refocuses on his opponent. Kolax already knows he's going to be defeated, but he wouldn't die without trying to gain some advantage. Kolax throws another punch. Brick catches Kolax's wrist, and then turns, twisting his body away from Kolax, and rapidly slams Kolax's hyperextended elbow over his shoulder. Richie and Tech wince from the sound of Kolax's bones cracking over Brick's shoulder. Kolax bends over and lets out a grunt filled with agony as his face tenses up from the pain. Brick stands up with momentum and smashes his elbow into Kolax's face, sending him falling backward onto the destroyed entertainment center.

As quickly as he can, Kolax turns over and gets up onto his feet. He staggers into the kitchen, leaving behind him a trail of blood leaking from his face. Brick slowly follows behind him and watches as Kolax opens the kitchen drawer and pulls out a knife. With the knife in his left hand and his right arm dangling like the last leaf on a branch in autumn, Kolax shouts, "Come on, muthafucka!" Pointing the knife at Brick, he lunges forward. Brick grabs Kolax's hand and chops him in his throat. Choking, Kolax falls to his knees, and Brick kicks him in the head. He flies backward, still holding the knife in his left hand. Brick takes Kolax's hand with the knife in it and slowly forces it into the side of Kolax's right thigh. He then covers Kolax's mouth to muffle the screams as he slowly removes the knife before plunging it into Kolax's left thigh, stopping only when the knife hits the floor. Brick then puts more pressure on Kolax's mouth and twists the knife. Kolax thrashes on the floor from the excruciating pain. Brick quickly pulls the knife from Kolax's leg and uses his jeans to wipe it clean. He then uncovers Kolax's mouth, twirls the knife in his hand, and uses the handle of the knife to knock out Kolax's front teeth.

Richie walks into the kitchen with Tech following close behind him. "Kolax!" yells Richie, standing over him while screwing the silencer onto his 9mm handgun. "I'll give it to you," he says bending down over him, "You're a tough motherfucka. You're the first person who fought Brick and kept their teeth… Well, never mind. Just when I thought you couldn't get any uglier. You had a good run." Richie pats Kolax's chest with the tip of his silencer.

"You have kids?" Kolax lies on the floor in silence, staring blankly into Richie's eyes. "They probably wouldn't be college material anyway. Maurice wanted proof of death, Mr. Loose End himself, and that's what we're going to give him." Richie places the silencer directly under Kolax's chin. Brick steps back to avoid the splatter as Richie pulls the trigger.

* * *

Damawi parks her vehicle exactly where Richie entered her car a few nights before and stopped her from doing something she would've regretted. She picks up her phone and texts Jordan: "Come outside." A few minutes later, the front door opens, and Jordan walks right over to the car. Damawi rolls down the passenger side window as Jordan approaches. "What you need?" asks Jordan.

"Nothing," says Damawi. "The man I was with the other night sent me over here to check on you." As Damawi gets a closer look at Jordan's face, she notices that the black eye is healing well, but now she has a busted lip. "What happened to your lip?"

"You know how the streets be," Jordan says.

"Hmmmm, I do, but the streets won't do that, just whatever situation you're in. Come to the driver's side." Jordan walks around the back of the car and up to the driver's side. Damawi gently grabs Jordan's chin and tilts her head upward to take a closer look at her wound.

"Are you free tomorrow?" asks Damawi.

"I have to work."

"Where do you work?" Jordan shrugs her shoulders, and Damawi understands exactly what she means.

"If you have some time tomorrow to talk, would you like to do that?"

"You gotta do all this to buy some drugs?"

"Well, this is how he likes to conduct business." Damawi reaches into her armrest and gives Jordan another one-hundred-dollar bill.

"What's this for?" asks Jordan.

"Your time. It's the most precious thing on this earth. How you spend it is entirely up to you. Text me if you'd like to talk." Damawi raises her window, and Jordan steps back as she watches Damawi pull away from the curb and leave. She stands in the street until she sees Damawi's car turn the corner; she then looks at the money in her hand before turning around and heading back into the house.

* * *

Brick carries Kolax's body outside into the alley and places it in the back of the van while Richie and Tech straighten up the house the best they could. After everyone is loaded up, they head back to Chicago to meet up with Maurice. They left the autonomous car outside of Kolax's house so it can meet up with the sixteen-wheeler before heading to New York. On the ride to Chicago, Richie sits in silence, thinking about his dream and the events that took place. The thought of losing his crew to one of his bad decisions is unacceptable. If he doesn't go around Felix, financially, it will hurt the movement, and the other organizations will just seek product elsewhere. There's a long way to go before the black communities could strive without him, so this seemed like the only route. He knows that finding another supplier could provoke a war. Not bending to Felix's demands would end in war as well. *I have no choice but to stay the course*, Richie thinks to himself. They arrive in Chicago early the next morning, and Richie calls an associate about meeting up shortly for a favor.

When Dr. James sees the headlights from the van illuminate his curvy driveway, he steps outside to meet Richie, who immediately hops out of the van as soon as it's parked. They talk silently away from the van for a few minutes at first, then the doctor makes his way over to the van. "Okay, I'm gonna give you this shot. It should help with the pain and make you relax. It'll last for a while, so you'll be fine."

"See, Brick, nothing to worry about. I know you don't like needles, but we gotta do what we must." Brick winces when the needle goes in, puts on his jacket, and shakes his head as he walks around the front of the van to the passenger side. "Dr. James, thanks brother. I owe you one."

"Nah, Richie. Anything for the cause." They shake hands, and Richie heads for the driver's side of the van and gets in behind the wheel. Richie then texts Maurice and tells him to meet them at the spot in an hour. Richie pulls up to the back of Up In Smoke. Moments later, Maurice pulls up behind the van. Richie looks in the side view mirror and sees someone in the passenger seat of Maurice's car. Maurice gets out, but the passenger stays. Richie and Tech then get out and meet Maurice at the back of the van. Neither Richie nor Maurice bother to exchange words. Richie just opens the van doors and shows Maurice Kolax's body stretched across the back of the van, the ceiling light highlighting Kolax's blood-covered face. Maurice looks at his arm and the wounds on his legs. "Did he go out like a soldier?"

"I told you he was a tough muthafucka." Maurice stares at the lifeless body of his long-standing friend. He then looks up to the front of the van to see Brick resting. "Say your goodbyes to your loose end. I need to get this done; I got people waiting." Maurice walks closer to the van, bends down close to Kolax's ear, and whispers, "I ain't want it to be this way, my G. Be with Spree." Maurice stands up straight, looks at Richie, and then heads back to his car. Richie closes the van doors and hops in to drive over to Lloyd's.

After dropping off Brick and Tech, Richie pulls the van into Josephine's parking lot and parks it around back. He walks to his car and sees a black envelope under one of his windshield wipers. He looks around before picking up the envelope and opening it. Inside is a card that reads:

El Muerte Lenta Cartel
Pedro Alejandro Gamboa
El Dorado Airport, Columbia
February 22, 2023

Richie's heart skips a beat. This could be the beginning of the end. *Why does he want to meet with me so soon?* he wonders. A thousand scenarios flash across his mind as he puts the card back into the envelope and sits inside his car. He takes a deep breath and says aloud, "It will all come out in the wash."

* * *

Leon Russell's lawyer walks into Chief Watkins's office where Detective Coles is already there waiting. The lawyer sits down and immediately goes to work on getting his client a deal if the tapes were found and released to the authorities. "I can't promise that it will keep him out of jail, but it might determine how long," says Chief Watkins. "Right now, he's looking at five years. If he gets us those tapes, and they're in an acceptable condition and not tampered with or altered, we can have a conversation. You have twenty-four hours to produce something or he'll be prosecuted to the fullest." The lawyer stands up and shakes hands with Detective Coles and Chief Watkins. Detective Coles waits until the lawyer exits and closes the door before speaking. "You think those tapes will miraculously show up?"

"I do," says Chief Watkins. "Russell isn't the jail type. Once his fellow Black inmates find out that he's a cop who protected four

White cops by tampering with evidence to hide the possible murder of a Black kid, he won't last a day, and he knows it. It'll show up. Keep Neeley informed Brian."

* * *

Richie's sleep is interrupted by the sound of his phone ringing. He grabs his phone from the nightstand and looks at the screen before answering. "Brian, what's good?"

"All is well, Richie. You got a minute?"

"I got two for you, Brian. Go."

"Javari Lewis's crime scene was dirty. A detective tampered with the evidence, but we won't know if it was a clean kill or not until we get those tapes."

"Who was the detective?"

"Leon Russell. We spoke about him before."

"Sounds familiar."

"He was the detective that was questioning your employees." Richie sits up in his bed.

"No shit! Is there any connection?" asks Richie.

"No connection. Just a nosey asshole who's a crooked cop. I'll let you know when I have more. He either has to shit those tapes out or face five years in prison."

"Okay. Thanks, Brian. Let me know what happens."

Richie lies back in bed and tries to go back to sleep. About fifteen minutes later, he gets a video call from Arielle. He sits up on one elbow and answers the call. "What's up, A? Oh, you looking as beautiful as ever."

"Thank you, Richie. I'm about to go live. I just wanted to talk to you before I did this."

"You got this, A. The team put positive energy into the universe for you."

"I'm so nervous. I can't believe there are so many people, politicians, and business owners supporting me."

"This is your calling, A; this is what you were made to do. I want you to be confident in front of that camera. Remember what we talked about. Say what your agenda will be as prime minister and don't let the media draw you in. Did they give you the scripted questions?"

"They did. They're even adding in a special segment."

"That's awesome! I'm proud of you. I'll be watching." They say their goodbyes, and Richie hops out of bed and heads to the living room to turn on his satellite TV to tune into Channel 3 Believe in Belize. He then walks into the kitchen, singing to himself.

* * *

T.K. and KAP are standing outside watching the truck back up past the security gates and head toward the backyard. T.K. looks at the truck and shakes his head. "I hope this twenty-foot container ain't filled front to back, top to bottom," says T.K. They walk to the back of the house to where the crew is waiting to unload. Two Latino men with semi-automatic handguns holstered on their waists hop out the front of the truck to open the doors in the back. One of the Latino men presses a button on a remote control, and the crew watches as the tailgate travels into the roof.

"Man, this is a lot of snort," says KAP. T.K. jumps up into the truck and takes a look. "This is much more than we got last time but not too bad," says T.K. He jumps down and walks over to the men. "Habla inglés?" They nod yes. "What are y'all's names?" asks T.K.

"I'm Paco, and this is Manuel."

"If you guys help us unload and reload, dinner is on us." The two men nod their heads in agreement, and everyone prepares to unload the product.

* * *

Arielle stands behind the curtain, waiting to hear her name called. When the show host, Rolanda Evans, introduces her, the crowd gives Arielle a warm welcome as she walks from behind the curtain and onto the stage. She doesn't seem nervous at all and even looks as if she belongs in the political arena. While Rolanda asks her various questions about her life growing up and her education, Arielle looks very comfortable and confident answering each and every question. Richie watches amazed at how well she answers the questions and lets the viewers know that she's cut from the same cloth as everyone else. She's a person who has struggled and has the same family issues as most families. People will be able to identify with her for sure. Richie also learned a lot about Arielle from watching the segment. He had no idea that her dad was a stunt double for Sidney Poitier back in the day. They show a picture of Sidney holding Arielle when she was a little girl.

"Now to the nitty gritty. We need to get to the meat of this interview. You have something you would like to announce to the people of Belize?" asks Rolanda.

"Yes, I do." Arielle is about to share her announcement when she is cut off by Rolanda. "Hold that thought. We'll be right back after a break for our sponsors." Richie throws down his remote control. "What the fuck is this? American Idol? Damn man! They be pissing me off with that shit." Richie's phone vibrates, and he sees a text from T.K.: "It's a lot, but nothing we can't handle, but we need to store the rest. I had Tech deliver the sandwiches. They'll be here in an hour or two." Richie responds with a thumbs up.

The show returns from commercial break, and he scoots up to the edge of the couch. "So, what is it that you would like to tell the people of Belize?" asks Rolanda.

"Well, for the upcoming election for prime minister, I'll be running as an independent under my established party called the J.U.S. Party. J.U.S. stands for, Join, Unite, and Sustain." She gets a standing ovation from the crowd.

"Congratulations, Arielle! What will your agenda be for the people of Belize?"

"I have many items, but these are my top three: One, provide better education for our youth and establish a coalition with the United States and Europe to send our children abroad to gain experiences and understand the history of different countries to help diversify their social portfolios. Education is the key to bridging the gaps. This will make it easier to broker deals with different countries that will benefit the people of Belize as a whole. Two, education is the seed that will grow entrepreneurs that help create jobs and in turn stimulate the economy. Once elected, I would immediately create jobs to help beautify the country of Belize. Better roads, infrastructure, and more opportunities for the middle and lower class to work. When you are working, you spend your money with established businesses. Three, I will stop the drugs from entering into our country. There is no home here in Belize for drugs. Narcotics are killing our beautiful people and countering my goals and politicians' goals of the past. I will stop this."

Richie smiles proudly as the audience cheers louder than before. Rolanda claps along with the crowd and continues, "So, I told you we have a special segment we would like to share with you and the people watching, and we would like your comment on it." Rolanda waves a hand to the screen behind her, and on it is the car that Ren, Kay, and Arielle's protégé, Chantel, were in when they were murdered. Then follows a picture of Arielle with all of them together at her school's opening. Finally, they show a picture of Ren, Kay, and Chantel as kids. The camera pans back to Arielle and Rolanda. Arielle sits there stunned, and Richie knows that look. She's coming apart. "So, we did some research, and we believe these beautiful ladies were killed in a hit involving mistaken identity over some narcotic operation," says Rolanda. "Is there anything you would like to add to my statement?" Richie stands up and shouts at the television, "Don't do it, A! Don't let them draw you in!"

"Yes. Those were my girlfriends. I've known two of them since the third grade, and the other was a recent protégé of mine. It saddens me to know that they were brutally killed for absolutely nothing. As prime minister, I will go hard after those who spill blood in the streets of Belize."

"Is there anyone in particular you're referring to?" asks Rolanda.

"Don't do it, A. Don't you fucking do it!" shouts Richie.

"Yes, his name is Felix Navarro." Richie closes his eyes and tilts his head toward the ceiling. "I'm not saying he's responsible, but he is someone who will be on my radar whether he's responsible or not. With the help of the US Embassy, I will bring him to justice."

Richie plops down on the couch. He knows she has just signed a death warrant for the crew and their families.

* * *

The doors open to Felix's entertainment room. He is surrounded by ladies, food, and drinks. In walks one of his guards holding a phone. "Boss, I think you need to look at this!" He starts a video and hands Felix his phone. Curious, Felix watches the last few moments of Arielle's interview. Suddenly, he slams the phone down enraged. "I thought she was dead! Where are those fucking idiots?!"

"We don't know, boss. We've tried to get in contact with them over the last few days but nothing."

"Kill their entire families and their neighbors! I want her dead now! Send some men to Belize and bring her corpse to me! And after the product gets disbursed, send some men to Chicago too! I want that nigger's fucking head on a stick!"

* * *

Damawi gets a text from Jordan telling her she wants to meet, followed by the address. She gets excited that Jordan has accepted her invitation to meet up. She gets in her car and heads for the address provided. About thirty minutes later, Damawi arrives at the destination, but she doesn't see Jordan anywhere. She gets another text from Jordan: "I see you. Turn down the alley."

Aloud, Damawi says, "What? I'm not going down no alley." Damawi is about to pull off when she gets a call from a number she doesn't recognize. "Hello?" answers Damawi.

"Hey, it's Jordan. I don't have my phone. Can we meet me at Harold's Chicken off Cottage Grove?"

"Sure." Damawi quickly drives off and heads up the road to Harold's Chicken. When she parks, Jordan walks out of the restaurant and comes to her passenger side door. Damawi rolls down the window. "You trying to set me up?" Jordan doesn't answer; she just looks at the 9mm laying in Damawi's lap. "You're a beautiful girl, but I'll fly that head. You understand me?"

"Yes. My boyfriend took my phone after our first texts. I don't want to do you no harm." Damawi unlocks the door, and Jordan gets in. Damawi then drives off, and they ride in silence for a few blocks. When Damawi feels safe again, she looks at Jordan and asks, "Why didn't you let me get got?" Jordan shrugged her shoulders. "I didn't think you deserved that. I think you're a nice lady." Damawi takes Jordan through the city, and they exchange small talk until Damawi stops at a downtown restaurant to eat. "Man, I ain't never been in a place like this," says Jordan when they walk through the doors. "Oh yeah?" asks Damawi. "The food here is amazing."

They are seated at a booth in the back away from people so they can talk comfortably. "So, Ms. D. Why am I here?" Damawi reaches into her purse and pulls out a newspaper article from the Chicago Guardian. She places it on the table, opens it up, and turns it around so Jordan can read it. Damawi taps the first line in the article, and Jordan reads it aloud, "Four white policemen are accused of shooting Javari Lewis, a Virginia State University football player and promising NFL prospect, at Abdul's Corner Store on 66th and Morgan. The cashier, Ahmad Nazari, was killed during a robbery shortly before the police arrived on scene. If you have any additional information on anyone involved with this matter, please contact the authorities immediately." Jordan raises her head up slowly and asks, "What does this have to do with me?"

"I don't know," says Damawi. "You tell me."

"What does this have to do with you?" asks Jordan.

"This young man was my nephew. A great kid. He went into this corner store and probably walked into a robbery with three people. Two of the guys were Roland Outlaw and Curtis Walker." Jordan looks as if she's seen a ghost. "The third person was a female. You know who that could've been?" Jordan holds her face with her hands and starts crying. "I didn't know they were gonna hurt anybody, and I didn't know your nephew was killed until the next day," cries Jordan, speaking through her hands.

"I can't sleep thinking about my nephew. My sister won't talk to me because she believes I'm responsible for his death. So I need to put my energy into something or somebody before I lose my mind. So, we're going to sit here and have an open conversation until I get an idea of who you are underneath the bruises and the pain, and then we'll go from there. Agreed?" Jordan nods her head in agreement, and they begin to converse as they look over the menu.

* * *

T.K., KAP, the rest of the crew, and the Latino men are finished unloading the truck, and the transportation vehicles are set to leave the next day to deliver the product to all the organizations. The extra product was placed inside the boathouse and will be loaded into the submarines, then put out to sea until the organizations request a re-up. Everyone goes into the house to get cleaned up for dinner. Evelyn and Barbara have already set the dinner table, and the food is ready, waiting on the table. Halfway through supper, KAP receives a text. He looks at it, puts his fork down, and excuses himself from the table. After a brief moment, he returns and calmly sits down. KAP then looks at T.K. and asks, "You not full, T.K.? We got more work to do outside. You keep eating, and I'm gonna have to strap up to lift you from the table." T.K. moves back from the table, rubbing his chest.

"Man, you right. This food was awesome ladies," says T.K.

Barbara looks at his plate and responds, "You didn't even finish, baby."

"I'm stuffed. Anybody need anything from the kitchen?" asks T.K.

"I'll get it, baby," says Evelyn.

"Nah, I need to walk and get this food to digest. I'm full." T.K. gets up and goes into the kitchen briefly and then comes back and sits down. The table is quiet, and everyone continues eating. Paco's phone vibrates; he looks at it for a few seconds, puts it back in his pocket, then keeps eating. KAP and T.K. quickly glance at each other without anyone noticing and then focus their attention on the food on their plates. Manuel's phone then vibrates. He stops eating, looks at it under the table for a few seconds, looks at Paco, and then puts his phone in his pocket.

"Paco, can you pass me the salt." asks KAP. When Paco reaches for the salt shaker, T.K. pulls his weapon up from underneath the table and shoots Manuel in the side of the head. Manuel dramatically falls from his chair sideways and hits the floor. Evelyn and Barbara scream, and everyone pushes back from the table. Paco reaches down under the table, trying to grab his gun holstered on his waist, but KAP already has his arm extended with his weapon ready to fire. He pulls the trigger, and the bullet penetrates the bone in Paco's eye socket, sending his head back as his body falls sideways off his chair.

Barbara and Evelyn scream frantically. "Ladies, ladies, ladies! Please calm down," says T.K. "It's over now, and we're okay; we're fine." KAP tosses T.K. his phone, and he reads Richie's text message: "If Felix's men are there, kill them immediately! I'll explain later." KAP puts his gun on his lap and starts to eat again. "Hey T.K., what do you think Richie would say right now if he was here?" asks KAP between bites. T.K. thinks for a second.

"I don't know. What?"

"He'd say, 'This food is delicious, but next time, I think we should do Mexican.'"

CHAPTER 11

T.K., KAP, and the crew spent nearly the whole night loading the submarine with the excess product. Around midnight, Edward stops to take a break, wondering if Barbara and Evelyn are cleaning up the mess T.K. and KAP left behind. "Yo, T.K., you think the ladies are cleaning up the dining room?" asks KAP. T.K. shrugs, so they both sneak into the house through the backdoor near the kitchen. They hide out in the hallway just outside the dining room to listen in on Barbara and Edward's conversation.

"No, no, and no! I ain't cleaning up nobody's blood!" says Barbara. "My job is to cook and clean whatever it is I mess up. I don't do brains and blood."

"Come on, baby. Now, it ain't much. Please just do it for me," says Edward.

"Shiiiiit! Just do it?" Barbara looks down at Edward's feet. "You the one got on Nikes. You just do it. Gone, Edward, gone nah." She walks off into the kitchen and side-eyes T.K. on the way. "Up in here blowing peoples' brains out. They popped it; they can mop it! Good night, Edward."

T.K. and KAP walk back to the boathouse laughing. "Elmer, Barbara got your brother by the balls, dude," says KAP.

Elmer smiles, then responds, "Ya balls will come up missing too after ten, fifteen years of marriage." Everyone laughs.

"How much more we got to go before we can get these subs outta here?" asks KAP.

"One sub is done," says Elmer.

"Well, let's get the bodies and put them on the top so Tech can take them out to sea with the subs. Once they get far enough out, the subs will submerge and the current can take the bodies away," says T.K. KAP's phone rings, and he looks at it and then points the phone's screen in T.K.'s direction. "Hey, T.K., it's Richie." They both walk out of the boathouse to take the call.

"Richie, what's going on?" asks KAP, answering the call.

"Where's T.K.?" asks Richie concerned.

"He's here." Richie exhales.

"Listen, A had her interview earlier, and she was doing great until the interviewer showed her a picture of her, Ren, and Kay when they were younger. Then she went fucking Tupac."

"Get the fuck outta here!" says KAP. "What she do?"

"She said Felix whole birth name on TV and was like she coming to get his ass two seconds after she gets sworn in."

"Stop playing!" says KAP and T.K. in unison.

"I wish I was. So, he's coming for us, and he's coming hard. We going back to how we came into the game. Be ready at all times. Where are the bodies?"

"They going out to sea with the subs in a few," responds T.K.

"Okay, finish up there, then come back to Chicago immediately after the crew gets on the road. Tech already has the autonomous car waiting at a rendezvous point to be loaded and head to New York. This situation is going to be very unpredictable and highly volatile. Pair up for extra security. I'll call D to close down Josephine's until further notice." KAP ends the call, and he and T.K. get to work.

Richie has called Arielle a few times, but she is too emotional to talk because she is too torn up about her emotional collapse on national television. A few hours later, she calls him after she has settled down. "Richie, I feel sick."

"A, it's done. Can't take it back now. We need to come up with a contingency plan in case everything goes south. First, you need to get twenty-four-hour security around you. Get with those politicians that's supporting you and tell them you are at risk based off the content of your interview. Only leave your place of hiding when necessary. I got the connect information you left for me on my car. Whoever gave it to you…"

"Richie, I don't have that information yet," says Arielle.

"What!?" asks Richie, confused. He pauses and thinks to himself, *I've talked to Marble Head since then, and he ain't said nothing about it.* "Are you sure? What about Phillip?"

"No, Phillip doesn't have the reach, and he don't know anyone there to leave something on your car."

"Hmmm. Well, we need to focus on getting those things done, A. It's life or death." Richie hangs up with Arielle and texts Tech: "I need you to dig up any info you can on Pedro Alejandro Gamboa from the El Muerte Lenta Cartel." Tech replies: "Got it!"

Richie understands that it's a high probability that he will not live past his trip to Columbia, so he texts his attorney and tells him to activate his will in five days if he doesn't hear from him before then. He takes out a letter from his desk that he wrote to his family back when he returned to the game just in case he met his demise. He puts it in an envelope and places it on top of his suitcase. Before Arielle's interview, Richie believed he had a seventy percent chance of leaving Columbia with some kind of resolution. But bringing attention to any branch of the cocaine tree was a guaranteed death wish. After sitting on his couch for a couple hours, replaying what happened in his head and trying to find a loophole or a solution to help the situation, he gets a text from Tech that breaks him out of his trance. "There's no information available on the FBI or the CIA database on anyone named Pedro Alejandro Gamboa or on an El Muerte Lenta Cartel."

Richie replies, "Thanks, Tech." He then just sits on his couch, looking through his living room window at the Chicago skyline, knowing he's going into a situation completely blind.

* * *

Leon Russell's lawyer returns to Chief Watkins's office where the District Attorney, Internal Affairs agents, Detective Coles, and Detective Neeley are all waiting. His lawyer brought the tapes with him, along with the device that would play the videos. They all sit in silence and watch the video from inside the store and the one from outside the store. They came to the conclusion that the sound of the soda exploding could have prompted the officers to fire. "Although the headlights from the cars provided some lighting, it may not have been enough for clear visibility," says the lawyer.

"That's true," says Detective Coles, "but from the time the cashier hit the alert button until the time the officers arrived at the scene, there's no way that any suspect would still be in the store." Chief Watkins doubles down on Detective Coles's theory.

"Not only that, but those officers should've come forward immediately after your client tampered with the crime scene, not when Internal Affairs got involved. I'm suspending those men without pay until the investigation is closed. If they're exonerated for the shooting, I'll let them resign."

"They could still face jail time for integrity violations," chimes in the District Attorney. "The mayor has no appetite for this bullshit. They made their beds, and they will lie in them."

"Alright, so Mr. Russell's lawyer and the DA can figure out their fate. My detectives and I will analyze the video from inside the store, the rest of you can analyze the shooting of Javari Lewis," says Chief Watkins, wrapping up the meeting.

* * *

The next morning, Richie is packed and waiting for T.K. and KAP to take him to the airport. He's watching the news on the couch when he gets a notification that visitors have arrived. He looks at the camera and approves the notification. His front door opens, and KAP, T.K., Damawi, and Brick walk through the door one after the other. "I'm happy to see y'all, but this isn't what we talked about," says Richie.

KAP nods and responds, "True, but everyone in here would take this risk every day of the week to see you off, brother."

"I appreciate it," says Richie, "but only T.K. and KAP will be taking me to the airport."

Damawi emerges from the background and asks, "Can I talk to you alone, Richie?" Richie extends his arm in the direction of his bedroom. She walks in front of him and then slowly turns around after he closes the door behind them. She immediately starts to sob. "This is sooo fucked up. I didn't see this coming. I have so much to say to you but with so little time." Damawi closes her eyes, sending tears rolling down her cheeks. Richie walks over to her and places his hands on her cheeks, using his thumbs to wipe away her tears. "So do I," says Richie. He looks down for a second to gather his thoughts and then looks up to express how he feels, but she beats him to it.

"Listen, I know who you are as a leader, but I wish I could learn more about the man behind the movement. I'm not going to put any negative vibes into the universe. So, when you make it back here, I hope you make changing some of your rules a priority." She wraps her arms around Richie and hugs him tightly. He can feel her body shaking, the same shake he felt when Javari was killed. She kisses him on the cheek and walks out the room.

Richie stands there for a moment, then follows behind her. Brick is standing in the hallway next to Richie's bedroom doorway. Richie stops in front of Brick, and they stare at each other. At that moment, Brick thinks about Richie moving his bed next to his while he was in the hospital. Richie remembers the countless hours of combat and weight training, and how Brick helped him overcome his back issues to be able to lead the team. Brick's eyes start to fill with tears, and Richie hits him across the chest with his forearm to stop him from crying. They both crack a smile as Richie walks around him.

"You guys ready?" asks Richie.

"Yeah," says T.K., picking up Richie's carry-on luggage. Before they walk out the door, Richie walks over to his table and grabs two envelopes.

"Drop this off to Maurice when you leave." Brick looks confused but nods.

They all get on the elevator and head down to their cars together. They ride in silence during the descent to the parking garage level. No hugs or last-minute goodbyes. When they step off the elevator, Damawi gets into Brick's truck to head to H2H, and Richie hops in KAP's SUV with T.K. to head to the airport. Three of Felix's men are parked on the street in a black sedan across from the parking garage. They've been waiting outside since last night, waiting for Richie to show himself. When they see the two vehicles leaving the garage, they pull away from the curb and follow them. The cars drive in the same direction for a while.

"Which one should we follow?" asks the driver.

"Follow the first one. The second one is normally security," says one of the passengers. Brick and KAP both merge onto the expressway and drive close together until they finally go their separate ways. Felix's men continue to follow the first vehicle. They each have their weapons locked and loaded, ready to kill Richie at first sight. They didn't care at all about potential witnesses or possibly hurting innocent bystanders. They only focused on following Felix's orders exactly as instructed for fear of retaliation. They follow the vehicle for miles until it finally makes a stop, and they have a chance to execute Richie. Felix's men park a short distance from the vehicle and watch intensely for any clear shot of Richie. When the driver's side door opens, they pull away from the curb and drive by slowly, looking inside the vehicle trying to get a glimpse of the driver. They roll down their windows and point the tips of their guns out the window, ready to let loose a massive number of rounds. Brick steps out of the truck to scan the area before he walks up to the building. The driver nearly comes to a complete stop until the front passenger says, "Hold your fire. There's a female inside."

* * *

KAP pulls up to ticketing, and Richie exits the back of the vehicle and pulls his carry-on luggage out from the seat beside him. KAP and T.K. get out of the SUV together, and they all stand on the sidewalk by the vehicle. "The excess product is in the sub?" asks Richie.

"Yes, and out to sea. We all good," says T.K. "We put Felix's men on top of the sub so they can float out once the sub submerges."

"Cool," says Richie. "I'll see you guys in a few days. If I don't, KAP, you got the helm." Richie then hands T.K. an envelope. "Make sure my mom gets this. She'll know what to do." Just as T.K. is about to say something, an Airport Security Specialist breaks up the conversation. "Hey, you guys can't park here. This area is for—"

"Man, if you don't get the fuck up outta here!" says KAP. The Security Specialist squints his eyes at them and then moves along.

T.K. says, "We're going to lay low. Tech is—"

"I don't want to know," interjects Richie, "just in case I'm forced to talk." T.K. shakes his head. "You sure about this? We can fight."

Richie responds by opening his arms for a group hug. As they embrace, Richie whispers, "The movement is bigger than just one person, brothers. Carry it on for as long as you can." They group hug for what seems like minutes. Finally, they separate, and Richie grabs his carry-on, walks inside the terminal, and doesn't look back.

* * *

Felix's men are waiting on the street outside of H2H's office, watching Brick and Damawi. The driver calls Felix and informs him that Richie isn't in the truck, but members of his team are. "Do you want us to continue to follow them, boss?" asks the driver.

"Yes, but have Julio stay there in case the person can be of some assistance."

"Do you want the address?"

"Yes. Let me find out who this is, and I'll contact you with instructions."

Damawi remains in the truck while Brick drops the envelope on the doorstep. Before Brick walks back to his truck, Julio slips out of the back of the black sedan and ducks down behind another vehicle. When Brick pulls out of H2H's parking lot and passes the black sedan, the driver pulls off to continue following Brick and Damawi.

* * *

Chief Watkins, Detective Coles, and Detective Neeley are still analyzing the corner store video after hours of watching it on repeat. The clarity of the video is good enough for them to clearly see that the shooter has a tattoo on his right wrist. His jacket was a bit small, so when he extended his arm to shoot the cashier, his panther tattoo was clearly visible. Detective Neeley examines the clothing and boots of the second assailant and determines his height and weight by comparing him to the height of the cabinets. The third assailant was rather short and slim but wore baggy clothes, which hindered them from getting an accurate description.

"This could be a female by the way she moves," says Detective Coles.

"You may be right," says Chief Watkins. "Check the database on the guy with the tattoo. If it's not a new one, we can easily identify him if he's in the system."

* * *

Maurice and Elder are in the office drinking coffee and exchanging small talk when they're interrupted by a knock on the door. "Come in!" says Maurice. Evan, a young lookout, opens the door with an envelope. "What you got, lil nigga?" Evan walks in and hands Maurice the envelope. "Who gave you this?"

"This big ass dude dropped it off at the door," responds Evan.

"Aight, get yo lil ass back downstairs," says Maurice.

Maurice opens the envelope, pulls out the letter from inside, and starts reading it. "Get the fuck outta here," he says, throwing the letter on the floor. Elder picks up the letter and reads it aloud: "To Elder, the product is on the way to NY as you read this letter to Handley because his reading skills ain't changed since the sixth grade. Anyways, I sent them extras for their participation in the movement. A note has been sent with the product informing them of this. If they want to share profits with you, it's on them." Elder covers his smile with his hand, so Maurice doesn't notice. "Man, this guy is the epitome of pettiness," says Elder. Maurice shakes his head in disbelief.

About twenty minutes later, there's another knock at the door. Maurice looks at the camera and sees a Latino man standing behind Evan just outside the door. Maurice stands up and pulls out his weapon. "May I help you?" asks Maurice. Julio looks up at the camera and shows him a cell phone. "Are you packing?" asks Maurice. Julio holds his hands up. "Evan, he clean?" Evan gives him the thumbs up into the camera. "Come in, slowly," says Maurice, pointing his weapon toward the door.

Julio walks over to the table, presses the speakerphone button on his phone, and slides it across the desk.

"Man, who the fuck is this?" asks Maurice.

"Hello, my friend."

"I don't have no fucking friends. Who the fuck is this before I send this chalupa looking muthafucka back across that wall stiff?"

"My name is Felix, Felix Navarro. I would like to offer you a business opportunity." Maurice lowers his weapon and puts it in the back of his pants. Maurice and Elder both sit down and scoot their chairs up to the table.

"I'm listening."

* * *

Richie lands at the El Dorado Airport in Columbia in the early afternoon, full of nervous energy. As he walks off the plane onto the platform, he relaxes slightly from the warmth of the beautiful Columbian weather, which is very different from the brutal February winter he left behind in Chicago. He walks through customs and out to the front of the airport. He has no clue who left him the information to Felix's supplier, but it's irrelevant at this point. He stands outside, frequently looking behind him, expecting to be clubbed over the head, blindfolded, and pushed into the back of a truck like his experience with Felix. Instead, two white Range Rovers pull up, and the second one stops right where Richie is standing. A tall, athletic-build Columbian man gets out of the front passenger seat, opens the back door of the vehicle, then walks over to Richie and grabs his carry-on luggage, putting it in the trunk. Richie cautiously walks over to the SUV and looks inside before getting in and closing the door. Once the front passenger gets in, the first Range Rover pulls away from the curb, and the second one promptly follows.

They drive for nearly two hours through the beautiful countryside of Columbia. The person sitting next to Richie is a little overweight and falling asleep during the trip. If his job is to keep an eye on Richie, he surely isn't doing a good job of that. *He probably the boss's in-law or some shit like that*, thinks Richie. His head repeatedly leans on Richie's shoulder. Every time the SUV hits a bump or makes a sharp turn, he wakes up, giving Richie's shoulder a break. Thirty seconds later, however, he's back at it. Richie grew tired of fighting for his space, so he just let the man rest.

* * *

Julio left immediately after Maurice and Felix finished their conversation. "Richie's ass is out, and I'm in goddammit! Elder, this shit will take us to the next level." Elder pauses with reservations before responding.

"This is going to be way harder than you think. We don't have the connections to push that much weight outside of Chicago and New York."

"We'll take those connections from one of Richie's people by force. We help Felix murder that nigga, and his people will work for us, or they will follow right behind his ass. We can get the lords to fill in."

"Maurice, do you really think those lords will continue the movement?"

"Fuck that movement! I'm the movement! Ion care bout that black power bullshit," says Maurice as he stands up and walks to the other side of the table. Elder walks over to Maurice and puts his hands on his shoulder.

"Son, we're not staffed to take this responsibility. I know how much you hate Richie, but if Richie is having issues with this guy… this ain't our lane." Maurice aggressively pushes Elder's hand off his shoulders and walks away.

"E, we doing this shit. Period."

* * *

Felix phones the men following Brick and Damawi. When the driver answers, Felix simply says, "Kill them," and hangs up. The driver immediately speeds up to pull alongside Brick's vehicle, but the thick traffic is detering him from getting close enough. The driver continues maneuvering the black sedan through cars, trying to get close enough to give the passenger a clear shot. Meanwhile, Damawi is talking to Brick about Richie and how worried she is about this situation. As she's talking, she notices he's paying attention to the conversation, but also constantly looking at his side mirror.

"What's wrong, Brick?" He looks at his rear-view mirror, then points to the passenger side mirror. Damawi looks in her side view mirror and leans forward slightly. "Is that the same car that was parked across the street from H2H? You think it was the same one?" asks Damawi. Brick reaches across her legs, opens the glove box, and pulls out his Glock pistol. Damawi taps her purse, indicating she has her gun as well. She then picks up her phone and calls KAP.

"What's up, D?"

"Hey, we got two of Felix's men following us."

"Where you guys at?"

"We left H2H and was headed back downtown. Where are you?"

"We just dropped Richie off. Headed back to the city. Where you taking them cause it's way too early to be on some murder shit in these streets." Damawi looks at Brick, who looks at her and then thinks for a second. Finally, he utters, "home."

"He said—"

"We heard him. We'll be there as soon as we can to help with the bodies." KAP hangs up and then starts racing toward Brick's house. Once Felix's hitmen finally catch up to Brick, they decide to just follow behind Brick's truck to see where he's headed. Brick had plenty of chances to evade them, but he didn't want to give them another opportunity to murder someone in the crew.

Twenty minutes later, Brick pulls into his driveway, then opens and enters the garage. Felix's hitmen drive past his house and then circle back. Brick gets out of his car, grabs the trash can from inside his garage, and rolls it out to the curb. He wants to give the men a false indication that he doesn't know he was followed. He then opens the car door for Damawi and leads her into the house, leaving the garage door open. Once they're inside the house, he immediately walks over to his hallway closet and hands Damawi a 9MM pistol with a silencer, and he grabs a large steel knife. He then walks over to the living room window and peeks through his mini blinds to see the men exiting the black sedan with assault rifles. He quickly determines that the hallway leading to the kitchen will be the perfect place to dominate the fight because it's narrow, and it would be hard to maneuver those weapons in that tight space. Brick moves Damawi to the hallway closet before walking into the kitchen and turning on the lights and the faucet. He then stands behind the refrigerator next to the hallway and waits with his knife in hand. The hitmen walk into the garage slowly and open the door to the house. Damawi hears the door open and holds her breath as the men step inside the house. Their shadows pass underneath the doorway, and she stands perfectly still with the gun pressed tightly against her chest. The hitmen automatically move in the direction of the running water toward the kitchen. When Brick hears the floorboard creak, he knows they're halfway to the kitchen. Brick quitely reaches into his pocket, grabs his cell phone, and dials Damawi's number and then slowly returns the phone to his pocket.

Damawi's ringtone echoes from the hallway closet. "Shit, shit, shit, shit," whispers Damawi, reaching into her coat pocket to silence her phone. Both men quickly turn in the direction of the closet, and Brick stealthily comes from around the refrigerator and throws his knife smoothly into the back of one of the hitmen's neck. He falls forward onto the other hitman's legs in front of him, knocking him off balance. When he regains his footing, he turns around to check on his associate and is met by Brick, who jumps and tackles him to the floor, landing on top of him. He had no chance. Brick grabs the barrel of the gun, snatches the weapon from the man, and strikes him in the face with the end of the gun, knocking him unconscious. He then removes the clip and throws the weapon on the living room couch. Brick walks over to the first guy and pulls the knife from the back of his neck. He then turns him over and watches as the man chokes on his own blood, suffering. Brick then suddenly stomps the man in his face, his jaw caving into his throat. Brick grabs the deceased hitman by his feet and drags his body into the kitchen. Damawi tries to come out of the closet, but the unconscious hitman is blocking the door. Brick comes back and drags him to the kitchen as well.

Damawi cautiously comes out of the closet and walks into the kitchen. She sees the guy with his jaw caved in and immediately looks away. She reaches in her coat pocket and looks at her phone to see who called. "Really?" she asks, looking at Brick with her head tilted sideways. Brick shrugs his shoulders. He then turns to wake up the unconscious but still alive hitman. He fills a cup with water and throws it in his face, startling the man awake. When he opens his eyes and sees Brick, he promptly tries to get away. Brick grabs him by his neck and pulls him up onto his feet. Brick then looks at Damawi and nods.

"Who sent you? Felix, right?" asks Damawi. He doesn't answer. Brick headbutts the hitman, smashing his bridge bone and flattening his nose. "Ahhhhhhhhhhh!" the man screams out as blood flows from his nose and onto his body and the floor. Damawi asks again: "Who sent you? Felix, right?"

He nods yes.

"How many of you are here?"

"Just us two." Brick grabs his knife and jams it into the lying man's shoulder, leaving it embedded. "Ahhhhhhhhhh, fuck!!!!" Damawi raises his eyebrows at him.

"Three."

"Where is the other guy?"

"We left him where you dropped off that package."

"Why?"

"Felix wanted Julio to find out who was there and if he could replace Richie."

"Do you have a picture of him?"

"No, I don't." Brick grabs the knife and twists it. "Aargh!" Brick then holds his hand out, asking Damawi for the weapon with the silencer. She reaches to hand it to him but quickly pulls it back. Brick looks at her confused, then watches as she presses the gun into the hitman's chest and pulls the trigger, shooting him directly in his heart. Brick releases his grip and lets the hitman collapse to the floor. Damawi hands Brick the gun, steps over the deceased hitman, and heads into the living room.

Minutes later, KAP and T.K. arrive at Brick's house. They park in the driveway in front of the still open garage. They also see the hitmen's black sedan still parked outside. "Well, that's a good sign," says KAP as he and T.K. get out of the car and head into the garage. When they walk through the door into the house, Damawi is sitting on the living room couch.

"You good?" asks T.K.

"Yeah, I'm good." They both then turn to look down the hall, and they watch as Brick prepares to put the men in garbage bags, getting them ready to be taken to Lloyd's. KAP immediately walks over to help Brick get them ready to transport when darkness falls. KAP throws T.K. the hitman's phone, and he starts going through it, looking at messages and calls as he walks over to sit down with Damawi. "The guy said there's still one more person out there," says Damawi. "He went to talk to Maurice to see if he could replace Richie. He's not coming back," she says as tears well up in her eyes. Suddenly, she starts wailing uncontrollably.

Brick and KAP walk into the living room to check on Damawi. The men all look at each other. At that moment, they all feel like Richie will die in Columbia. And if there was any secret as to how Damawi truly felt about Richie, it was solidified at that very moment. Brick and KAP walk back into the kitchen to finish up. T.K. wraps one arm around Damawi, allowing her to cry on his shoulder while he continues looking through the phone for any clues that could help them identify and locate this third person.

* * *

Richie arrives at Pedro Alejandro Gamboa's mansion just after noon. It's exactly what he expected it to be: gorgeous. From the front, it seems as long as a city block. He's eager to see more of it, but his mind is currently focused more on the outcome of this trip. They exit the vehicles as soon as the drivers spot two golf carts coming from the back of the estate. The men driving the carts are wearing black suits with pistols holstered on their waists while the passenger in the first cart is wearing clothes that fit the stature of a drug lord. He's wearing a turquoise-colored shirt with a tan-colored pattern of an exotic bird, matching tan pants, and turquoise loafers. The overweight man who slept on Richie's shoulder stands next to Richie, sweating to death. The golf cart pulls up right in front of Richie, and the well-dressed man gets out of the golf cart with a towel and a glass of water, walks over to the overweight man, and whispers in his ear. All the men leave in the golf cart except the well-dressed man and the two armed guards.

Richie is totally confused. The well-dressed man then walks over to Richie and introduces himself. "Hi, my name is Enrique. Follow me please." Richie follows Enrique without hesitation as the two armed guards follow behind them. As they get closer to the mansion, Richie realizes that the guards' suits look similar to the ones from his dream. Anxiety starts to set in, but Richie doesn't let it show. He continues to walk with confidence through the front doors of the mansion. "We'll escort you to your room. If you need to call or text anyone, do it now because you won't be allowed to once you're in your room," says Enrique, leading Richie through the mansion and to a guest room. Richie shakes his head and hands his phone to Enrique. "Are you sure? You'll be waiting for quite awhile. We're waiting for another guest to join you and Mr. Gamboa for dinner tomorrow." Richie thinks to himself, *Tomorrow?!* before shaking his head again. Enrique then opens the door to Richie's guest room, and he enters in front of a servant who rolls his carry-on luggage into the room and places it near the foot of the bed. "There are beverages and prepared meals in the refrigerator if you get hungry or thirsty," says Enrique. Richie looks over his shoulder and sees two men in suits holding machine guns posted outside his room door. "I will come and get you when the guest arrives," says Enrique as he and the servant leave and shut the door. Richie hears keys jingling and the sound of the door being looked from the outside. Richie sits on the chair next to the bed and thinks to himself, *Fuck!!*

* * *

Later that evening, Damawi backs the hitmen's car up into the garage and pushes the button to open the trunk, so the guys can load the bodies inside. Once the bodies are loaded, Damawi gets out, so that T.K. can deliver the bodies to Lloyd's to get rid of them. Brick, KAP, and Damawi then hop into Brick's truck and follow T.K. to the funeral home. The hitman's phone rings, and KAP just lets it go to voicemail, assuming it's the third hitman calling. He doesn't leave a message, so KAP texts him: "Where are you?" No response. "We need to find this guy before he finds one of us?" Still no response. He turns around to the back seat to ask Damawi a question and sees her looking in her phone. "What are you doing, D?" She slowly looks up. "I know you're tempted to text him to see if he's okay. We all want to, but we can't. I'm sure we'll hear from him soon enough. If it was some way he could communicate with us, he would." Damawi puts her phone in her pocket, lies her head back on the seat rest, and closes her eyes.

When they arrive at Lloyd's, they drive around to the back of the building. Lloyd and his nephew meet them outside to grab the bodies from the trunk. T.K. throws Lloyd the keys to the car and asks him to take it to Smitty's when they're done. They all hop back in Brick's truck to head back to his house. "We gonna stay together until we hear from Richie or until this other guy rears his little head. Since we don't know what that conversation with Maurice was about, kill anybody that look like, associated with, in, or around H2H without hesitation," says KAP.

"Good," says T.K., "Cause I told Lloyd to be available to us twenty-four seven."

* * *

The next morning, Arielle is getting ready to go into town for a meeting with her newly appointed campaign manager and her staff. Phillip is at her house trying to talk her into postponing it, but she insists on moving forward with her plans. "Arielle, are you sure about this?"

"Yes, I'm positive. Richie put me in this position to make change. The schools, businesses… it wouldn't have happened if it wasn't for him. He's over in Columbia right now, and we don't know if he's going to make it back alive. If I stop now, and he dies, it will be in vain. I have no more fear of dying."

"A, listen—"

"Phillip, I'm either going with you or without!" Phillip nods and tells the security team to get ready to leave in five minutes. They grab their weapons, load the cars, and head for the city.

Arielle makes it to the meeting safely thanks to her security team, who provided the perfect coverage she needed to remain safe. This meeting is the start of her life in politics, and she couldn't miss it. The campaign manager and her staff lay out their plans for campaign finances, Arielle's political party convention, and a possible deputy prime minister. Her being young, intelligent, and charismatic will definitely help her draw people in to support her plans, and the campaign manager plans to highlight all those qualities. Her being a beautiful woman of color would give the voters of Belize a better image of what a fresh start should look like. Arielle is very much engaged and more determined than ever before. She now understands what Richie saw in her, and she's going to do everything in her power to fulfill his prophecy.

* * *

Richie didn't sleep well at all the night before. He woke up early that morning, worked out in the room, showered, and waited for his fate. That afternoon, he finally hears the sound of keys outside his door. His heart rate spikes, knowing that this was the beginning of the end. The crew would have to move forward with the movement minus one. The door opens, and Richie pops up from the foot of the bed. "Our guest has arrived. Mr. Gamboa will see you now," says Enrique, gesturing for Richie to exit the room. Richie walks through the doorway and follows Enrique and the two armed men to meet with Mr. Gamboa and this unknown guest. Richie can hear his heart beating in his ears as the anxiety grows with each step toward his demise. Enrique leads him through the mansion, over polished marble floors and past ornate sculptures and vases, and then outside onto a huge patio with white marble floors. He scans beyond the deck and gasps slightly at the beautiful scenery full of beautiful, lush grass and groves of passionfruit trees. It looks exactly like in his dream when Brick was torn apart by horses.

When his eyes land on the swimming pool, he quickly looks away, avoiding the replay of that portion of the dream in his mind. As he continues to follow Enrique, he wonders if his dream is really a premonition of what is going to happen to his crew once he's gone. He slows his pace, not looking to bring about the end so soon. "Mr. Richie, please keep up. We can't keep Mr. Gamboa waiting any longer. He's already irritated that his guest arrived a day late." Two guards are standing directly behind Mr. Gamboa, blocking Richie's view of the man sitting at the dinner table. As Enrique escorts Richie to his seat, he walks past Mr. Gamboa, determined not to look at his face until he's standing directly in front of him.

* * *

After three hours, Arielle finishes up her meeting with her campaign team. The security team quickly escorts her from the building to her vehicle, which is the second one in a trio of black Chevrolet Tahoes. As soon as everyone is in their designated vehicle, they proceed to returning Arielle to her safe house in the countryside. When they exit the city and turn onto a two-lane road, the convoy picks up speed, determined to return Arielle safely. Suddenly, two black sedans turn onto the road behind the trailing vehicle in Arielle's convoy, quickly gaining speed until the first vehicle rams into the back of the third SUV. The security team's driver swerves, struggling to maintain control of the vehicle. One of the passenger guards grabs the radio and informs the other guards, "We have two vehicles behind us! The lead vehicle is ramming us! Go, go, go!!"

The first two Tahoes speed off as the third one slams on its brakes, attempting to slow down the black sedans behind it and give the rest of the convoy a chance to distance themselves from the threat. A Latino man in the first black sedan comes through the sunroof with a submachine gun as the car pulls alongside the stopped SUV. The security guards attempt to shoot the men in the sedan, but the Tahoe gets riddled with bullets before anyone in the SUV can even fire their weapon. The second sedan slides into the opposite lane and drives past the stopped vehicles to continue the chase. Arielle's lead security vehicle watches as the sedan comes speeding up the highway behind the convoy and radios Arielle's car. "We're going to have to stop and take a stand." The lead vehicle slows down, allowing Arielle's vehicle to take the lead, then the two-car convoy stops. Both security teams exit the two SUVs, leaving Arielle and Phillip in the lead car. Two of the security guards position themselves at the back of Arielle's car while the rest of the team takes cover behind the trail car. The two black sedans catch up to the convoy, then they park the sedans at an angle, blocking the road.

* * *

When Richie makes it to his seat, he looks up and sees the man from the Range Rover who was resting his head on his shoulders. "Sit down, Richie," commands Mr. Gamboa. Richie sits down, and the two guards who walked over with him stand behind him. "Are you shocked it's me?"

"No, I'm not," says Richie.

"Why is that so?"

"Any man can come from humble beginnings to be a king. The way a person dresses has very little to do with their mind or the person's capabilities. So, it doesn't surprise me. Anyone can wear the crown if that's what they choose to do."

"I like that, I like that. Well, Richie, it seems we have a huge problem. We now have politics involved in our business and that I cannot live with. I don't think it can be worked out, so something must be done."

* * *

The Latino men jump out of the black sedans and immediately start shooting their submachine guns at the black Tahoes while they advance toward the vehicles. Arielle's security team is outmanned and outgunned, dropping like flies with every second that goes by. The first SUV is destroyed, and bullets are now reaching Arielle and Phillip's car. Phillip covers Arielle with his body as shattered glass rains down on top of them. Phillip holds her as tight as he can while they both sob, knowing it's the end. The gunshots suddenly stop, and Arielle and Phillip hold their breaths, waiting for Felix's men to approach the car. They listen with quiet panic as the sound of boots stepping on glass gets closer and closer. Just as Phillip raises his head to get a peek at how close the men are to their vehicle, gunshots ring out from every direction, sending Phillip back on top of Arielle.

* * *

Richie sits and stares at Mr. Gamboa until he's distracted by the waiter to his left, who is pushing over a cart with a stainless-steel serving tray that matches the one from his dream. He feels himself getting more and more nervous as the tray gets closer and closer. "Our guest has arrived," announces Mr. Gamboa. Richie is too focused on the tray to notice anyone other than the waiter walking up to the table. The waiter carefully removes the tray from the cart and places it between Richie and Mr. Gamboa. "Ahh, my apologies for keeping you waiting for so long, Richie. For that, please do the honors." Richie's hands are sweaty and somewhat shaky. He wipes his hands on his thighs to dry them off and extends his arm over the tray. He grabs the handle and hesitates for one breath before removing the cover.

* * *

For nearly a minute, the sound of machine guns surround the SUV before they suddenly stop again. Phillip had no thoughts of raising up this time to see what was next. They remain crotched down as the sounds of dress shoes clacking against the concrete gets louder and louder. "I am so sorry, Phillip. Richie..." cries Arielle, trying to talk through panic and fear.

"I love you, sis. I wouldn't have this any other way." The left passenger side door opens slowly. "Ms. Arielle McCallister?" calls a voice from outside the SUV.

"Yes, that's me," answers Arielle, slightly confused. Phillip lifts up his body from on top of hers, so she can raise up to see who she's responding to. She looks up and sees a tall man wearing a black suit waiting by the door. He steps to the side so that Arielle and Phillip can exit the vehicle. When they step out, they're shocked at the sight of dead bodies, broken glass, and bullet casings everywhere. There are six men wearing black suits surrounding the SUV. One of the men approaches Arielle and calmly says, "We work for Mr. Pedro Gamboa. We need you to come with us."

* * *

Richie lifts the cover up gradually, keeping his eyes focused solely on the cover until he rests it on the table to his right. He takes another deep breath before he shifts his eyes back to the tray. He's shocked and relieved to see Felix's head served on the platter with flowers around it.

CHAPTER 12

"So, what's going through your mind right now, Richie?" Richie thinks for a second, then responds, "I usually eat dessert after the main course, but I think I'll make an exception this time." He grabs his fork from the table and moves it toward Felix's head. Mr. Gamboa bursts out into a loud laugh. "I was told you have comical responses at times like this. I like it!" He looks at the waiter and waves him over. The waiter covers the tray and carries it away. "You know why Felix's head is on that platter?" asks Mr. Gamboa.

"I have an idea, but I'd rather not assume," responds Richie.

"Felix and I have been at odds for quite some time. El Muerte Lenta means Slow Death. His time was up long ago; today, it expired. The way Felix handles business...so outdated. People who rule with an iron fist destroys one's motivation to go that extra mile. You circumvented his organization for a resolution for your cause. So, now we're here. You're just as valuable to my organization as you are to your organization. Felix's actions affected your business, his business, and most importantly, my business." The waiter comes back with a Cuban cigar for Mr. Gamboa. He puts it in his mouth and lights it before walking away. "So, Richie, we have this cutie pie Belizean politician. I believe she's a part of your organization, correct?"

"She is."

"Is she still an ally?"

"Yes. Felix attempted to kill her but killed her best friends and a protégé instead. She's fine, just lost control for a second. The interviewer used her emotions against us. She can open a lot of doors for us if she wins."

"I see. Felix sent men to kill her today, but we stopped him. Her death would have put us deeper in the thoughts of people that don't need to think about us." Richie nods in agreement. The waiters bring over a five-course Columbian meal, including bandeja paisa, arepas, fritanga, and empanadas, neatly place everything on the table, and fill the glasses with champagne. Members of the Gamboa family and Enrique take their seats at the table with Richie and Mr. Gamboa, who then raises his glass in a toast to his new business relationship with Richie. Everyone around the table raises their glasses and takes a sip of champagne before they begin eating.

"Is there anything more we can do to help her, Richie?"

"She'll need security from this day forward."

"Consider it done!"

* * *

Maurice and Elder are in the office discussing how their organization will flourish once Richie is gone. "Maurice, in order for you to advance in the drug game on this level, you need allies outside of the street world. Business men that can set you up so your money can't be tracked. Every kingpin started from the bottom in the game and survived through the trials and tribulations that come with it. So, when they make it to that level, they have seen the failures of the people that came before them and capitalized on their mistakes. We're not ready for this."

"Well, we need to get ready because when Felix comes calling—"

"Son, I know you want to be the man your father wanted you to be. You'll get there, just not like this." Just then, Karimah walks into the office, and Maurice and Elder cut their conversation short. "What's up, fam?" asks Karimah.

"What's up? Have a seat," says Maurice. "I need to tell you guys something." She takes a seat and gives Maurice her undivided attention. Maurice pauses for a second to help with the dramatic effect. "I got word that Kolax was killed the other night." Elder and Karimah look at him shocked.

"What?! I haven't heard shit from my peoples down there. Where did you get this news from?" asks Karimah.

"I got peoples there who I asked to check on him from time to time, and they said they seen three dudes carrying his body out the house into a van."

"Who the fuck is responsible for killing my cousin?!" shouted Karimah.

"Niggas saying it was Richie." Elder instantly frowns, disappointed in what Maurice is doing. "If you got something to say, E, speak on it," says Maurice.

"Richie has always been a man of his word; plus, he removed Kolax off the police radar for those murders. I can't believe that." Maurice becomes noticeably irritated.

"What the fuck? You cheerleading for that nigga now? You got a hat that says, 'Fan of Richie' on it?" asks Maurice. Elder just sits there quietly as Maurice goes on his rant. When he gets no reaction from Elder, Maurice looks at Karimah and says, "This nigga secretly working at Josephine's as a waitress n shit! He did that shit, and he gonna get got." Karimah covers her face, devastated by the death of her cousin. "Yeah, that nigga will get dealt with," says Karimah. She stands up and smacks Elder's coffee cup off the table and into the wall, splattering coffee all over the furniture, the wall, and the carpet. She walks out of the office enraged.

* * *

As Richie and members of the El Muerte Lenta Cartel continue to enjoy dinner, Mr. Gamboa continues his conversation with Richie. "An old friend told me about your cause; I can respect it. Your famous black leaders who have taken center stage, screaming their cause through religious organizations and from a mountain top, assassinated. You do it quietly, so the gringos will never see you coming. I want to see you win, Richie. You win, I win..." He scans the room, looking at his team, "we all win. If your people really knew their history and capabilities, you wouldn't need my assistance. So, I know you have to get back to Chicago. I know your people are awaiting your return. Don't worry about prices and logistics right now. I imagine you will be extremely happy with our business arrangements. Your point of contact is Enrique. He is my voice." Enrique returns Richie's cell phone. "He is available to you any time. When you're ready to leave, Enrique will take you to my airport."

Richie smiles, feeling content with his new business arrangement.

* * *

Detective Neeley walks into Detective Cole's office and drops three files onto his desk, spreading them all apart. "What's this, Neeley?"

"I entered the tattoo into our database and came up with a Curtis Walker. His known associate is Roland Outlaw, and he has a child with a Jordan McVeigh. Not saying she's one of the mopes in the store that night, but the person's body looks the female type."

"Good work, Neeley. Let's look into Curtis first. The tattoo could be the nail in his coffin, but let's bring him in, rattle his cage, and see what he gives us."

* * *

Karimah comes back into the office to speak with Maurice. "Yo, I gotta have him. I just called my people, and they said Kolax car still outside. They broke into his house, and his crib was a mess. TV and entertainment set smashed in with a trail of blood leading to the kitchen. Put me on him." Maurice stands up from behind his desk, walks over, and sits on the front edge of the desk. "No doubt. I'll let you at him in due time. Let me finish working out the meeting with the lords, double down with them, and I'll let you lead the hunt. Cool?"

Karimah nods and asks, "When this meeting taking place?"

"Tonight. Just waiting on a couple more calls to confirm. Don't worry; you'll get your chance soon." Karimah gives Maurice some dap and heads downstairs. She sees Elder talking to one of the youngins and asks, "Yo E, can I holla at you?"

"Give me a second, K," says Elder as he finishes his conversation with the youngin. "So whatever stresses the US like the job market, what the President may or may not say, or if any of the big businesses take a hit, it will affect your stocks." The youngin shakes his head in understanding, and Elder rubs his hand across the top of his head before he walks over to Karimah. "What's up, K?"

"Did you and Kolax have beef or something?"

"Not at all. He was a standup guy who got shit done. I just don't think Richie is involved with Kolax death."

"If not him, then who you think?"

"I don't know."

"Well until another muthafucka name comes into the mix, it's Richie. So, I don't know how y'all do it in Chicago, but in the Lou, we ask questions after the fact. You hear me? Save your questions and analogies after we peel his shit back. I need you behind Maurice and me on this shit." She walks off without giving Elder a chance to respond. He shakes his head in disappointment, then walks back over to the youngin.

* * *

Richie is headed to the airport with Enrique and two of his men in one of the same white Range Rovers that picked him up. "Mr. Gamboa is really happy to have you directly under him, no middleman. I can tell he really likes you. Reach out to us once you are ready to receive a shipment. I understand Felix gave you shipments from other people who are no longer available."

"We plan to expand to other states, and we will. I'm going to have to grow my team before I can do that. We both know good people are hard to find."

"I understand. We'll make this transition for you as smooth as possible." The Range Rover goes through the secured gate and parks on the runway alongside the jet. A female flight attendant walks to the back of the vehicle and takes Richie's carry-on luggage from the trunk and onto the plane. "Is there anything else we may need to assist you with?" asks Enrique.

"Yes, as a matter of fact, there is. I need two more submarines. They can be gutted, but the hull has to be in perfect condition."

Enrique rubs his chin and responds, "I will look into it."

"I'll be back soon to check in with you and Mr. Gamboa."

"We'll be looking forward to it." They shake hands as one of Mr. Gamboa's men opens the car door for Richie to exit the SUV. As soon as Richie enters the plane, the doors close behind him. He takes his seat and watches the Range Rover drive out of the gate. He leans back into his seat, feeling rejuvenated and ready to continue the movement. He reaches into his pocket for his phone to call the crew. *Fuck*, he thinks, realizing he left his phone. The plane is headed down the runway, and Richie looks out the window, watching the views of Columbia speed by as the plane picks up speed and lifts up from the ground. He closes his eyes, content to be heading to the same ole place, his sweet home, Chicago.

* * *

T.K. comes downstairs into Brick's living room where the crew is sitting around watching TV. "Hey, I figured out who the third person is," says T.K. The crew jumps up to hear what he's discovered. "The dude had the third guy's contact information in his phone as Nino Perra, which means bitch boy. I looked at his text messages, and there's a text between him and the other two at O'Hare. His real name is Julio, and I believe he's related to Felix somehow. Nephew maybe. So...that means he probably isn't leaving and won't stop, even if they have to send more people here to finish what they started." The room is filled with silence because the more they find out, the more it solidifies Richie's demise. "Well, we have a picture of him now, so it won't be a surprise if he rolls up," finishes T.K., showing each of them the guy's picture on the phone. After everyone takes a look, he goes back upstairs, and the crew resumes watching TV and staring at their phones.

* * *

Maurice walks into the conference room where his crew is waiting for him to start the meeting. "Elder, we got everybody?" asks Maurice. Elder nods, so Maurice starts talking. "I appreciate everyone showing up on such short notice. I know y'all got shit to do, so I'll be quick. I'm about to flood Chicago with coke, and I need some help pushing it. We'll start with Chicago, then move it to other states. If you know peoples in other states that needs it, they'll get it from us. We can build an empire on this shit here. It's pure, and the prices is cheap. We'll corner the market and profit big time."

"Where did this connect come from?" asks Kenyatta White from the South Side Vice Lords. Everyone promptly shifts their attention from Kenyatta to Maurice for answers.

"It's Richie's old connect.

"Richie Swaggazine from that entertainment company that do comedy shows and shit?" asks Jose Rayo from the Cobra Stones.

"Yeah, that's him," confirms Maurice.

"That pretty dude push weight?" asks Jose Rayo.

"Don't let dem cardigan sweaters and dem gators fool you. He's a monster with it, but his time is over. His connect got a bounty on him and his whole crew," gloats Maurice.

"That won't be easy. His crew was cleaning out dem D boys like it was nothing a few years ago. They some straight up murderers," says Kenyatta.

"Look, the faster we get him and his crew out the way, the quicker we can get this money. Let's join in on the bounty and off them niggas." Everyone sits quiet for a moment, thinking. Maurice looks at Derrick Brooks, Lord of the South Side Vice Lords. "We ain't heard from you, D. What's up?"

"Man, this is hard for me. I use to work for his Uncle Marble Head when I was a youngin. He was a muthafucka, but he was fair. I have no problem merc'n his nephew, but it's gonna have to put us on some next level shit, and it has to be organized. I don't think too many people in this room have the experience dealing and moving the weight Richie moves. So, let's have another meeting soon. We need to see numbers."

"Before we meet again, Richie at the very least need to be dead and gone," says Maurice. "So if one of you get a line on him…" Maurice takes his hand and slides his index finger across his throat, imitating slitting a throat with a knife. The thought of creating more wealth for their organizations outweighed the uncertainties of what was offered to them. Everyone seemed hesitant to remove Richie, except Kenyatta.

"We'll handle that shit," says Kenyatta confidently.

"Aight, then it's done," says Maurice.

* * *

Richie's flight lands in Chicago, and it feels so good for him to walk on Chicago's soil once again. Since he left his phone in Columbia and is a product of technology, he doesn't remember anyone's number in the crew by heart. Once he gets through customs, he heads out to catch a cab to take him home. While riding through the city, he thinks of all the things he will like to discuss with Mr. Gamboa when he returns to Columbia. He still plans to distance himself from the drug game once he pushes his movement throughout the US, once he finds another suitable replacement of course. This is a discussion he will need to have with Mr. Gamboa next time he sees him. After a thirty-minute ride, the cab driver pulls up to the front of Richie's building. He pays the cab driver and then gets out, relieved to finally be home.

"Mr. Richie, welcome back!" says William, the doorman.

"Thanks, William, glad to be back. What time are you done for tonight?" asks Richie.

"Two hours to go, and I'll be homebound,"

"Great. William, I lost my phone. Can you help me with the elevator?"

"Sure thing!" says William, walking Richie to the elevator.

"You know you still ain't showed me that new deck you put on the back porch," says Richie, pressing the number for his floor.

"You're right. I'm so sorry about that."

"Uh huh. If it's as good as you say it is, I'll pay you to put one on the back of my mom's house. She could use a bigger deck."

"Okay, Mr. Richie. I'll show you; I promise." When they arrive at Richie's floor, William puts his thumb on the fingerprint reader to authenticate access. "Thanks, William! Have a good night," says Richie, stepping off the elevator and walking down the narrow corridor to his front door. "You too, Mr. Richie!" calls out William as he presses the button to return to the lobby. Richie presses his thumb against the fingerprint authenticator on his front door and walks into his condo. Once inside, he steps over his piled up mail and newspapers and heads straight to his bedroom to get his other phone, so he can call his crew. He rolls his carry-on luggage into his closet and grabs the extra phone from the top shelf of the closet. It's dead, so he plugs it up and runs to the kitchen to grab a bottle of water.

* * *

Julio, who's been waiting in a car outside of Richie's house for two days, perks up when he sees the taxi pull up to the front. He's close enough to the building to recognize Richie as soon as he gets out of the car. He calls Felix for the third time, no answer. Julio sits and watches through the glass doors as Richie and the doorman get onto the elevator. When he sees the doorman return to the lobby, he exits the car and enters the building carrying a half empty pizza box.

"Hello, welcome to Vista Tower Luxury Condominiums. My name is William. How can I serve you?"

"How do I visit someone that lives here?"

"Well sir, they would have to give me authorization for you to come up."

"I see, I see. Well, what if they weren't home, and I was on the list but I lost my access?"

"Well, if the guest didn't put you on the finger scan or the face recognition, I can give you access."

"Really? Technology is so great. Do you use a finger or face, William?"

"I use finger recognition."

"Nice. Last question: Are you a cheese or pepperoni guy?"

"Pepperoni of course!"

"This is your lucky day." Julio opens the pizza box, pulls out a 9mm Glock, and shoots William in his right eye, sending him falling backward into his chair.

* * *

Richie goes back into his room to check the charge on the phone. It's now charged enough to make a call, so he picks it up and scrolls through his contacts. He finds who he wants to call and hits send.

"Hello."

"If I was to change some of my rules, which ones would you prefer?" asks Richie. Damawi, who was lying on the bed in the guest room, sits up immediately at the sound of Richie's voice. "Richie, oh my God! Is this you?"

"Yeah, it's me. Where is the rest of the crew?"

"We're all here at Brick's house."

"Really? Okay, I'll call KAP now, but one day I would like an answer to my question." He hangs up, and Damawi collapses back onto the bed, relieved to know he's still alive.

"I'm getting a call from Richie's phone," says KAP, sitting on the living room couch with Brick. T.K. comes running from the kitchen to the living room, and they all gather around the phone. Damawi wipes the tears from her face as she heads downstairs to join the guys. KAP takes a deep breath and answers it. "Hello?"

"KAP, how's the crew?"

Excited and relieved, KAP stands up while everyone else sits on the couch listening to the call. "We good, B! Where you at?"

"I'm home. I left my phone in Columbia, and of course, I don't memorize numbers. I'm glad I synced my contacts on my other phone. So, what's the business?"

* * *

Julio walks behind the front desk, pushes William's chair up to the desk, and presses his thumb on the fingerprint scanner to access the residence list. "Seventy-fifth floor," says Julio when he finds Richie's name. He's about to walk over to the elevator until he sees the fingerprint access panel on the wall. He looks down at William, then back at the access panel.

* * *

"So, one of Felix's hitmen is still out there," says T.K. "I believe his name is Julio." T.K. sends Richie the photo.

Richie looks at it and responds, "He doesn't look familiar to me."

"So, what's the play, Richie?" asks KAP.

"We need to link up and discuss what moves we need to make with Felix's guy still out there. Plus our next moves with Maurice and the future with the new connect." Richie hears the elevator ding. "Hold on. I think William's coming to tell me about his back deck." Richie walks over to the door still holding the phone up to his ear. He slowly opens the door with his free hand as he calls out, "Hey Will, this is a bad time. We can talk about your—" The barrel of a gun is thrust into the small opening in the door and right into Richie's face. Richie drops the phone as he steps to the right and grabs the assailant's wrist. The gun fires. Richie grabs the barrel of the gun with his right hand and twists it away from his body, bending the assailant's fingers backward as Richie gains control of the weapon. Still listening on the other end of the phone, the crew all look at each other confused and worried. "Was that a gunshot?" asks KAP. The crew jumps up and runs out to the garage, hoping to get to Richie in time. Richie slides the barrel of the gun backward to clear the bullet from the chamber and then removes the clip. He kicks the bullet on the floor behind him and throws the clip and weapon behind him too.

"Julio, right?" Richie then looks behind the assailant to see William slumped down in his desk chair, blood oozing from his eye.

"Julio Navarro." The crew is still listening as they pile into Brick's truck.

"Well, Julio, I'm sure you've been trying to contact ole Uncle Felix. You'll be seeing him soon enough." Richie inhales deeply as his mind takes him back to when Brick was training him. The last few months of training, Brick would sneak up on him in the house and launch an attack to see how fast and efficiently he could counter it. The last attack happened one day when Richie had just come home from work. "Yo, big dawg!" Richie called out as he walked through the door. He scanned the room briefly for Brick, dropping his bags by the door before going through the mail on the counter. Then he walked over to the refrigerator and looked around for something to cook. He didn't see anything in the fridge, and he said, "Okay, cool," then stood up to look in the freezer. Brick darted out from the side of the refrigerator at the exact moment Richie opened the freezer door, slamming it into Brick's face. The force stopped Brick temporarily, but he continued to charge Richie, who simply stepped back, stuck his foot out, and used Brick's momentum to push him by. Brick tripped and slid across the floor on his stomach. Richie grabbed the freezer door and looked inside. "Let's see...we can go with asparagus, baked potatoes, and salmon. The salmon is frozen, so it'll take some time to thaw. Or, we could just go with pizza. What you think, big dawg?" Richie looked at Brick, who had rolled onto his back and raised his middle finger.

Richie and Julio stand there, staring and measuring each other up. Richie widens his stance, awaiting any physical interaction. Julio strikes first, throwing a right-handed punch straight for Richie's face. Richie knocks it away, then immediately returns fire, blasting Julio in the face with a right hook. "Fast, ain't I?" asks Richie. Julio attempts another punch. Richie smoothly blocks it; his reflexes making Julio look like he's moving in slow motion. Richie counters with a kick to Julio's face, sending him flying backward into the wall. Julio regains his balance and wipes away the blood seeping from his mouth. Richie moves forward with his hands held up, guarding his face. With his teeth clenched, blood filling the spaces in between them, Julio rushes forward, slamming his head into Richie's abdomen. His bullish aggression is effective; Richie collapses over Julio's shoulder. Julio pushes Richie's body into the accent table, which forces him to stand straight up. Julio jumps up, slamming his head into Richie's chin. His teeth slam together, sending Richie reeling as a shock wave of pain rushes to his neck and jaw.

Julio charges again with arms outstretched, attempting to gouge Richie's eyes. Richie grabs and pulls Julio's arms, slamming his knee into his abdomen. The collision folds Julio's body forward, emptying his lungs. Richie grabs the back of Julio's head and slams it into his knee, dislocating his nose. Julio stumbles backward as blood gushes from his nose and onto Richie's expensive Mediterranean rug. He hits the floor, his back thumping from the impact, and he quickly rolls over onto one knee. He swiftly pops his nose back into place. Before he can stand up, Richie swings his right leg at Julio's face. Swerving to the right, Julio grabs Richie's leg and traps it between his left arm and shoulder, then punches at his groin. Richie catches Julio's hand and then drops to the floor. He brings his left knee to his shoulder, then launches his foot into Julio's jaw. Julio grunts loudly as he grabs his jaw and drops face-forward onto the floor. Richie rolls over and rises to his feet.

"Come on. Let's not keep Uncle Felix waiting," says Richie. Slowly rising to his feet, using the door handle as a crutch, Julio makes his last stand. Richie waits patiently for Julio to make a move. He wants to punish him before he sends him to the afterlife and completes the end of Felix's reign. Julio became Felix in Richie's eyes. It was time for him to pay for the senseless murders of Chris, Janine, Ren, and Kay, and the attempt on the lives of his crew. Staggering forward, Julio throws a punch. It was sloppy and slow. Richie grabs Julio's wrist and pulls him close, pushing the inside of his elbow down with his forearm. Julio tries to counter

Richie's force by straightening his arm. Richie puts his hand underneath Julio's elbow, moving upward against Julio's force. The bone snaps like a twig. Richie continues pulling Julio's wrist down until bone rips through the skin. Screaming in agonizing pain, Julio falls to his knees, holding his right arm as more of his blood splatters onto Richie's rug.

Richie kicks Julio over and gets on top of him. He glances at William, an older gentleman so close to retirement. There was no reason for him to die, leaving a wife behind to sort out life without her husband. This angered Richie the most because he knew this would bring unwanted attention from the police, especially his Uncle Swift who would now watch his every move. But death came to his doorstep and invited itself in. Richie welcomed it with open arms, toyed with it, but it would leave without him. He puts one hand behind Julio's head and the other on his chin. He twists Julio's head slowly. Julio tries to hold his neck steady and grabs at Richie's arm, continuing to fight for his life. Richie continues twisting, pushing Julio's neck muscles to their limits. He knows that death is certain, so he relaxes and lets Richie have his way. A loud snap echoes throughout the hallway. Richie releases Julio's head, letting it fall to the floor. He stands up, steps over the lifeless body and grabs his phone.

"How far are you guys?"

"About ten minutes out," responds T.K.

"Is Tech still in Chicago?"

"Yeah, he's here."

"Get him here asap."

* * *

The doorbell rings. JoAnn, Richie's mom, is upstairs checking on Marble Head. "Who the hell..." she says as she heads downstairs. "Who could be coming by here this time of night?"

She opens the door and sees a man she's known for many years. She has a quick flashback to when they were high school sweethearts before Marble Head and Swift ran him off. "Well, well, well. Look what the dog brought in," says JoAnn, greeting her visitor.

"JoAnn, you look just as beautiful as you did in high school."

"Thank you, Mr. Edwards," says JoAnn, blushing. "I see you're still handsome and fit. I guess all those times my brothers were chasing you away paid off." They both share a brief smile. "So, what brings you by here?"

"I need to talk to Marble Head. It's very important." She invites him into the house and walks him upstairs. "Stay here," she says before opening Marble Head's bedroom door.

"Who was that at the door?" asks Marble Head. JoAnn stands to the side as Marble Head leans forward in his recliner to see who this guest could be. The man walks through the doorway. Marble Head sits back in his chair and puts his TV on mute. He places the remote control on his leg, puts his hand in the pocket on the side of the recliner, and grabs his weapon.

"How can I help you, Elder?"

* * *

The crew finally arrives at Richie's condo. They step off the elevator surprised to see the doorman slumped in his chair outside of Richie's front door. They walk up to Richie's open door and immediately see Julio lying on his back with his face nearly parallel to the floor. Richie is in the kitchen pouring himself a cup of tea. "Anybody want tea? I have honey in the cabinet." No one answers. "Where's Tech?"

"He should be here in a few minutes," responds KAP.

"Good! We have about an hour to decide how to move forward with this situation."

"You okay?" asks Damawi.

"I'm fine," replies Richie. She walks over to him and hugs him. The rest of the crew follow suit. They're happy to have him back. Tech walks through the door. "What the hell went on here?"

"Tech, can you access the building's security system and erase all the footage for today?"

"I have my stuff in the car. I'll take a look." Tech hurries back downstairs.

"What are you thinking, Richie?" asks T.K.

"My uncle is already suspicious of me. This would permanently put me on his radar. We have to clean this up as much as possible. A dead doorman downstairs is better than a dead doorman and an unknown man with his neck broken in my hallway. Feel me?"

Tech calls Richie's phone from his car downstairs. "This system is basic. I can erase everything and put my trojan horse in the system, so no one can access it. So how this works is—"

"How long will it take?" asks Richie, interrupting Tech before he geeks out.

"Ten, fifteen minutes tops."

"Okay, do your thing. I would love to hear about your horse later, Tech. KAP, take Mr. William back downstairs and put him back behind his desk. We have about an hour before his relief comes. D, check the elevator for blood and prints; wipe the access buttons clean and tidy up the hallway. Let's move fast." Brick grabs Julio's feet and drags him out of the doorway. He wraps the body up in garbage bags and drops it down the garbage shoot.

Forty-five minutes later, everyone's tasks are complete. Before they depart, Brick and the crew drive around the back of the building and retrieve Julio's body. As Brick drives past Richie's condo, the team watches as William's replacement walks inside of the building. "Has anybody noticed how Richie acts after he kills someone? The dude offered us tea, bruh," says KAP, shaking his head.

"When we went through that crew a few years back, he was throwing bodies down the stairs like stuffed laundry bags, making a game out the shit," says T.K.

"He be on some other shit," says KAP.

"I swear if Richie was just a few shades lighter, he'd be a serial killer," adds T.K.

* * *

Chicago police officers respond to a call about a murder at the Vista Tower Luxury Condominiums. They quickly clear the area and secure the crime scene while they wait for the homicide detectives to arrive. Moments later, Detective Coles arrives with Detectives Neeley and Teddy Cooper, a new detective assigned under Detective Coles. They walk into the lobby and see the victim in his chair with a white sheet over his body. Detectives Neeley and Cooper walk over to the police officers who first arrived on scene, asking them about what they found and who called it in. Detective Coles walks behind the counter to view the body. He removes the sheet and says, "Now this is just fucked up. A man can't even go to work and earn a living these days." He pulls out a sticky note, writes on it, rolls it up, and places it in the victim's hand. He puts the sheet back over him and steps away.

"Cooper, front and center." Detective Cooper quickly walks over to Detective Coles, followed by Detective Neeley. "This is your first case, correct?"

"Yes, sir," replies Detective Cooper.

"I want you to look over the body for any clues that might help us." Detective Cooper promptly walks over to the body and removes the sheet. After carefully scanning the body, he notices a piece of paper rolled up in the victim's right hand. "Detective, detective!" calls out Detective Cooper. Detectives Coles and

Neeley walk over to Detective Cooper. "Look, there's a piece of paper in his right hand."

"Do you have your gloves and tweezers?" asks Detective Coles.

"Yes, sir!"

"Well, retrieve it, detective. It could be a major clue." Detective Cooper quickly takes his rubber gloves from his coat pocket, puts them on, and grabs his tweezers. With a steady hand, he carefully removes the paper from the victim's hand. Detective Neeley stands by wondering if this note could really help the case. "Open it," commands Detective Coles. Cooper opens the note and reads it aloud: "FUCK YOU ROOKIE." Detective Cooper stands there dumbfounded. Detective Neeley covers his mouth and walks away, trying not to laugh in the rookie's face.

Chief Watkins arrives at the scene, and Detective Coles walks over to meet him just outside of the entrance. "What's up, boss?"

"What do we have?"

"Doorman took one to the face. The video recording has been wiped clean. It's like it never existed. The only thing we have is a half empty Pizzeria Uno box, a shell casing, and the round that's still inside the victim's head."

"Okay, let Detective Neeley take charge of the crime scene. Come with me; I want to check on my nephew." Chief Watkins puts his badge in the scanner and takes the elevator to the seventy-fifth floor. Richie is still in the kitchen when he hears a knock on the door. He opens the door. "Uncle Swift, what's going on?" Detective Coles looks from Richie to Chief Watkins, shocked and confused. He had no idea they were related. "The doorman downstairs was killed, just checking on you."

"Come on in and have a seat," says Richie.

"Oh, this is Detective Brian Coles, my lead detective."

"How are you, detective? Can I get you anything?" asks Richie as they shake hands.

"No, no. I'm fine," says Detective Coles. "Nice place you got here."

Chief Watkins proceeds to ask Richie a series of questions concerning guests and residents and all the security measures they have in place in case of matters like this. After a few minutes, Detective Coles stands up. "Boss, I'm going to head downstairs and check on my detectives." He walks over to the door behind Chief Watkins and signals Richie to call him.

Ten minutes later and after a cup of coffee, Uncle Swift gets up to leave and meet with Detective Coles. Richie walks him to the door. "Thanks Uncle Swift for checking on me."

"No problem, nephew. Just make sure you stay safe. Do you have a weapon?"

"I do."

"Good." Uncle Swift turns around and looks over Richie's shoulder toward the kitchen.

"Can you bring me a chair, Richie?"

"Sure, unc." Richie walks to the kitchen for a chair. Uncle Swift yells for him to bring a butter knife too. Richie thinks, *What the hell he need a chair and a butter knife for?* Richie returns with the items. "Thanks, nephew." Uncle Swift takes the chair and puts it against the wall near the entrance to the kitchen. He steps on it and sticks the butter knife into a hole in the wall. A bullet hole left from Julio's weapon. Richie screams internally, *FUCK!* Uncle Swift digs the round out of the wall and steps down. "Now, this is odd," says Uncle Swift. He puts the round in a bag, then puts it in his coat pocket. Richie stands there staring at his uncle speechless. *If he matches that round with the one in William's head...,* thinks Richie. Uncle Swift walks out the door and pushes the down button. Richie stares at his uncle's back while he silently waits for the elevator. The doors open, and Chief Watkins steps in. Before the door closes, he looks at Richie. "Tell my sister I said hi." The doors close, and the elevator descends to the lobby.

* * *

Just before midnight, Richie calls Detective Coles. "Brian, can you talk?"

"I'm clear," says Brian. "The million-dollar question is why didn't you tell me that chief is your uncle? That would've been good information to know."

"Brian, if I would've told you that, you would've moved differently. I need you all the way in." Brian had no response because he knew Richie was right. He wouldn't have been as forthcoming. Working directly for Richie's uncle, who's known as the executioner throughout the police force, would give anyone second thoughts about supporting any cause outside of police work. "So, what you got for me, Brian?"

"I got a few things. Detective Russell did dirty the crime scene. He removed the tapes from the recorders. His lawyer turned them in. He's being charged and facing jail time. The recordings show three assailants, two males and a female. We're looking for a Curtis Walker. The tattoo in the video is identical to his file. He has a kid with a chick named Jordan McVeigh, who we suspect was also one of the assailants, and a Roland Outlaw, a known associate. We believe Curtis and Roland were tipped off that we're looking for them. We have Jordan, but she's not talking."

"This is great news, Brian. Thanks, and keep me posted."

"Question before we hang up. What was it like growing up with the chief as your uncle?"

"Always serious, laughs maybe once or twice a year. I haven't confirmed it, but I heard he wears his holster when he has sex." They both laugh.

"That's funny. If I hear anything, Richie, I'll call you."

* * *

The next morning, the crew gather at Josephine's for a meeting. They're all in the party room discussing Richie's trip, filling him in on what happened while he was away, and making plans for the organization now that they're working directly with Mr. Gamboa. They also decide to reopen Josephine's for business and to relax security measures until further notice. After the meeting, Richie asks Damawi to stay behind. "When was the last time you spoke to Jordan?" Richie asks.

"She called me the other day, but we had a lot going on. So, I ain't call her back yet."

"Well, she was picked up by the police the other day, and they're questioning her about the corner store incident and her two friends. Did you know she had a baby by Curtis?"

"Yes, she told me."

"So, what do you think? Is she worth saving?"

"Everyone is worth saving, Richie. You should know that better than anybody."

"Okay, if Curtis folds when the police catch up to him, the best we can do is to provide good representation. Call Alex and have him send one of his lawyer buddies to get her out of there." Damawi nods, and they head into her office to discuss the upcoming play, The Sweetest Temptation, which will be premiering in a few weeks. "Are we sold out?" asks Richie.

"Yes. Friday night and both plays for Saturday are sold out. Sunday, we have about one-thousand seats available," says Damawi.

"Okay, great. We'll sell out Sunday on that Friday because it's payday weekend. Watch. Hold on, D," says Richie as his phone rings. "A, what's going on?" Damawi's phone rings too, so Richie leaves her office and calls T.K. into the party room to listen to his and Arielle's call. As soon as T.K. closes the door, Richie puts the phone on speaker. Arielle goes on to tell Richie and T.K. about how Mr. Gamboa's people saved her and Phillip from Felix's failed assassination attempt and how they're continuing to provide security to protect her and her team. She talks about how she's trying to build her brand to expand support for her agenda throughout Belize. She's lost ground due to the second attempt on her life because the people are fearful that the drug cartels will bring more violence to Belize in order to stop her agenda. Unfortunately, her team can't seem to come up with a strategy that will ensure voters will stay the course and support her agenda until election day.

"What you think, T.K.?" asks Richie.

"Well, your biggest opponent isn't the Democratic Party; it's fear. Politicians use fear to discourage certain agendas. I remember when they pumped fear into people when President Obama ran for office. The Clintons said that because he was black, he could get assassinated like Kennedy did. Somehow, we have to put the focus from you onto something else," advises T.K.

"So how did the word get out about what happened?" asks Richie.

"The Democratic Party started releasing it to the public the next day after it happened and has been keeping it in the news," responds Arielle.

"What have you done to combat what they're doing?" asks T.K.

"We're trying to come up with a strategy, but—" starts Arielle.

"Who was the lady that interviewed you?" Richie asks, interrupting her excuses.

"Her name was Rolanda Evans," says Arielle. "I have an idea. I'll call you back." Richie hangs up with Arielle and immediately calls Enrique to explain the situation and what he wants to do to turn the tides on Arielle's situation. Enrique wouldn't be able to do what Richie wanted without approval, so he goes and gets Mr. Gamboa on the phone.

"Richie, I didn't think we would be talking so soon?"

"Me either, Pedro, but I wanted to run this by you to ensure what I want to do won't affect your name and our business."

"Okay, go ahead." Richie explains his idea. After listening intently to the idea, Mr. Gamboa responds, "It doesn't affect me, Richie, but our logistics will change. Are you okay with that?"

"Yes, I planned on coming straight to you for a while, and after she wins, we can go back to the original arrangement. But I think this move will keep her on top until the polls open next year."

"Okay, Richie, I will do my part."

"Thanks, Pedro."

* * *

That afternoon, Jordan steps outside with the lawyer as Damawi's car pulls up to the police station. "Here's my card, Ms. McVeigh. I'll call you to come to my office in a day or so," says the lawyer, Maximus Price, a young black man in a navy Tom Ford suit. "Thank you," says Jordan. She walks over to Damawi's car and sticks her head in the passenger side window. "Did you send a lawyer to get me out?"

"I did," confirms Damawi. "Get in. Let's talk." Jordan obeys, and Damawi drives off, headed back downtown. "So, you know they have the video showing your baby daddy killing the clerk along with you and the other guy. It's only a matter of time before they catch him."

"They won't. He's smart," says Jordan a little too quickly.

"So smart that he didn't cover up his tattoo. That's how the police figured it out. It's not if he gets caught; it's when he gets caught. And when he gets caught, that's when you go down for accessory to murder and robbery. If there's ever a time when you need to take my advice, young lady, it needs to be today. If you love your son like I know you do, you have to protect him by any means necessary."

"I love my son with all my heart, Ms. D."

"Well tell me how you can love and protect him while you're in jail?" Jordan drops her head to her chest because she doesn't have an answer. "He'll be in the foster care system, and you already know how that will be for him. You're protecting a man who has no respect for you or your well-being."

"He respects me at times."

"At times? Jordan, he puts his hands on you."

"He just going through some things. He told me he'll change."

"Baby, the only thing he'll change is the hands he puts on you. He'll never change. He'll just change women once you have nothing else to give." When Damawi pulls into Josephine's parking lot, Jordan asks, "Who's Josephine?"

"It's my favorite aunt."

So, you own this?" asks Jordan, surprised. Damawi cuts her eyes at Jordan because she is frustrated with Jordan and so many of the young queens who are in similar situations. She simply nods her head yes before getting out of the car. As they walk through the door, Jordan is amazed at how the club looks on the inside. She is used to the hood clubs and the hole-in-the-wall spots where all the drug dealers and hood rats hang out. Damawi leads Jordan to her office and says, "Sit down," as she closes the door. "How many times has he put you to the hospital?" asks Damawi, walking over to her desk. Jordan pauses before she answers.

"Five times," replies Jordan.

"Really? Five times? What for?"

"Black eyes, bruised ribs, a concussion, and I've had two anxiety attacks."

Damawi gets up from behind her desk and sits in the chair next to Jordan, looking directly in her eyes. "Jordan, sweetheart, that's not love. You haven't experienced real love. Love don't put you in the hospital. He's been abusive the whole time y'all been together. How long did it take after you started dating for him to put his hands on you? Did he hit you while you were pregnant or afterwards? Has he done it in front of Amari?" Jordan starts to cry, answering Damawi's questions through her sobs. "I just wanted my son to have his dad in his life."

"Follow me, Jordan." Damawi leads Jordan out of her office onto the balcony overlooking the club. "You see that gentleman right there?" asks Damawi, pointing at Richie, who is sitting at a table on the first floor. "His father was in and out, mostly out, of his life since he was one years old."

"He's the guy that was with you in the car that night."

"Yup, that's him. You see that gentleman over there?" Damawi points at KAP. "His dad was murdered when he was two. He doesn't even remember his dad. And that's T.K.; his father passed when he was barely a teenager. They all feel the effects from not having a father, but they had good men around them. It takes a village. They may not be perfect, but they are successful black men." Jordan nods her head, understanding what Damawi is getting at. They walk back into Damawi's office. "So, you have two choices, Jordan: Protect your son or go to jail. Your son will be fine. Put good men around him, and he will flourish. But if you don't protect him, he'll turn out just like his dad."

"Why are you helping me? You said I was responsible for killing your nephew. Why help?"

"You are, along with your baby daddy and his friend... and so am I. So are those cops who gunned him down. As well as the systemic racism that kills so many of us. But I need you to be a success story so my nephew wouldn't have died in vain. Take one, make one. You got thirty minutes to decide." Damawi walks out of her office and leaves Jordan there to think about her offer.

Marble Head texts Richie, telling him they need to talk. Richie replies: "I'll be there later tonight." He then looks up at the team and announces, "I'm making a food run. My treat. What's the pick?"

"Let's do Joe's. I feel like some seafood," suggests T.K. Richie gets everyone's approval and jots down their orders.

"What about Brick?" asks KAP, looking over at Brick, who's asleep in a booth.

"Don't wake him," says Richie. "I got him."

"They deliver?" asks KAP.

"They do, but that's too many hands on my food. The person cooking it, another person that puts it in the to-go boxes, the cashier, and then the driver. It'll taste different when we get it. I'm gonna pick it up."

KAP laughs. "Man, I never thought about it that way. I'll drive."

They hop into KAP's SUV and head for Joe's. "So, our shipments all made it to their destinations. The New York cats were tripping off the autonomous car, bruh," says KAP.

"I'm sure they were. I'm still tripping," jokes Richie.

"But yo, we thought you wasn't coming back for real tho. You went like a real G."

"Me either. I thought I was done for. But you held it down when I was gone. It may not mean as much to you now, but once we get back to normal, it's yours. You can have the keys."

"Man, that means the world to me, my dude!! Straight up!" says KAP, excited.

"I'll find more organizations just like ours and push the movement all over the country. Just give me time," says Richie. They shake hands, and KAP gets emotional.

"I love you, dude, just know that," says KAP as he pulls up to a stoplight.

Richie smiles and says, "I love you too, bro." Something in the side mirror catches KAP's eye. He glances over his shoulder out the window and sees a black truck driving up slowly alongside them with a man hanging out the passenger side. His upper torso is sticking out the window, and he's holding an assault rifle.

"Richie, get down!!!"

CHAPTER 13

Broken glass rains down like hail throughout the SUV as bullets penetrate the vehicle from all sides. Richie ducks down, removes his seat belt, and opens the passenger side door, falling out of the vehicle to avoid the onslaught of bullets. KAP unfastens his seat belt and tries to jump out the passenger side door with Richie. KAP screams as multiple bullets penetrate his back. He folds over as he continues to make his way over the center console out the passenger door. He finally slides out the vehicle and lands onto Richie's legs. "I'm hit, I'm hit! Aww fuck, I'm hit!" Richie leans back and looks underneath KAP's truck, watching as the gunmen's vehicle slowly passes by. He knows they're going to attempt to finish the job. The back of KAP's shirt is soaked with blood. Richie rolls KAP off of his legs and sees blood spots on his shoulder and chest, getting bigger by the second. Richie sneaks inside KAP's SUV and grabs a gun out of the glove box. He slides away from the vehicle and lies flat on his stomach, tracking the vehicle and waiting for the gunmen inside. KAP lies on the ground next to Richie, gasping for air. Richie listens as the gunmen step out of their vehicle and walk over to KAP's SUV. One of them opens the back passenger door on the driver side, checking to see if Richie and KAP are dead.

Richie pops up from the side of the vehicle, catching the gunman off guard. When the man raises his gun to fire, Richie already has him in his sights and pulls the trigger. The bullet strikes the gunman in the neck, and he collapses into the back seat, clinching his bloody neck. The other gunman opens fire, spraying the area with bullets. Richie ducks down and makes his way around the back of the SUV toward the driver side. There's a car stopped behind him; the driver frozen from shock. The driver has her hands up while the passenger is recording the fire fight with his phone. Richie peeks around KAP's vehicle, watching as the getaway driver pulls the wounded gunman into the backseat. "Come on, come on! Let's get the fuck up outta here!" screams the driver as he runs around the front of the vehicle and jumps in the driver's seat. The other gunman walks backward to the front passenger seat, trying to prevent Richie from sneaking up on him. When he finally turns around to get in the vehicle, Richie fires two shots, hitting the gunman in the back.

The truck pulls off with him barely in the car; the door closes onto his body as they drive away out of control. Richie turns his focus on the car behind him. He approaches the driver's side with his gun pointing directly at her. Everyone in the car screams as he smashes the driver side window with the butt of the gun. "Erase it," Richie screams, now aiming his gun at the guy in the passenger seat. He nervously erases the recording. "Give it here." He promptly hands Richie the phone. Richie looks at the driver and calmly says, "Wallet." She reaches down and grabs her wallet from the side of the door. "Driver's license." A nervous wreck, she opens her wallet and hands him her license. "What did we just see? Nothing, right?" They both frantically nod their heads. "I'll be in touch."

Richie runs back over to KAP. Blood is flowing onto the concrete. Faintly, KAP utters, "Ahh fuck." Richie lifts up his shirt and sees bullet holes in his chest and shoulder. He grabs some napkins from his center console and presses some against the chest wound. "Ahhhhhh!" cries out KAP. "Put pressure on this," says Richie as he replaces his hand with KAP's. He then rolls him over and pulls up his shirt to check out his back. Richie sees the wound and thinks, *Fuck!* He pushes the rest of the napkins into the wound. KAP screams. "I know it hurts dude, but I gotta slow down the bleeding." Richie returns KAP to lying on his back. "I need you to help me pull you up," says Richie. Richie opens the back passenger door then grabs KAP's shirt at each shoulder, pulling him up and into the truck. KAP, in agonizing pain, uses whatever strength he has left to help himself to his feet. Once KAP is secure in the back seat, Richie runs to the driver's side and takes off toward Northwestern Memorial Hospital.

* * *

Detectives Coles and Neeley arrive at Josephine's to speak with Jordan. She's in the party room waiting with Damawi and the lawyer, Maximus Price. Gina leads the detectives up to the room. When everyone has introduced themselves, they all sit down to listen to Jordan recap, off the record, what happened on the night of the corner store robbery. After she finishes with her story, the detectives and Maximus Price go into Damawi's office to call the district attorney for a deal. "So, what do you think will happen?" asks Jordan.

"Maximus is a good lawyer," responds Damawi. "He'll work out a deal that will help you. If you know Curtis and Roland's whereabouts, that would definitely help your case." Damawi's phone vibrates. It's a text to the crew from Richie: "911 Taking KAP to Northwestern Memorial." She immediately stands up and walks out of the room, leaving a confused Jordan behind. T.K. and Brick are running up the stairs toward her to see if she got the news.

"Yo, we bout to head that way," says T.K.

"I'll be there as soon as I finish up here," says Damawi. Brick and T.K. run back downstairs and rush to the hospital.

"What's going on, Ms. D? Is everything okay?" asks Jordan, standing in the doorway.

"Jordan, let's just focus on you right now, sweetheart." Maximus walks back into the party room. "The DA is willing to play ball, but Jordan, you have to be transparent with every single thing they want to know about Curtis, Roland, any gang and drug activity from your neighborhood, and other robberies or murders that you know about or been involved in. Your testimony will remain anonymous to protect you, so you and Amari can have a life. If you don't provide everything they're asking, then the deal is off. I hope you understand."

"I do," replies Jordan.

"What's the next step?" asks Damawi.

"We have to go to the station with the detectives to get a sworn statement for the DA. Will your son be good while you're at the station?" asks Maximus.

"Yeah, he's with my aunt."

"Good. Let's go." Maximus and Jordan leave for the police station with the detectives. Damawi runs to her office and grabs the power of attorney paperwork for KAP. She faxes it over to hospital admissions and then puts the original in her purse to take to the hospital with her.

* * *

Brick and T.K. arrive at the emergency room and immediately spot Richie in the waiting area. "Yo! What happened?" asks T.K. Richie quickly and quietly recaps the attempted hit on him and KAP. "Who do you think this came from?" asks T.K.

"If not Felix, then I have no idea," says Richie.

"It could've come from Maurice," suggests T.K. "One of Felix's men did say that Felix was looking for Maurice to take over."

"Maurice doesn't have the crew, the knowledge, or the means to do what we do." Tech walks in, panicked. "How's KAP? What the fuck happened?" he asks frantically. Damawi walks up, and T.K. walks with Tech and her outside to explain what he knows. Brick and Richie just sit there quietly. Nearly two hours pass, and there's still no word on KAP's condition. Richie steps outside to get some air and try to clear his thoughts. As soon as he takes a deep breath, messages and missed call notifications flood his phone. He checks his phone and sees four missed calls and a text message from

Marble Head. He calls him back. "Nephew, I thought you was coming by here tonight. We need to talk."

"I know, unc. Listen, KAP got hit two hours ago. He's in bad shape. I'm with the crew at Northwest. What's up?"

"Damn, sorry to hear that. I hope he pulls through. I just wanted to tell you about this visit I had today." Marble Head tells Richie about Elder's visit, not in great detail but enough for Richie to connect the dots on who made the hit and why. Richie is furious. "What's your move?" asks Marble Head.

"Everybody goes!"

"What about Elder?"

"What about him? Did you give him any info that I need to know about?" asks Richie, very short on patience.

"Nah, I just let him do all the talking."

"We'll see," says Richie.

"Nephew, if you dance, they'll know who's throwing the party. Then you'll have all the vice lords coming to the dance. Let me make some phone calls to see if this can be handled—"

"No, unc," Richie interrupts. "Then who's next to party? The Cobra Stones? The Disciples? We have to put the word out again because obviously, they forgot."

"I understand, nephew. Be careful."

* * *

Kenyatta calls Maurice to give him an update on the situation. "Yo, we came at Richie. He took two of ours, but we got his man though."

"That nigga got nine lives! What his peoples look like?"

"Muscled up, playboy, brown-skinned nigga."

"Oh shit! That's KAP. Good shit. So, he knows it was you?"

"Nah, we ain't leave no bodies behind."

"Good. When you sending another round at him?"

"In a couple days. Letting it die down. We come too soon, and he'll be expecting it. You heard from the connect?"

"Nah, he'll pop his head in I'm sure. He got people looking for that nigga too. He won't show until he dead."

"Aight," says Kenyatta, "I'll let you know when we gone snap."

* * *

Tech comes outside. "Richie, the ER doctor is here."

"Unc, I'll talk with you later." He runs back inside as the crew surrounds the doctor. "Hi, I'm Doctor Kirkpatrick, one of the doctors that's stabilized Mr. Pettaway."

"How's he doing?" asks Damawi.

"We've stabilized him enough for surgery. Does he have any medical history we should be concerned about that wasn't included in his power of attorney?"

"Not that I'm aware of," replies Damawi.

"Well, we're moving him upstairs for surgery. Since information was given to the detectives already, you can go upstairs to the waiting area while we operate."

"Is he going to be alright, doc?" asks Richie.

"Sorry, the OR surgeon will be better suited to answer that question." The doctor walks away, and the crew gathers their things and heads upstairs. Once upstairs, the team sits away from everyone in the waiting area to discuss what Marble Head told Richie. "So, how are we going to respond?" asks T.K.

"Once we get the word that KAP is out of surgery, we're going to annihilate Kenyatta and his front line within forty-eight hours. Maurice within forty-eight hours after that. Tech, get the drones prepared to take flight once we leave here."

"You know I'm on it."

After three hours, Richie and Tech are the only ones still sitting in the waiting area while the rest of the crew is off wandering around. Damawi is standing just a few feet away, leaning against a wall and looking through her phone. "You know, life sure is short," says Tech. "And regardless of what happens in that operating room, I can say that KAP lived a full life."

"I agree with that, but let's not go there," says Richie.

"You see that woman right there? She loves you." Tech pauses to look Richie in the eyes. "The whole team knows it. One thing I know from being involved with what we do: life is short. That could be you in that room getting operated on. What if you didn't make it, and you leave here not knowing what could have happened, and you leave her feeling the same? No one cares about your 'rule' but you, dude. You're about the movement; I get it. But who's for Richie? Even Martin and Malcolm had wives. I know you think I'm just this genius, sexual tyrannosaurus with a huge penis, but I know some shit. Just my two cents." Richie doesn't say anything. They continue to look at each other and then Richie pushes his fist out toward Tech, who smiles big and bumps Richie's fist, harder than what was required. They go back to sitting in silence, and Richie and Tech both look over at Damawi.

"Hey, Richie."

"What's up, Tech?"

"Can I watch?"

The surgeon comes out to the waiting area and calls out for the Pettaway family. Richie and Tech walk over to where Damawi is standing, and T.K. and Brick walk up from around the corner. "What's up, James? How's KAP?" asks Richie.

"Well, Richie, he was shot four times. One in his left shoulder, two in his back and one in his buttocks. The bullet that went into his left buttocks hit and fractured his pelvic bone before it ricocheted and exited out the side. The shot to his left shoulder went clean through. Those issues have been addressed. The remaining two shots entered through his upper back. One went straight through, missing all major organs and arteries. The second one, however, did some damage. We did a CT scan of his chest and abdomen, and found that the bullet punctured his right lung and left bullet fragments in the right side of his chest. He also had some internal bleeding in his abdomen. Luckily, we were able to stop the internal bleeding, so he's out of danger now, and we're patching him up. He'll pull through and make a full recovery, but he has a long road ahead of him."

"Thanks, James," says Richie.

"We'll move him into a room in a few more hours. He won't be responsive until tomorrow, so come back at noon. He needs his rest."

* * *

It's nighttime, and Rolanda Evans is walking to her car, leaving the Channel 3 news studio to head home. Right before she reaches for her door handle, a black sedan with tinted windows pulls up alongside her. The back window rolls down, and it's Arielle sitting in the back seat. One of her security guards exits the vehicle and holds open the door, so Rolanda can get in. "Sorry, Ms. McCallister, I don't have time to talk to you. I have to hurry home to my child." The guard opens his blazer, showing Rolanda his gun holstered on his waist. Her mind quickly changes, and she does a quick scan of the area before getting into the back seat with Arielle. The guard hops in the front, and they drive away. "You set me up," starts Arielle. "You didn't tell me about your surprise segment because you wanted an emotional response for your viewers, and it almost got me and someone I care dearly about killed."

"That wasn't my intentions," says Rolanda. "I just wanted the people of Belize to see a different side of you."

"Well, they did, and I'm losing support because of you. So that was all your doing."

"No, my manager said it would be a good idea."

"Marc is a devoted democrat, Rolanda. We're both Black women trying to advance in a male-dominated world. You sold me out. But I promise you this. I will win this election, and when I do, I'll cut you so deep you won't be able to interview a brick wall. And If I lose…" Arielle's security turns around, pulls his shades down to show his eyes, and stares at Arielle briefly before turning back around.

"What do you need me to do?" asks Rolanda.

* * *

After KAP's successful surgery, he's transferred to his recovery room. Once the crew gets confirmation that he has been moved, Richie encourages everyone to go home and get some rest. "The detectives are staying here until KAP wakes up to ask questions. He's safe," says Richie, trying to reassure the crew and himself that KAP will be okay. "Tech, when you wake up in the morning, get all the personal information you can on Kenyatta White. We need those drones following his every move until we strike. The gunmen were driving a dark blue Lincoln Navigator, so see if you can find out who was in there."

"Okay, boss."

"I'll wait for D to finish up paperwork and head home. Remember, we got people looking for us, so be smart. Tech, stay at Brick's." Brick, Tech, and T.K. head to rest up at Brick's house while Richie waits for Damawi to finish up with admissions. When she comes back to the waiting area, she asks, "Where is everyone?"

"They're headed over Brick's. We have to stay teamed up, so... you ready?"

"Yea. I'm so glad KAP's going to be okay. I understand we doing this for the greater good, but this part of it I can do without." As soon as they walk outside the emergency room doors, Richie detours over to the bushes and picks up KAP's gun. He looks around, checking for any passersby, and puts the gun in the back of his pants. They get into her car and leave for Richie's house. Twenty-minutes later, they pull into his parking garage, park, and take the elevator to his place. The Vista Tower's security guard stationed inside the elevator stands by until Richie goes inside and clears the condo. "You want something to eat?" asks Richie, walking into the kitchen.

"No, I'm fine. You need to get out those clothes," says Damawi, staring at Richie's blood-stained clothing. They both look at each other then look away awkwardly.

"You're right. Mi casa, es su casa," says Richie as he heads to his bedroom to get ready for a shower. He closes his bedroom door then looks down at the amount of KAP's blood on his shirt. He pulls it off and then looks at his pants; it's the same. Splotches of KAP's blood are all over his pants. He takes them off, puts on his robe, and goes into the kitchen to throw away the bloody clothing. Damawi is gone. He looks down the hall toward the other bedroom and sees the light on. He turns around and walks back into his bedroom and into the bathroom, immediately taking off his robe. He turns the water up as hot as he can bear it; steam fogs up the glass surrounding the shower as he steps in. Water runs down the back of his neck, and he watches as the bloody water rolls over his body and down the drain. He replays the shootout in his mind. Thinking about how he almost lost KAP makes him reminisce on when they first met back in the navy well over twenty years ago.

Richie went to the club on base his first night there after reporting to his second duty station in Norfolk, VA. Three dudes were standing outside the bathroom talking about how they were going to bum rush this dude named Pettaway in the parking lot when the club closed. That was a normal after-the-club activity on post, so he paid it no mind. When Richie entered the bathroom, there was a guy standing in there on the phone. "Well, how the fuck did he find out? Why he all up in your photos? Did he say it was big?" Richie laughed, and the guy looked at Richie and laughed as well. "He coming up here? Let em come! I ain't worried about that clown! You still coming over? Why? You scared? Ahh, you be bullshitting. I'll call you later." The guy hung up the phone as Richie was washing his hands. He was heading out the door when Richie called out, "Yo, bruh, yo name Pettaway?"

Caught off guard, the guy responded, "Yeah. Why? What's up?"

"It's three dudes waiting outside the bathroom saying they gone tune yo ass up in the parking lot when the club close."

"Straight up? What they look like?"

"Them niggas in the gym fo sho, but that ain't got shit to do with nothing. Hearts prolly pump kool-aid."

"True dat. What's your name, B?"

"I'm Richie."

"Aight, dude. I'm Kali." They shook hands.

"Aight, let's walk out like we been cool, and let's see how them niggas carry it," said Richie.

Richie smiles thinking about their friendship. He's finishing up washing his body when he hears the bathroom door open. He glances over his shoulder, knowing exactly who it is. Coasting through the steam, Damawi quietly enters the bathroom and makes her way to the shower. Richie turns fully around to watch as Damawi, fully naked, walks over to him. His heart rate increases as he scans her chocolate, athletic body. Her breasts are perky and muscular with large areolas two shades darker than her chocolate complexion. Her nipples are already erect; radars searching for pleasure. She takes her time getting to the shower. Richie doesn't rush her as he's enjoying the view. Her toned abdomen and leg muscles flex with each step she takes. Richie stares intensely into her eyes, like two laser beams piercing Damawi's confidence.

She avoids his gaze and instead scans his body as he stands back, allowing her to see him fully. She envisions him penetrating her as her eyes travel down his long chiseled chest over his sculpted abdomen and down to his manhood nestled between muscular thighs. Richie walks backward under the waterfall-style showerhead, the water flowing over his body, until his back touches the glass wall. Damawi follows him through the waterfall, her short bob now wet and wavy. Her breasts press into his abdomen as he wraps his arms around her waist. She gently strokes his chin, bruised from the fight a day prior.

"Which rules do you want to change?" asks Richie. She stands on her tiptoes, launching her face toward his and grabbing the back of his head the moment their lips touch. Their tongues intertwine, Damawi sucking on Richie's tongue whenever he pushes it into her mouth. Richie pulls back and tries to speak. "Which rules—" She pulls him back to her and kisses him deeply. Richie feels the blood flowing downward as his manhood begins to rise. Damawi's pearl tingles as she feels his masculine energy against her body. Suddenly, she breaks away, then walks backward into the waterfall. He follows her, keeping his eyes connected to hers. She turns around to walk out the shower, and he stares at her inverted heart-shaped ass and quietly utters, "Damn." He's said it in his mind many times before when she walks away. Damawi grabs a towel from the rack and heads into his bedroom. He grabs a towel too, drying his body off as he quickly moves to catch up with her. She is baiting her big fish.

Richie walks through the doorway to his bedroom; Damawi isn't there. He scans the room, noticing she lit the candles throughout, looking for her chocolate body. He whispers to himself, "Where did she go?" Surprisingly, she wraps her arms around his waist from behind, startling Richie and making him jump slightly from her quiet attack. She licks the back of his neck, then kisses along the same trail. Richie smiles. She pushes him forward with enough strength to move him a few feet. When he turns around, she closes in, pressing her body against his. She returns to her tiptoes, putting her hands behind his head and forcing it down until his lips meet hers. She runs her tongue across his lips, sucks on his bottom lip, and then releases it. She pushes on his chest, forcing Richie to fall onto the bed. He lands on his back and uses his elbows to push himself backward to the middle of the bed. She climbs onto the bed slowly while she slides her hands between his legs, pushing them apart so her body can fit between them. She has control over him now, her puppet on a string. Their eyes connect as she slowly crawls between his legs, gathering saliva in her mouth, preparing her tongue to be slippery and warm. Placing her hands on the outside of his thighs, she lowers her head to the base of his manhood and gently licks upward along the shaft until she reaches the tip. She rotates her tongue around the crown, sending tingling sensations throughout his manhood. He inhales deeply as he bites his lower lip.

"Let's talk about your rule: mixing business…" She returns to the base and slowly licks upward once more, covering the underside of his shaft entirely with her saliva. "…with pleasure," she says before gently sucking on the tip of his manhood. Richie closes his eyes and opens his mouth slightly, trying to breath through the pleasure her tongue brings him. She repeats her exploits. "Do you agree with removing it?" Damawi asks between licks.

"Yes," replies Richie, meeting her eyes.

"Don't I handle my business and your business well."

"Yes, you always do." She grips the base of his manhood with her right hand and moves it downward toward his jewels, standing his erection straight up. Her business persona hid the sexual prowess she now displays. Richie often wondered how making love to her would be. He believed her to be submissive, intimidated, soft. He was wrong. He couldn't have imagined that she would be so confident and skilled. He was eager to see what more she had to offer.

"You know I want you, Richie. Can we have business and pleasure?" She gathers more saliva in her mouth and licks around his tip once more before fully inserting him into her mouth. His back arches and his toes curl as he inhales deeply through clenched teeth. He watches her as the light from the candles makes his shaft glisten as she moves hungrily up and down his manhood. Richie attempts to put his hands on her head, but she grabs them and pins them both to his sides. She continues to devour him handsfree, going deeper and deeper until her lips are touching the base of his shaft. She releases his hands and starts stroking his manhood. She returns to sucking slowly on the tip, pausing only to ask, "Can we do both?"

"Yes," is all Richie can say. Never breaking her rhythm, Damawi slowly rotates her body from between his legs until his head is between her knees, and he's in the perfect position to taste her sweet nectar. She's dripping wet, and he's eager to get a taste. He lightly licks her juicy lips, and she moans as she continues pleasing him. He tightly grips her cheeks as he pulls her pearl into his mouth. Her body immediately starts to shake, and she tilts her head up, letting out a passionate moan. Richie uses his tongue to toy with her pearl, knowing he now has control over her. Damawi is unable to continue working her magic as her orgasms flow one after another.

Damawi breaks away from the sixty-nine and turns around to face him. Before he can react, she quickly straddles him and smoothly slides his manhood inside of her. Richie arches his back to help her take all of him in. Her eyes close, and her head tilts back as she releases a soft moan into the air. "Uh huh," says Richie, gripping her booty with both hands. She presses her hands into his chest, rocking her hips back and forth as the curve in his manhood rubbed perfectly against her G-spot. Her queensway gripped him tightly with every orgasm.

Richie releases his grip on her booty, and he wraps one arm around her back, pulling her close so he can pull her sweet nipples into his mouth. Damawi lets out a series of moans as her juices come splashing down. She pushes against his chest and away from his mouth, trying to gain some control. He lifts up onto his elbows and grabs her throat and lightly squeezes. Her body shudders unexpectedly. She likes the power, feeling submissive to her boss. He pulls her forward and licks her lips. She continues to rock her hips on his love muscle. He whispers to her, "Go slower. Feel every vein, every inch." The feeling is so intense she tries to stop to gather herself. "No, no, keep stroking. This the dick you ordered, right?"

"Yes," she says in a light moan.

"Is this that dick you dreamed about?"

"Yes!" He sucks in air through clenched teeth as he feels his orgasm knocking at the door. He pulls her close and kisses her deeply as he explodes inside of her, and she shudders from one last orgasm. She collapses onto his chest, still moving her hips. He wraps his arms around her back and squeezes her tightly, getting her to calm down. He then pushes up on her shoulders and kisses the sides of her neck and face. She feels her nectar soaked into his beard against her face. She licks it, then pushes her tongue into his mouth.

Damawi is shocked she actually caught her big fish. The guys she's dated before were nothing compared to Richie. He is her dream man; the one she's been praying for. He's handsome, sexy, focused, intelligent, caring, and committed to his community. Everything she's ever wanted in a man. She lies on top of Richie, completely content. They exchange soft kisses until they both drift off to sleep.

"Yes, yes, yes! Give it to me! Yes…" Richie, tired of hearing the screams coming from his uncle's room, grabbed his Etch A Sketch and went outside onto the front porch to get away. Later, Marble Head came outside, fixing his pants. "Good dick is like Wonder Woman's lasso. Once you put it on dat ass, all the emotions and truths come out and shit. You ready, nephew?" Bzzzzzz, Bzzzzzz, Bzzzzzz. Richie's phone vibrates, interrupting his dream. He carefully moves Damawi off of him and then scans the room for his phone, following the sound of the vibration. When he finds it on the chaise longue, he picks it up and answers the call. "What's up, Tech?"

"Good morning, boss man. I found our guy early this morning. I have the drone sitting on the top of his roof right now. The blue Navigator left about seven minutes ago, probably parked there all night."

"Okay, Tech, good stuff. We'll meet up today to discuss the way forward."

"Sooooooooooooo, how was your night?" Richie looks at Damawi, still sleeping.

"Tell the guys we'll meet up at one at the hospital to check on KAP."

"Okay, I will. Sooooooooooooo—" Richie hangs up. He crawls back into bed and on top of Damawi as she begins to wake up. She raises her head, kisses him, and then stares into his eyes.

"What?" asks Richie, rolling off to her side.

"You have any regrets?"

"Only that we didn't do this sooner." Damawi smiles.

"We can keep us quiet until things level out," she says before kissing him and rolling out of bed. She grabs her towel from the floor and heads into the bathroom to shower. He checks the time on his phone and then follows her.

* * *

The crew piles into KAP's room at Northwestern Memorial to check on his health. He's awake and coherent, happy to see everyone. "What's up?" asks KAP.

"What's up, fam? How you feeling?" asks Richie.

"Like I got hit by a truck, dude. My throat is sore. But I got some good drugs in me, so I'm cool."

"Good. You need anything?"

"Can you stop them cops from constantly coming in here asking me about that shit. I don't remember nothing, man. What happened?"

"We'll talk about it later, bruh. Get some rest." The nurse comes into the room and asks everyone to leave because they need to check his wounds, and he needs his rest. The crew says their goodbyes and heads out. "Richie! Richie!" calls out KAP. Richie turns around, and KAP looks at the nurse. "Ma'am, can you give me a minute please?" The nurse steps away, allowing KAP and Richie a moment alone.

"What's up, brother?"

"Thank you, bro. The doc told me what you did with them napkins. I was losing blood. He said I probably wouldn't be here if it wasn't for that."

"A kidney, a lung, anything you needed to keep you here, it was yours." Richie bends down and kisses KAP on the forehead. "Your peoples on the way here from Cleveland." He starts to walk out. "Oh, I almost forgot." Richie pulls out a napkin he didn't use for KAP's wounds and shows it to him. On it is written, "Sharon 773-444-2333." They both smile as Richie places the napkin on KAP's bedside tray and walks out.

Downstairs in the lobby, Richie explains to the crew how they're going to go after Kenyatta and his crew. "Tech, keep your drone on the vehicle. Whenever it leaves, T.K. and I will strike when the opportunity presents itself. Depending on how many people are in the truck, we'll use the autonomous vehicle to transport them to Lloyd's. If more than three, we'll just have to leave little to no evidence for forensics. Tech, you and D will be at my place. Brick, you ride solo during the first strike then rendezvous and head to Kenyatta's house and go from there."

"The video cameras are already set up in the club to make it seem like we've been there all day, so we can have an alibi. This is close to the hit on you and KAP, so, just in case we're questioned, I got us covered," says Tech. Richie, T.K., and Brick head to Joshephine's to get the vehicles, and Damawi and Tech head to Richie's place.

* * *

"Welcome back to Believe in Belize. I'm Rolanda Evans and next to me is a surprise special guest, Prime Minister Candidate Arielle McCallister. How are you doing, Arielle?"

"I am well, Rolanda! Thank you for inviting me back on the show. What a surprise." Rolanda has an uncomfortable pause.

"So, there were rumors surrounding an attempt on your life because you called out a well-known drug lord on this show. Would you like to share what events took place with that situation?"

"I would. Thank you. Whenever you go against the norm, or you try to make changes for the better, there are people who don't like change and go with the status quo or like situations to stay the same because of the probable involvement that leads to a corruptive outcome. I'm not one of those people. So, yes, there was an assassination attempt on my life. Fortunately, it was a failed attempt. Fortunately, Mr. Felix Navarro was present when this happened. Unfortunately, he will not be called to justice because he is dead." A picture of Felix's lifeless body displays on the screen in the background. The audience gasps.

"My security team handled that situation excellently. Fortunately, I was able to have a short conversation with Mr. Navarro before his transition, and he wanted to clear his conscience before his departure. He said that there was a political agenda by the Democratic Party to have me assassinated because I would learn of the corrupted political officials that are currently serving in our government, and I'm a huge threat to their agenda. I want the people of Belize to know my life is precious, but no more precious than yours. My life's calling is to serve the beautiful people of Belize and be an open book to all, even the ones who don't vote for me when those polls open. We cannot fear death. We must be fearless in righting the wrongs of corrupt individuals. Fredrick Douglas once said, 'if there is no struggle, there is…'" The audience joins in, "no progress!"

"When I'm elected prime minister, there won't be any drugs coming into, across, or from this great Country of Belize. I will defend us by any means necessary."

* * *

Nightfall touches down in Chicago. Richie, Brick, and T.K. are near Kenyatta's house, waiting to make a move. Tech has been hovering the drone around the house trying to get a body count. They all have communication devices in their ears, so Tech can feed them information on their targets. "I think it's about nine guys in the house," says Tech through their earpieces. "It looks like they just finished up with a meeting."

"Okay, get ready. They're heading out," says Richie, looking at T.K. and Brick.

"It's four guys and one of them is a really big guy," says Tech.

"Is he driving?" asks Richie.

"No, front side passenger."

"Okay, Let's get them away from the house so the news won't get back too soon. Then we'll box them in."

"Okay, they'll be passing you guys in about thirty seconds." Tech lands the drone on Brick's truck while T.K. and Richie move to the end of the block. When the Navigator passes by, T.K. pulls onto the road behind them, followed by Brick.

The Navigator drives for about twenty minutes before it pulls into the driveway of another house. As Richie's crew drives by the house, the drone takes off, scanning the area. "We're going to take them down in the house," says Richie. T.K. and Brick park their vehicles in the alley just past the house. They all grab their weapons and attach the silencers, then put on their all-black masks and gloves. "Tech, what do you see?" asks Richie.

"The house barely has furniture in it."

"It's a stash house," says T.K. "When we take them down, we have to rob them too." They quietly approach the back of the house and check the patio door. It's open, so they walk onto the porch and up to the back door. "Locked," announces Richie. T.K. pulls out his tools and starts to pick the lock. After a few seconds, he whispers, "I got it."

"When you hear the doorbell ring, enter," says Richie as he starts making his way off the porch. He runs to the front of the house, walks up the stairs, and rings the doorbell frantically. He then steps to the side of the doorframe where the door opens outward. "Who the fuck is ringing the doorbell like they fucking crazy?" screams the big guy from inside the house. "Gino, go see who the fuck that is."

T.K. and Brick slowly enter through the backdoor and stand inside the hallway, which is dark and off to the side of the kitchen. Richie tucks his gun close to his chest as he hears footsteps coming toward the front door. Gino looks out the front window, checking for the cops, then heads to the front door. A voice coming from the back of the house yells, "Who is it?"

"Some fiend ass nigga trying to get a bump. Yo, we ain't serving tonight, homie," says Gino through the door.

"I'm going outta town, baby. I need a lil something to get me there. I'll pay extra," says Richie, imitating a drug addict. Gino takes his gun out and opens the door as he yells, "Ion give a fu—" Richie swiftly comes around the door and sticks his 9mm in Gino's face. He then smoothly grabs Gino's gun with his free hand and twists the barrel away from him. Gino's fingers get stuck in the trigger loop, and he snatches his fingers out quickly to keep them from breaking. "Shhhhh. Turn around," says Richie. Gino puts his hands up and turns around slowly. Richie shoves the gun into the back of his head and pushes him forward into the living room. "Richie's in," says Tech. T.K. peeks around the corner of the hallway, checking for any movement. He hears voices in the kitchen, but he can't see anyone. Richie is standing at the front door with Gino, waiting.

"What the fuck taking Gino so long," asks one of the dudes in the kitchen. He gets off the bar stool and heads for the front door. "What the fuck? Nigga, who the fuck is you?!" Richie moves his gun up to Gino's shoulder and fires. The bullet strikes the other guy in the nose. The sound of his body hitting the floor alerts the others, and the two men in the kitchen grab their weapons and start running toward the living room. T.K. charges the guys from the behind and shoots the person trailing to the living room in the back of the head. "Drop your weapon!" commands T.K. "No one else has to die." The guy promptly drops his weapon. Richie puts the tip of the silencer on the back of Gino's neck and pulls the trigger.

"Okay, no one else after Gino," says Richie. Brick follows behind T.K., looking for someone to kill. There's only one man standing. "Brick, you feel left out don't cha, big dawg?" Richie takes a deep breath. "Sorry bro, we uphold equal shares in the murder game." He gives Brick the nod, and Brick slowly raises his weapon toward the remaining guy. Richie fires and shoots the man in the head, leaving Brick without a kill. "Man, that's so fucked up!" says T.K., laughing. Brick looks at Richie, scowls, and walks away. "Brick, Brick! Wait! He still moving, Brick." He ignores Richie and goes into the kitchen to look for the stash. Richie looks at T.K. and shrugs his shoulders. He then goes to check upstairs while T.K. searches the living room. Brick grunts loudly from the kitchen. "Hey Richie, Brick found it," calls out T.K. from the living room. Richie runs downstairs to the kitchen. Brick dumps some bags out onto the table; they're full of money. "What are we going to do with the money?" asks T.K.

"One bag will go to my doorman's family," responds Richie, "and the other to whatever KAP wants."

CHAPTER 14

Richie and the crew head over to Kenyatta's place to give him and his people a permanent dirt nap. They park nearly a block away from the home. "Tech, let the bird fly," says Richie. The drone takes off from the back of Brick's truck, travels up the block, and slowly circles around the house, checking if it's occupied. After ten minutes, Tech reports, "I don't see anybody in the house or the basement. There are three cars parked outside, but the house is totally dark. I think you should go check it out."

"Okay, keep the drone on location. We'll be there in a few."

Richie, Brick, and T.K. walk up the alley into Kenyatta's backyard. "Let's make a way for Tech to take a look from the inside," says T.K. Tech hovers the drone over to the crew and lands it next to T.K.'s feet. "Hey T.K., turn the drone upside down and push the button in the center," directs Tech. T.K. follows Tech's instructions, and a smaller drone disconnects from the top of the drone. Brick punches out a window in the back of the house. Tech powers up the smaller drone and activates the night vision as T.K. puts it through the window. They wait. Three minutes later, Tech reports, "Ummm, you can just go on in. I don't think we'll have any more problems out of these assholes."

Richie, Brick, and T.K. look at each, intrigued by Tech's report. They walk into the house with their guns held close to their chests, slowly scanning each room as they walk through the kitchen, the family room, and into the dining room. Brick opens the door to the basement and heads downstairs with T.K. while Richie stands by the door. When he hears them coming back upstairs, Richie starts moving toward the front of the house. He finds the drone hovering over the living room. "Check it out," says Tech as he switches on a light on the drone. The light shines across the floor, revealing five dead bodies lying next to each other. "Hey, turn the lights on," says Richie. Brick turns the lights on in the dining room, and T.K. finds the light switch to the living room.

"What da fuck happened here?" asks Richie. Brick and T.K. start scanning the house, looking for clues as to what could've happened. They find blood streaks on the floor leading from different rooms in the house to the area where the bodies are lined up. Richie walks over to the bodies, all lying face down, looking for Kenyatta. He turns over one that has a huge hole in the back of his head. Jackpot. Kenyetta was shot in his forehead at point blank range. Lying on the floor underneath Kenyatta is his cell phone. Richie grabs it and puts it in his pocket. The bodies are still warm with blood oozing from the bullet wounds. *Whoever did this probably left just before we got here*, thinks Richie.

Brick and T.K. cautiously head upstairs while Richie continues checking the bodies for cell phones or anything that could help them make sense of what happened. "It's clear," says T.K. Tech lands the small drone in T.K.'s hand, so he can reconnect it to the larger one. Richie takes Kenyatta's phone from his pocket and looks through his text messages with Maurice. He fully understands the takeover attempt now. "I don't know what the hell happened here, or why, but—" The sound of a silenced weapon goes off, causing Richie and T.K. to bend down and draw their weapons. Richie then turns around and sees Brick standing over one of the dead men, putting a couple rounds into his chest. Richie stands up and frowns at Brick. "Really?!" Brick shrugs his shoulders. "We good now?" Before Brick can reply, they're startled by bullets flying into the house, shattering the windows and filling the room with glass.

Everyone hits the floor, covering their heads to avoid being struck by bullets and shards of glass. Crawling on his knees and elbows, over dead bodies, Richie makes his way to the corner of a window and carefully peeks out to get a look at who's firing at them. Two men dressed in black Dickies coveralls are firing automatic rifles at the house while two other men hop into a black minivan. The two men firing walk backward toward the van, never taking their eyes off the house or pausing the shooting until they get to the open van door. Once they all pile into the vehicle, Richie lets off shots as the minivan drives away, putting bullet holes in the trunk and back window. "Tech, get that drone airborne!" shouts T.K. The drone takes off from the floor and exits through one of the living room windows. They all jump up off the floor and run out through the back of the house to their van. Brick hops in the driver seat and speeds off, following directions from Tech. "They're heading north on MLK. You need to catch them. This is a single rotor drone, not built for high speeds." Brick accelerates, taking a left onto MLK almost running through a red light. "There they go right there!" says T.K., pointing at the van as it makes a left onto 79th street, heading for the freeway. "Brick, let em go." Frustrated, Brick looks at Richie. "We wearing all black, face masks, and gloves with weapons in the van. Not worth the risk," says Richie. Brick nods then slows down the van and pulls over to wait for the drone to return.

"Any ideas who they were?" asks Richie.

"Whoever they were probably thought that the rest of Kenyatta's crew came by, and they wanted to body everyone he's associated with. No way they knew it was us," says T.K. Richie nods at T.K.'s assessment. "What's the play?" asks T.K.

Richie thinks for a second. "Tech, did you get the license plate?"

"I did, but there's no information available."

"Well, we don't know what we don't know. All the details will come out in the wash in due time." After the drone lands on the roof, Brick heads back to the alley near Kenyatta's to get his truck. Richie reaches into his pocket, pulls out Kenyatta's phone and looks through his text messages. He turns around to T.K. and smiles.

* * *

Maurice gets a late-night text message. Lying in bed, he reaches over and grabs his phone off the nightstand and reads a message from Kenyatta: "We got that nigga," followed by a picture of Richie lying lifeless in the street. "Let me know when you wanna meet. I'll reach out to the rest of the lords." Maurice smiles and texts back: "Good shit. Let's meet up tomorrow at seven in my office." He puts his phone back on his nightstand and looks down at his pleasure for the night.

"Why da fuck you stop? That muthafucka ain't gone suck itself."

* * *

The next morning, Richie is awakened by the vibration of his cell phone. He rolls over and grabs it off the nightstand. "Good morning, Brian."

"Richie, just wanted to give you an update on Jordan." Richie puts his phone on speaker and lays it on his pillow. "She confessed to the robbery and gave us information on her accomplices, Curtis Walker and Roland Outlaw, as well as their whereabouts. We picked them up this morning. She also gave up information on the drug and gang activities in her neighborhood. Good information, but nothing we can use right now. The DA agreed to a strict five-year probational period for her. She has a number of probation requirements she must meet. She breaks it, she'll serve her time effective immediately.

"Brian, thanks for the news and the help."

"No problem, Richie, but I do have a question. How did you find her?"

"I know people, Brian, just like you do."

"Well, whoever you know, tell them thank you. Your uncle, the superintendent, and the mayor were getting a lot of smoke behind this case. Well, I know it's early, and I don't want to keep you.

Hopefully Jordan can start a new life and stay on the straight and narrow. Goodbye, Richie."

"Later, Brian." Richie puts his phone down and looks at Damawi. She holds the side of his face and kisses him. "Thanks, baby." She puts her head back on the side of his chest and smiles.

* * *

Later that evening, Richie and Brick leave the hospital after checking in on KAP and head to H2H's office. It's a quiet ride. Richie is looking out the window, people watching, and thinking about how the night might end. He ponders on all the events that have occured since his birthday. Shortly after that night, he lost some good people and some great friends. KAP was nearly killed. Richie tried to work with Maurice, but due to his greed and mentality, it all comes down to this. Seeing the demise of Maurice will be bittersweet, but there's always a Maurice lurking around the corner. Brick pulls into H2H's parking lot five minutes before seven and parks. None of his little guards are present. *He must be real comfortable thinking his childhood nemesis is dead*, thinks Richie, smiling.

Maurice and Karimah are in the conference room waiting for the lords to arrive. They bought food and alcohol to celebrate the downfall of Richie and his crew. "This shit finna be monumental. We gone take over Chicago, K, and I'm taking you with me. Once we get rid of the mute, take that fucking club over...ain't no stopping us."

"No doubt," says Karimah.

"Let me see where these niggas at, man. It's almost that time."

Richie reaches into the glove box and pulls out his Desert Eagle pistol, which he named One Less. He only uses it for special occasions like this one. Bzzz, Bzzz. Richie pulls out Kenyatta's phone and reads the message from Maurice. "It's on," says Richie to Brick. He texts Maurice: "On the way up." He then looks at Brick, and says, "Come up in ten minutes."

"Aight, Kenyatta n dem on they way up," says Maurice. Richie racks his gun, checking to make sure there's one in the chamber, and walks up the stairs. The conference room door is open, so Richie walks right in with One Less ready to make it one less Maurice in the world. When they see Richie walk into the room, Maurice and Karimah stare at him as if they're looking at a ghost. They both stand up, and Karimah immediately reaches for her gun. "Don't do it. I'll send you the fuck home." Richie walks over to her and takes her weapon from the back of her pants. He then runs his hands down her legs, checking for any additional weapons, and pushes her down in her seat. He walks over to Maurice and says, "Hey, boo boo. You missed me?" He checks Maurice for weapons too, then pushes him down in his seat. Maurice just sits there staring at Richie in disbelief.

Richie steps backward away from them down to the head of the conference table and removes his coat. "Are these chairs clean? This is a two-thousand-dollar coat, so. Well, I'll make an exception due to the nature of this meeting." He reaches in the pocket and tosses a leather pouch onto the table. He then gently lays his coat on the chair next to him as he takes a seat. He opens his leather pouch, pulls out a Cuban cigar, and lights it. He takes a couple of puffs and kicks his feet up on the table, crossing them and placing One Less in his lap. Maurice and Karimah look at each other and then back at Richie.

"So, where should I start? I'm sure you have a lot of things running through your mind. Let me see... Felix is dead, Kenyatta's peoples dead, Kenyatta..." Richie pauses to take a small pull from his cigar. "I didn't do it, but, dead. I'll take credit for it though. Don't tell anyone." He takes a big pull from his cigar and blows the smoke up into the air. "I'm sorry. I didn't even ask. Can I smoke in here?"

"So, what's next, nigga?" asks Maurice.

"Well, that's entirely up to you. I won't kill you if you confess to Karimah that it was you that sent me to kill Kolax."

"I ain't confessing to some bullshit I ain't do. That was all you, homie!"

"What a shame. Still lying seconds away from death." Richie smiles when he hears Brick coming up the stairs. "Well, it looks like Brick is going to have the honor of sending you to the afterlife."

"Whatever, nigga! You always getting that fucking mute to do your dirty work."

Brick comes into the conference room and stands by the door. He then stares Maurice in the eyes as he reaches back through the doorway to help Maurice's long-lost friend, who's currently recovering from injuries, through the doorway. "Kolax!"says Karimah as she stands up, confused. "What the fuck is going on?" Surprised, Maurice slumps back in his chair, and Richie replays that night's events in his head when he walked back into Kolax's kitchen after Brick sent him knocking on death's front door.

* * *

"Maurice wanted proof of death, Mr. Loose End himself, and that's what we're going to give him." Richie placed the silencer directly under Kolax's chin. Brick stepped back to avoid the splatter. Richie cocked the hammer back as Kolax closed his eyes and held his breath, bracing for death. Richie pulled the trigger. The hammer slammed against the firing pin, but the gun didn't fire. "Wait a minute…" said Richie. When Richie released the pressure of the gun from his chin, Kolax's heart started racing, and his breathing was heavy. "How well do you know the New York and New Jersey connects?"

Between panicked gulps for air, Kolax replied, "They my peoples."

"So, if you called them right now and told them Maurice is out, they'd listen?

"Yeah, they my peoples."

"Okay, okay." Richie took the weapon away from under Kolax's chin and sat next to him. "What about Maurice's fraudulent passport and credit cards business. You know them peoples too?" Kolax nodded rapidly. "I need you to be very clear," said Richie. "Besides the gang lords, are his other customers terrorists?"

"Yes."

"I tell you what. I'll give you proof that Maurice set you up and let you live if you turn over your East Coast connects and the names and locations of these terrorist groups. But, you leave Chicago for good. If I see you again, Brick will break his foot off in your ass once again. Then, I'll blow your brains out the top of your skull. Agreed?" Kolax nodded in agreement with Richie's demands.

When the team returned to Chicago, Dr. James gave Kolax a shot of Tracrium and a quick tutorial. "So this causes temporary paralysis and lowers blood pressure down to extremely low levels. It'll last about thirty minutes. Anyone looking at his injuries, with him being in this condition, will think he's dead."

* * *

Kolax looks at Maurice as tears fall from his eyes. "I kill't many muthafuckas for you, so you could be in this position. 'I ain't want it to be this way, my G. Be with Spree.' That's what the fuck you said to me!" Karimah steps away from Maurice and walks to the other end of the table to stand next to Kolax, staring at Maurice the whole time. She's furious at his betrayal of her cousin. She realizes that she would always be just a pawn in his world, and he would sell her out in a heartbeat, just like he did Kolax. She thought about her earlier conversation with Elder. He knew Maurice was on some bullshit, but she didn't listen. Richie puts One Less on the table and slides it toward Karimah. Brick hands Kolax his 9mm Glock. The room is dead silent as they all stare at Maurice. Kolax raises the gun at Maurice. "This is for Spree." He pulls the trigger, striking Maurice in the shoulder. "Ahh fuck!" He grabs his left shoulder, leaning forward from the pain. "Fuck you, nigga!" yells Maurice.

"This is for me." Kolax pulls the trigger again, hitting Maurice in his right shoulder.

"Ahhhhh, mutha fuck you!"

Karimah raises Richie's weapon. "Wait," says Richie. "Maurice, I'm going to dump your body in the same place my uncle put your father down. Safe travels, my nigga." Karimah pulls the trigger, and One Less explodes. The bullet flies from the barrel, through the air, headed in Maurice's direction. Maurice's life flashes through his mind. He sees himself as a kid standing next to his dad in the parking lot after a White Sox game. He hears Elder yell, "Smile," and a huge smile comes across his face before Elder immortalizes the memory. He remembers his father's funeral, sitting next to Elder and his mom, unable to look at his dad lying in the casket. He sees the first person he robbed, cheated, and killed. He pictures his mom's face when she picked him up from a detention center, disappointed.

He looks over Kolax's shoulder, and he sees his dad, waiting to reunite with him. He smiles right as the bullet hits him directly between his eyes; his head jerks backward as pieces of his skull and brain exits out the back, painting the wall red. His chair topples over, heading to the floor. The table catches his feet, leaving his chair suspended in the air on its two back legs.

Richie stands up and walks over to Kolax and Karimah. They hand Richie and Brick back their weapons, then Kolax wraps his arm around Karimah's shoulders. Richie walks over to where Maurice is lying still suspended in his chair. He pulls out his phone and calls his cleaning crew. "Raymond, I need your team at H2H's. Get here quick." He hangs up with Raymond and turns to Brick. "They'll be here in twenty-minutes. Brick, you hungry? I'm starving." Brick shrugs his shoulders. "I'm feeling like seafood," says Richie as he walks past Karimah and Kolax and smacks Brick on his chest. "Let's go, big dawg!" Brick nods. "I'm sure you two have some catching up to do. I'll let you have at it. We'll be back when my peoples finish up."

Two hours later, Richie and Brick return to H2H. The office is cleaner than it was before. Elder is now there, standing next to Kolax and Karimah in the parking lot. When Richie and Brick walk over, Elder asks, "Richie, can I talk to you for a moment?" They walk away from everybody. "I understand you two have had beef for a long time. I'm out the game, and I don't want any problems with you, Richie. I know this is part of the game, but please, don't take him to Pirie Park. Do it another way. He wasn't the best person, but him and his dad was all I had. He's my son." Richie ponders the request and places his hand on Elder's shoulder.

They arrive at Lloyd's as he's rolling Maurice's body inside. Richie follows behind Elder, who's emotional about the loss of his son. He raised Maurice since he was ten years old. He weeps as he watches them lift Maurice onto the platform. He looks at Maurice and places his hand on the side of what's left of his head. He whispers his goodbyes as Lloyd allows him to push the button to start the cremation process. Maurice's body slowly enters the crematory. When the door closes, the flames ignite. The man known as Maurice Alphonse Handley is no more. Ashes to ashes, dust to dust.

EPILOGUE

Five months later.
"Detective Neeley speaking. Really? Pirie Park? Okay, I'm on my way." His wife sits up next to him, yawning. "Honey, I gotta get to a crime scene."

"Really, babe? It's two in the morning. I don't like your new position."

"Love, even if Detective Coles didn't run off to play FBI, I would still have to get up." He gets dressed and kisses her goodbye before leaving. Thirty minutes later, he arrives at Pirie Park, where yellow Police tape and a tent set up around a body seems to be the norm. He walks through the Channel 7 News crew, under the yellow tape, and into the tent. Detective Trent Cooper and two patrolmen are there waiting for Detective Neeley to inspect the body. Before he could ask who the victim is, he looks down and immediately recognizes him. Former Detective Leon Russell is lying face up, naked, with his old police badge stabbed in his chest.

"Where's the witness that called this in?" asks Detective Neeley.

"We believe it's the person who did this," says Detective Cooper.

"What do you mean?"

"Well, dispatch got a call from a trap phone, and the person said in a deep voice, 'Come get this sellout ass nigga,' before hanging up." Detective Neeley stands there to think for a second and then asks the rookie detective a follow-up question. "So, what do you think happened after that?" Detective Cooper looks up at the top of the tent, trying to find the best philosophical answer he can conjure up. Detective Neeley stands there and smirks as he watches his subordinate think. "Well, we came and got him." Detective Neeley just shakes his head, amused at Cooper's failed attempt to impress his boss.

* * *

Days prior to Kolax leaving for Arizona, Richie and his new muscle paid him a visit at his hotel room. "Ko, what's up? You all set?"

"Yeah, I'll be leaving in a few days."

"A present before you go," said Richie, handing Kolax Leon Russell's file. Karimah then threw him a bag of money and hugged him as they headed for the door. "Pirie Park. You know how you do," said Richie. "Let K know when it's a done deal. Safe travels."

* * *

After the hit on the former detective, life finally normalized for Richie and the people close to him. As Karimah drives him to the airport, he looks out the window, reflecting on the last five months after Maurice's death. The crew has grown some, filling the shoes of the ones who transitioned, retired, or moved onto something greater. Elmer and Edward, the Jones brothers, along with their wives, Barbara and Evelyn, have retired. They received a severance package with an open invitation if their services are ever needed in the future. Tech and his team of geniuses finally got the fleet of autonomous vehicles running, drastically improving the logistics of the business. Evelyn has agreed to travel to New Orleans from time to time to cook after an onslaught of begging from Tech. Barbara, however, fully retired. After KAP and T.K. killed Felix's men, she made it very clear that she "don't fuck with nobody's blood."

Larry, Jeff, and William decided to continue loading and unloading the product. They now live in the mini New Orleans mansion full time. Marble Head is still Marble Head, staying in his room and watching cartoons and episodes of the *Three Stooges*. Elder goes by the house often to visit with him. They seem to be friends now, talking about old times and laughing about sexing the same chicks from back in the day. Time and age can help you bury the hatchet on any past issues. Big issues just seem to lose their sting overtime, but knowing Marble Head, he still checks for his forty-five whenever Elder stops by. Besides, Elder still has a thing for Richie's mom. Marble Head in general seems to be at peace.

Mr. William's family was devastated by his death. Unfortunately, he was in the right place but at the wrong time. Richie paid off his doorman's home and sent his wife three hundred thousand dollars in cash. He knows Mr. William's family would trade every penny to have their husband and father back.

Shortly after KAP left the hospital, Richie sent a package to the college kids who witnessed KAP's shooting. It had the driver and passenger's belongings in an envelope along with a card that showed a person holding up a finger over his lips and a receipt showing their zero tuition balance.

Spree's daughter, Spirit, is prospering in school. Her Aunt Natasha bought a home for them closer to the private school Spirit now attends. Richie is her godfather, and he and Damawi attended the grand opening ceremony for her daycare, Joyful Spirits. Natasha runs the day-to-day operations. Jordan's son, Amari, attends the daycare center. Jordan got her GED and now takes college classes and is avoiding trouble, so she doesn't violate her probation. She works at Josephine's for Gina, who now runs the club with Octavio as her right-hand man.

Comedians Micah "Bam-Bamm" White, Timmy Hall, and Big Sean Lawkins opened up some youth centers in Richmond, Baltimore, and Detroit. The centers provide a place for Black youth to put their energy and stay off the streets.

Chief of Detectives, Ronnie Watkins, a.k.a. Uncle Swift, retired from the police force. He opened up a business in Chicago to help police officers de-escalate potentially life-threatening situations within Black communities. He also started a Be-a-Cop Program, which recruits qualified people to serve and protect the communities they're from. Surprisingly, he is currently vacationing somewhere with his wife Beatrice.

Arielle is leading in all the election polls. She's seven months from the election, and it looks like she will be the first Black female prime minister in Belize. She deserves it and will do a great job serving her people. Mr. Gamboa and Richie agreed to move the pick-up point away from Belize and re-evaluate using that location until after Arielle gets elected. Richie's goal is to remove transportation from there altogether and make it a great place for American Black people to retire and visit. Arielle was able to help Phillip with his murder investigations, so he could get a passport. He will be leaving for Chicago immediately after the election.

Damawi now runs Swaggazine Entertainment and takes care of the organization's administrative requirements. She handed the club over to Gina, so she can spend more time mentoring Jordan. Her sister still doesn't speak to her much, so she needs something to occupy her mind. She's also handling the general operations of the organization while KAP completes rehab. Then he'll run the organization, and Richie will be an advisor while he continues pushing the movement to other states. Thanks to the East Coast connects, they now have people in Pennsylvania, Washington D.C., Maryland, and Virginia helping communities of color build esteem and wealth.

Twenty minutes later, Karimah pulls up to Midway International Airport. A private jet is waiting to take Richie to Columbia to meet with Enrique, Mr. Gamboa, and a special guest he's been talking about for the last two weeks. Richie prays it's not another head on a platter. Brick gets out the front passenger seat and opens Richie's door. Damawi slides out with him as Karimah stands just outside the car door scanning the area. Brick has been training her for the last few months, dishing out daily ass whippings. "Baby, I'll see you when you get back," says Damawi, kissing Richie. "I'll be in the morning of the comedy show," he says looking into her eyes, smiling. "See you in a few days, big dawg," says Richie to Brick as he pats him on the chest before entering the airport.

Richie walks through the regular security checks and climbs aboard Mr. Gamboa's private jet. T.K. and Tech are already seated and ready to tour Columbia. When they land, Enrique meets them at the airport. "That's yours, my friend. You will go home in that," says Enrique, pointing over to a beautiful burgundy and gold jet.

"Nice colors, Enrique. Thank you!"

"Man, you on some real pimp shit now, dude," says Tech. "I'll be balls deep in this shit every night. I'm masturbating on it going home. Any lube onboard?" Enrique looks at Richie.

"Just ignore him," says Richie. "We all do."

"What the fuck did I do?" asks Tech, throwing his hands up in the air.

Enrique smiles and then gestures for them to follow him down to the port. Docked against the pier are two submarines. "You done good, Enrique," says Richie. Tech takes off down the pier like a kid in a toy store. T.K. slowly walks behind him. He wants to check out the vessel and understand the load requirements. "Come, Richie. Our guest has limited time." They hop into the Range Rover to meet Mr. Gamboa and this mystery guest. "Enrique, I'm going to have to think about the jet. I want to be on the low if you know what I mean. That will bring too much attention. I hope you understand."

"I understand, Richie. No problem," says Enrique. "It was just a kind gesture from Mr. Gamboa." When they arrive at the mansion, Richie feels like he's seeing it for the first time. *I thought I was taking the walk of death when I was here months ago*, he thinks while walking through the palace. He follows Enrique onto the large patio where he sees Mr. Gamboa sitting with this mystery guest, who's wearing a large sun hat and sitting with his back to Richie. Mr. Gamboa waves to Richie as he gets closer to the table where he nearly had a nervous breakdown. Richie approaches the table, which already has a plate of food and drinks prepared for him. Mr. Gamboa's guest stands, his back still facing Richie.

When the mystery guest finally turns around, Richie stares at him in shock. Every unexplained thing that's happened in the last few months now made sense. The invitation from Mr. Gamboa left on his car. Kenyatta and his people being murdered by a team dressed in black coveralls that just disappeared after that night. Keeping Richie and his team out of harm's way directly or indirectly. Even taking evidence that could've very well caused unwanted attention and issues with pushing the movement forward. The man walks up to Richie, and they just continue staring at each other, mainly because Richie has no words.

"How's my brother and sister doing?"

"They're good," says Richie. "How's Aunt B doing?"

"She's great. She over there in the pool," says Uncle Swift. Richie turns and looks.

"Hey, nephew!!"

* * *

"Listen up! Before we take our seats and get started, I would like to give a round of applause to Special Agent Coles, the rookie. Within his first thirty days on the job, he's already brought down a terrorist cell that was involved in fake passports, credit cards, and driver's licenses based out of Boston and his hometown Chicago." Everyone claps. "Alright, we some got information from one of our informants, who is no longer with us, about a person of interest. Our informant told us that the person of interest is heavily involved in the narcotics game, but he's squeaky clean. Although he's not a top priority, we'll start watching him closely. The informant's name was Felix Navarro." His face displays on the huge screen. "The person of interest's name is…" Special Agent

Coles opens his folder. "Richmond Alexander Tomlinson. Also known as Richie Swaggazine. Business man, retired military, a highly decorated soldier. Special Agent Coles, you have the lead on this. I need you to report to me after thirty days with any relevant information pertaining to Mr. Tomlinson's involvement in the narcotics game."

"Roger that, sir, roger that."

I hope you enjoyed the *Emancipation of Limits*. This is the first book in a series written in reverse chronological order.

Stay tuned for the upcoming books:

THE PROCLAMATION OF A GOD.
Richie is stationed in Belize when he first makes contact with his connection Felix. After the partnership begins, Richie returns to Chicago to start his movement.

THE BEGINNING: THE REIGN OF MARBLE HEAD.
Marble Head is the leader in the game, and now he's pulled Richie into the game too.

If you're wondering if there will be a book after Emancipation of Limits, maybe...maybe not.

Visit my website for E of L acknowledgements and updates on future works.

www.apajturner.com